THICK AS THIEVES

Personal situations
with
THE JAM

"For those of you watching in black and white – this one's in Technicolor"

THICK AS THIEVES

Personal situations with

THE JAM

Ian Snowball & Stuart Deabill

visit our website at:
www.marshallcavendish.com/genref

Marshall Cavendish
Editions

The publisher acknowledges the sponsorship by Peckham Rye towards the publication of this book.

Peckham Rye®
LONDON

Copyright © 2012 Stuart Deabill and Ian Snowball
Published by Marshall Cavendish Editions
An imprint of Marshall Cavendish International
1 New Industrial Road, Singapore 536196
Email: genrefsales@sg.marshallcavendish.com
www.marshallcavendish.com/genref

Marshall Cavendish is a trademark of Times Publishing Limited

Other Marshall Cavendish offices: Marshall Cavendish Corporation. 99 White Plains Road, Tarrytown NY 10591–9001, USA • Marshall Cavendish International (Thailand) Co Ltd. 253 Asoke, 12th Floor, Sukhumvit 21 Road, Klongtoey Nua, Wattana, Bangkok 10110, Thailand • Marshall Cavendish (Malaysia) Sdn Bhd, Times Subang, Lot 46, Subang Hi-Tech Industrial Park, Batu Tiga, 40000 Shah Alam, Selangor Darul Ehsan, Malaysia

A CIP record for this book is available from the British Library.

ISBN 978 981 4398 06 0 (trade edition), 978 981 4398 29 9 (limited edition)

Design and picture research by Jon Abnett at Phoenix Photosetting
Typeset by Phoenix Photosetting, Chatham, Kent
Copy editor: Michael Spilling
Cartoons by Marty Street of The Cartoon Workshop, Wolverhampton
Printed and bound in the United Kingdom by Henry Ling Limited

Contents

List of Contributors:

Ady Croasdale was one if the co-founders of the Northern Soul scene down South. He runs Kent Records and the 6Ts Rhythm and Soul club.

Alwyn Clayden was a Polydor sleeve designer.

Andy Nykolyszyn is 44 and from Leicester. Despite occasionally being a 'Billy Hunt', he's morphed into a 'Saturday's Kid'/'Smithers-Jones' hybrid. He always knew that boy Weller had a future in showbiz…

Andy Winter became a Mod after having been influenced by "that film". A regular at rallies since the 1980s, he is a member of Burton Brewers Scooter Club and is a School Business Manager. He is married with two children and describes himself as part David Watts, part Mr Clean and part Smithers-Jones.

Ann Kerr is a mother of three children from Bathgate, West Lothian. She runs an unofficial Paul Weller forum: www. paulwellerchat.com.

Barry Goodwin is a reluctant glamour photographer, web designer and musician. He lived and worked forever and a day in Central London but has now escaped to the country and enjoys playing guitar, writing songs and drinking whisky in an old caravan/ studio with musical partner Tim.

Bill Smith was The Jam's sleeve designer, 1977–81.

Bob Collins played guitar with Medway indie outfit The Dentists in the mid 1980s. Bob continues to play and is currently co-writing a book on the Medway underground bands between the years 1977 and 1987.

Bob Gray grew up with Bruce on the Sheerwater estate and attended the same school as him and Paul. He emigrated to Canada in 1979 and has for the past 30 years been traveling worldwide as an international keynote speaker, entertaining and teaching human memory development (see www.memoryedge.com). He is also a Guinness World Record holder, still plays the piano, still loves R'n'B and still keeps in touch with Bruce.

Bob Manton was the lead singer of the Purple Hearts. Sounds from the band included 'Frustration' and 'Millions Like Us'. Bob continues to sing with the band today.

Brett 'Buddy' Ascott drummed for The Chords and continues to drum today. Songs by the band include 'Maybe Tomorrow' and 'Something's Missing'.

Caron Wheeler is a British R'n'B singer and was with The Jam on their farewell tour. Afterwards she went on to great success with R'n'B group Soul II Soul.

Chris Makris was born in 1954. He grew up during the 1960s and was a mad fan of British popular music, an interest that continues to this day. He currently teaches high school social studies and lives with his wife, daughter and son in Concord, New Hampshire, USA.

Chris Parry, producer, is the Polydor A&R man who signed The Jam.

Col Baker is a Modernist, cyclist and piss artist. His cues, lyrically, musically and politically, came from The Jam in the early 1980s. They've influenced the way he dresses — even now, 30 years later.

Dan Derlin lives in Kent. He owns a particular reggae record by Wayne Wade that he says he will leave to Ian Snowball in his will.

Daniel Ash is the lead singer/songwriter/guitarist with the band The Lost Boys.

Den Davis was inspired by the family love he witnessed following The Jam, and spent the next 30 years working with young people through football (as a Uefa coach/scout) and music with his charity, Impact England.

Dennis Munday was a Polydor A&R.

Derek D'Souza was born in '59. He loves music, photography, football and paintball, and is the proud owner of over fifty nicknames to date! He feels blessed to have good family and friends, especially his lovely wife, Krissie.

Diz is a lucky husband, proud father, suffering Pompey fan, grateful Weller/Jam fan, occasional DJ = life sorted.

Ed Mylles is currently in Whitehall looking for those responsible.

Eddie Piller was one of the founder members of Acid Jazz Records and continues to keep the label and book division going from strength to strength.

Elinor Crockford lives in the Medway towns. She would go and see The Jam in between gigs from The Prisoners, in which her brother Allan played bass.

Erland Johnson is a baker by day and a BHS trucker by night.

Garry Bushell was one of the earliest music journalists to write about The Jam. He has written several books that include *Dance Craze* and *Two Faced*.

Garry O'Connor was born Garry Morris in Hulme, Manchester, in 1962. He moved to Charlesworth, Derbyshire in 1970. Youngest of four and brought up on Pink Floyd, Zeppelin and Elton John, he bought Bowie's *Aladdin Sane* and soon discovered his own tastes. Then Punk hit. He saw The Jam in late '77/early '78 and did the whole Mod thing. Weller has been his deity ever since.

Gary Crowley has been a broadcaster for over three decades, still retains his youthful enthusiasm for up and coming artists and is one of Lisson Grove's favourite sons.

Gary Shail played 'Spider' in the 1979 film *Quadrophenia*. Gary caught on to the Punk idea very early on and also wrote the music for the classic 1983 TV programme *Johnny Jarvis*.

Gavin Anderson is 45 years old and retains the Mod ethic. He grew up in Leith, Edinburgh, and has been in London since 1989. All through his life the doctrine of clean living under difficult circumstances stayed with him.

Gavin Martin has been a professional writer for the last 35 years. Belfast-born, he founded the fanzine, *Alternative Ulster*, in 1977. Since moving to London in 1980 he has written for many publications, including *NME*, *The Guardian*, *The Independent*, *Uncut* and *Classic Rock*. He is currently *Daily Mirror* music critic and curator and host of his own live music/DJ/spoken word event, 'Talking Musical Revolutions'.

Gordon Waring is Liverpool born and bred. Despite serious health problems he has ridden Vespa and Lambretta scooters all over the country and has been a member of both The Cheshire Cats (Runcorn) and Goldhawks (Liverpool) scooter clubs. His other obsessions are clothes and music. He has little interest in the boring commercial clichés that surround the Mod scene and much prefers a more individual approach.

Guy Helliker is a sales manager from Staffordshire. The hard kids from the city schools in Portsmouth and Southampton had taken over the jukebox in the cafe with stuff like Saxon and Quo. Something had to be done, 50p got him eight plays, only one thing for it, 'Start!' and 'Liza Radley' four times each! A victory for the Andover kids. From that moment and for the next thirty plus years he was a Jam fan through and through.

James Papadamitres has written about all kinds of un/popular music for all kinds of pamphlets and periodicals. He used to put on the odd disco in Shoreditch many years ago, but since moving to Brighton he's been ploughing his less youthful energies into his radio show, 'The Séance', which he co-presents with Pete Wiggs of Saint Etienne fame.

James Tindley was born in North London in 1962. He lived for the next 45 years in and around London, massively influenced by the music of one Paul Weller and The Jam. At the tender age of 50, he now lives a slightly more sedentary existence by the beach in South Australia. Still lovin' the scene, still lovin' the music… once a Mod, always a Mod.

Jason Brummell has written a lovely book called *All About My Girl*. He is working on a follow up.

Jennie Baillie once ran and published the Mod fanzine *Double Breasted*. She lives in Scotland.

Jennie McKeown (Matthias) sang with 1980s outfit The Belle Stars. She continues to sing today.

Jim Tiddiman has been a Jam fan for 30 years and has a footlong tattoo along his spine showing the album cover of *Dig the New Breed*.

Joey Saunders has been stranded on a desert island since 1983 armed only with a turntable, seven albums, 18 singles, a Torquay United scarf and a typewriter.

John King has written several best-selling books that include *The Football Factory*, *Human Punk* and *White Trash*. John is a Chelsea supporter and lives in London.

John Reed is an author and journalist. Amongst John's literary works are a biography of Paul Weller called *My Ever Changing Moods*.

Johnny Chandler is currently Head of Product for Universal Music. A club and gig DJ for 20 years he has also written for *Mojo* and *Record Collector*, managed bands and broadcast extensively on BBC 94.9. He supports Aldershot Town FC.

Jon Abnett likes music, football, art and photography. He still recalls the first time he heard the 'Woking Wonders' and is just as passionate about their music to this day. He has advised on a freelance basis to book and magazine publishers and also record companies on various Jam/Weller related projects over the years.

Jon 'Ginny' is a Northern Jam fan.

Jonny Bance is a Leicester man, but don't hold that against him. At 38 he is far too young to have seen the best f**kin' band in the world storm the stage of the Granby or the De Montford halls, but his passion for them is second to none. He has watched *Quadrophenia* more times that he can remember, spins a few records on the radio and talks rubbish over the airwaves, puts students' worlds to rights with psychotherapy and can order a beer in several different languages.

Kate Butcher was one of the book's earliest contributors.

Keiko was born in Tokyo and first came over to the UK in 1978. She loves animals, especially cats, and good music.

Keith Thomas is a South London born-and-bred musician who has played with the acclaimed Jazz/Funk band, Second Image, as well as session work with numerous other bands, including The Jam and Julian Lennon.

Kev Stevens is a 56-year-old construction worker living in London. Originally from Newcastle, he has a love of all Max R'n'B and sweaty emotional gigs.

Mark 'Bax' Baxter has written several books in his time, some co-written with Paolo Hewitt, such as the *Fashion of Football*. His book, *The Mumper*, has been made into a film, retitled *Outside Bet*, starring Bob Hoskins.

Mark Hough is a Liverpool fan who grew up in Falkirk, Scotland, surrounded by music, football and Raleigh Chopper bikes.

Mark Smith has a way with words. He wears a suit well and lives in Kent. He is a Fulham supporter.

Mark Watkins is a Wolves fan currently living in Worcestershire.

Martin Carroll is editor of leading Weller website www.fridaystreet.com. He is now based in Chipping Campden, Gloucestershire.

Marty McAllister co-wrote a book called *To Be Someone* with Adam Cooper of Rowed Out Records. It's about the Irish Mod scene of the 1980s.

Matthew Priest always wanted to be healthy, wealthy and wise, just like his nan said. Unfortunately he became a drummer in a rock & roll band. Along the way he has played with Dodgy, The Lightning Seeds, The Icicle Works, The Electric Soft Parade and The Yellow Moon Band. Thankfully his life-long love of Northern Soul and Nina Simone has kept him sane.

Matteo Sedazzari is editor and founder of the online magazine, www.zani.co.uk, for contemporary culture. He resides in leafy Surrey. He first discovered The Jam in the spring of 1979, via his older brother's record collection. He finds The Jam as inspiring now as he did when he was a schoolboy in shorts.

Max Splodge is of the 'Two Pints of Lager and a Packet of Crisps, Please' fame. He still looks the same as he did back then.

Michael Patrick Hicks is a guitar tutor/journalism student. Marvin Gaye's 'What's Going On' changed his life and continues to shape it. He lives in Cardiff – where music surrounds his existence – and Weller is the soundtrack.

Mick Habeshaw Robinson was born Chelsea blue-blooded in West London. He started with stadium bands and worked his way down the musical ladder, passing through Acid House and St George by Duffer. He is now by the seaside running Hotel Pelirocco retirement home for rock & roll casualties.

Neil Pearce is by day a 53-year-old, greying/balding, slightly overweight (fat but knows where it's at) customer services assistant for John Lewis stores. By night he's a 53-year-old, greying/balding, slightly overweight drummer in a pub-level Blues band.

Neil Sheasby is a bass player and founder member of Midlands Rock 'n' Soul combo, the Stone Foundation. He owns far too many records and is still a devoted disciple of the holy trinity of football, clothes and music.

Pat Nevin played for Chelsea and Everton for much of his footballing career and is now an esteemed commentator for Radio 5 Live. His double nutmeg on Kevin Keegan in 1983 is still talked about in hushed tones round the pubs of Fulham Broadway.

Paul Baker is a West London boy and Chelsea fan. Now older and fatter, he's a drinker, grafter and mortgage payer who still keeps the faith.

Paul Gallagher is a DJ, writer and brother to a couple of rock & roll stars.

Paul May was born in Belfast in 1965. He trusts animals more than people, likes a drink, Chelsea FC and a good tune....

Paul 'Mez' Merrick, AKA DJ Sunflower, is 48 and resides in sunny Birmingham. He is partial to the Small Faces and the odd drop of port 'n' brandy. Keep right on!

Paul Thompson is a 51 year old Man of Kent and Gooner. Married to Yvonne with two teenage boys, Nick and Phil. The music of Paul, Bruce and Rick has been the soundtrack to his life for the last 35 years.

Pete 'Esso' Haynes was the drummer with early Punk band The Lurkers. He has written several books that include *God's Lonely Men* and *An Unlikely Fooligan*.

Pete Skidmore is a Jam fan through and through.

Pete Wilson was the The Jam's producer, 1981–82.

Phil Jones is a Liverpool author and ex editor of *Time For Action* and *The End* fanzines.

Phil Potter was born in Paddington, West London, in 1968. He left school with one 'O' level (Art), and has worked for the Royal Mail since 1990. He supports QPR, loves a nice curry, would love to have been around in the 1960s and longs to have his hair grow back.

Ray Gange is a DJ, artist and the original Rude Boy.

Richard 'Dickie' Lewellyn now lives in Germany but in his early years helped promote the UK Mod scene. He helped run The New Untouchables in the early days and is a massive Prisoners fan.

Richard Lewis lives in Cardiff and for his sins supports the football club, too.

Rob Haynes is a West London based purveyor of pop culture. Husband, father and a proud owner of a pair of Kenneth Monkou's shin pads.

Robert Peston works for BBC News as business editor and you can spot him on the television... a lot.

Simon Kortlang is the original Saturday's Kid. He spends his weekends shouting at Loftus Road, hammering round London on his scooter and trying to keep beer stains off his desert boots.

Steve Brookes was born in Paddington on 26th May 1958 and has spent the intervening years in a state of mild confusion and accumulating a vast collection of china cats.

Steve Butler was an East London/Essex Mod who joined the army in 1983 and lived in Australia for eight years. He now lives in West London as a photographer who covers entertainment/news stories, and travels extensively.

Steve Carver was born in Woking in 1955, and has never moved away. He still lives there today with his wife Ruth and young daughter Charlie. He was educated at Sheerwater Secondary

Thick As Thieves

School, where he unknowingly went to school with three lads who shook the world. He became best friends with Paul Weller in 1976 and watched his mate's climb to fame. He later worked for the group selling T-shirts and merchandise. He still thinks that The Jam are the best group he has ever seen…

Steve 'Meds' Medlin is 45 years young, lives in Wellingborough (see *Jeremy Kyle Show* for further details). Still Chelsea, still smart, still scootering… That will be all!

Steve O'Neill is 47 years old and lives in Ruislip with his wife and two kids. Steve is still active in the Mod scene and is the proud owner of a Lambretta SX scooter.

Steve V. Page discovered The Jam in 1978 after hearing *This is the Modern World* album. He lived in Shepherd's Bush as a kid and has a son called Stanley, whom he named after Stanley Bowles the footballer.

Steve Proctor is a London-based Liverpudlian and one of the UK's best-loved DJs from the Acid House era.

Tim Filor is 52 years old and has been following The Jam since buying 'All Around the World' at the same time as 'Pretty Vacant'. He became a Mod convert after seeing *Quadrophenia*. Today, he's a big fan of From the Jam — it's great to hear the old songs again and appreciate how special the Woking Wonders really were.

Tim Rolls is a Chelsea season ticket holder and blogger. He was lucky enough to be 19 and in London when Punk started. Still recovering.

Tony Beesley has written several books that include *This Is Our Generation Calling* and *Out Of Control*. Tony's books document the Punk era extremely well.

Tony Spence is a 46-year-old native of Belfast. From a pre-teen Punk rocker he accidentally drifted into Modernism through a love of The Jam. He has been involved in the Belfast Mod scene ever since, on and off at times, but just like in the best gangster movies, he isn't ever allowed to leave. He is a supporter of Cliftonville FC and works in Procurement for the NHS. He is currently to be found promoting Belfast's premier Northern Soul club, Heart and Soul.

Tracie Young was the vocalist on 'Beat Surrender' and went on have more hits as a solo artist. Tracie is now an acclaimed local radio DJ.

Vanessa Jayne Lindley-Blunt used to own a vintage clothes shop, Cuba, in London's New Oxford Sreet. She had two daughters, India and Ruby Saax, in the 1980s. More recently, she has returned to her roots and is currently in her third year at Newport University, doing a BA in Fashion.

Vic Falsetta went to school with Paul Weller. In his spare time he net minds for the 'Guildford Smoke' ice hockey team. More recently, he can be found promoting charity gigs in Woking.

Photo credits:

Barry Goodwin cover, iii, 76–79; Derek D'Souza ii, 1, 2, 131, 134–153, 187; Jo Jo Baldock v, xiii; Dennis Munday 4–5; Bill Smith 8; Bob Gray 10, 19; Jon Abnett 14, 23, 55, 101, 116, 168, 205, 212–218, 224; Steve Brookes 15–18; Marty Street 24, 48, 64, 96, 114, 154; Guy Helliker 27, 84, 118, 125, 162; Stu Deabill 28, 54, 132, 159; Col Baker 33; Gavin Frankland 66, 68, 71, 74–75, 88, 95, 105, 211, 223; Keiko 73, 110, 112; Christie's Images Ltd. 85; Chris Makris 91–92; Ken Watkins 99, 182; Greg Swatton 106; Neil Sheasby 109; Phil Potter 165; Den Davis 166–167, 170, 181; Kevin Styles 174, 179, 206; Barry Mason 177; Anita Hill 186; Paula Jones 188–204

All badges and tickets Gavin Frankland, unless indicated.

The authors and publishers would like to note that the majority of photographs featured in *Thick As Thieves* were shot by amateur photographers and most are 30–35 years old. The quality is consequently variable, reflecting the time lapse and the circumstances in which the photos were taken.

foreword

I'm always amazed at how young our audience was! I thought I was young, but looking back, a lot of our fans were just 12 or 13. Have a look at the front row of kids in The Tube TV performance we did. You'll see they were proper kids!

The Jam Army were committed, dedicated and ferocious. There was a tremendous sense of occasion at our gigs. There was also an air of violence and tension. But then so was our music, so we reflected off each other, as all great art does – though none of us would have called it that at the time. I am glad I was on stage and not in the audience, as most nights were fucking scary!

But young passions run high and passion it most definitely was. It was also very tribal, whether 'style' tribes or football ones. EVERY NIGHT would kick off and the sea would part in the middle and blood and beer would fly. Scary but always exciting.

Towards the end though, I'd had enough. I saw what the Thatcher gang were doing to the country and the working class and I thought, why do we have to fight each other when we could be fighting those fuckers? But it was divide and rule in motion and I had to move on.

God bless the Jam Army, almost every day of my life I have a person in their forties or fifties come up to me to say how much our music meant to them and telling me of their Jam gig experiences. They've never forgotten that gig or that song. That says an awful lot about how passionate those gigs and songs and kids were. That passion never withered or died.

Paul Weller, April 2012

THICK AS THIEVES

I am certain that many Jam fans have been cornered by somebody and asked: so what's your favourite Jam song? It's a tough question to answer because there are just simply too many fantastic songs to choose from. Whilst Stu and I were putting the book together there were certain songs that the contributors often mentioned, such as 'Thick As Thieves' and 'Saturday's Kids', for example. These songs encapsulated the essence and flavour that we wanted for our book. Those songs touched something in us that evoked memories of being young and all the buzz, energy, excitement and discoveries therein.

All of us will have tales to tell from any era about our teenage years but the song 'Thick As Thieves' has a deeper meaning for anyone who grew up in the late '70s/early '80s. Track 2 off The Jam's fourth album, *Setting Sons*, was part of Paul Weller's idea of a concept album, loosely based around three friends, growing up and then gently drifting apart as the adult world beckons and each friend takes their chosen path in life into the capital world. The album didn't quite materialise that way, as Weller either got bored or ran out of ideas, but songs like 'Thick As Thieves', 'Burning Sky' and 'Saturday's Kids' tell their own story.

'Thick As Thieves' has a beautiful poetic lilt that is far more relevant than anything Wordsworth produced. As Weller writes about a teenage friendship that was so close that nothing could come between "us or the world, no personal situations", we all identified with his description of the bonds we held so dear.

The song 'Saturday's Kids', describes a feeling, a unity and a celebration of youth that would have been chewing on mouthfuls of porridge or Golden Nuggets whilst watching Saturday morning breakfast television shows, like *The Banana Splits*, *Tiswas*, *Multi Coloured Swap Shop* and *Flashing Blade*.

After throwing the bowl in the sink for their mum to wash up, Levis or Sta-Prest were zipped on, feet were slipped into a pair of Hush Puppies or Adidas Sambas, a Lonsdale sweatshirt or Fred Perry polo was pulled on, before heading off down the local high street. They would loiter around town centres whilst trying their luck with birds that worked in Tesco and Woolworths, whilst nicking the pick 'n' mix or flicking through the latest 7" records; or they tried to get served in the pubs between 11am and 3pm, playing the one arm bandits and talking to girls that sipped Babycham. And who *was* the Jan that Paul Weller sung about?

Some of them would gravitate to the local parks, football grounds or wastelands to forget school and feel free and uninhibited, kicking a football between makeshift goal posts and generally just getting up to mischief by trading insults with rival street gangs, passing pedestrians or throwing stones at mates up a tree.

The girls would be in Top Shop or Chelsea Girl reeking of Charlie or Impulse perfume, singing along to the shop's radio while trying on a hundred tops, before buying just one; then popping into Our Price to buy the big record of the day before heading off home for their tea.

On their way home the kids would pass corner shops, butchers, greengrocers, fishmongers, off licences, broken fences, Austin Allegros, Ford Escorts, nosey neighbours or a mate fixing his Lambretta on the side of the road (again!).

Once indoors, it was time to catch Giant Haystacks having a staged tear up with Big Daddy on the TV, or listening to Peter O'Sullivan doing the racing commentary from Sandown Park (in between your dad's swearing as his big bet of the day is bringing up the rear). Then Dickie Davies or Frank Bough would be telling you Chelsea had beaten West Ham before having a Matey bubblebath and a pop at their older sister's terrible choice of music as she's getting ready for a night out at either America's, Tudors or Oscars with her new, dopey Soul Boy fella (whilst hoping she doesn't end up in the back of his fur-trimmed Cortina afterwards).

The Saturday's Kids lived their mainly uncomplicated lives to the soundtrack of the bands of the day. If they were old enough, they went to see The Jam play live at a City Hall, a Top Rank or an Apollo. Or they went to a house party, where cheap booze was downed and communal snogging with the opposite sex was undertaken before one your friends ends up with sick down their shirts, but not before pogoing to 'When You're Young' or 'In the City'.

For the younger kids, they settled down to watch Tom Baker in Doctor Who or Jimmy Saville fixing it for someone to sing with The Nolans, whilst chomping on a Texan or Lion bar. Then they were sent to their Jam poster-ridden bedroom because it's gone 10pm, and they're having a sneaky listen to *Setting Sons* through headphones – thinking of Emma who's still at college, trying to suppress the urge to shout out "Hello Hooray!", feeling genuine sorrow for the soldier in a pine overcoat being delivered to his mum – before nodding off and dreaming that they'll marry the girl next door....

Thick As Thieves is as much a celebration of the lives of The Jam's fans as it is of the band, and for many of us, we are still bound by the friendships that were forged all those years ago through the band's music. Little did we know back then that some of those friendships would stand the test of time – "all time" – just like our relationship with the Woking Wonders.

START!

My co-writer Stu came to me with the idea of doing a book about The Jam. I love The Jam: they stood for everything I believed in, influenced my dress sense as a teenager and their lyrics and tunes made life interesting. But Stu was a slightly older, committed borderline obsessive and felt that the time was right to put out a book to cover the Woking Wonders, but from a fan's point of view rather than from a balanced, dispassionate journalistic angle.

We were winding up our *Ronnie's to Ravers* book (about 50 years of London's club land) and not one to let the grass grow under my feet, I agreed. It was only then that it dawned on us that if we wanted to keep the book in line with the 35th anniversary since the release of 'In the City', we had to get a serious jog on to have the book ready for the publisher.

Stu got in touch with a certain Jon Abnett, whose encyclopaedic knowledge and 'Jam' contacts, along with his passion became invaluable, and as a result threw us some contact details for a publisher that he knew and had worked with previously on *The Jam Unseen* book by Twink. The publisher showed some interest and invited Stu and I to meet with him in the café above Foyles bookshop in Charing Cross Road. This was four days later.

The meeting went very well. Stu and I did our best to explain that our book was a work that would be built on and around what being a Jam fan was and what its legacy meant. The template idea for the book seemed sound enough and Stu and I also had some other ideas up our sleeves that we hoped would make our book even more original and interesting.

But the main thing we wanted to communicate to the publisher was that the book was simply a celebration of a brilliant band. A band we knew meant a great deal to many people – and the memoirs and content of the first interviews confirmed this. We left the meeting confident that we had shared our vision for the book accurately and that he understood and would support us.

This foreword also requires a nod towards most of the previous books on The Jam. All of them have something to offer. Some appear to be better written than others, or more informative, or have better photographs or whatever. But for a Jam fan they all count. I hadn't even read half of them until Stu turned up at my door holding a great big box full of books, programmes, posters and all sorts of things that contained some written words on The Jam. I spent the next week diving in and out of the box and discovering new things.

Previously my Jam bible had been Paolo Hewitt's *A Beat Concerto*. I bought the book when it was first released in 1983. I loved the book then for many reasons and still do. Then in Stu's box I came across *Sounds From the Street* by Graham Willmott and *About the Young Idea* by Mike Nicholls. I found these to be important books that helped inform my own research and knowledge of the band. So I spent weeks listening to, talking about, and writing about The Jam.

This book doesn't aim to retell stories already written about hundreds of times before. It doesn't attempt to look for more meanings or hidden agendas behind the songs, or dissect them into pieces. The intention of the book is to be by the fans, for the fans, old and new, and to attempt to provide different angles on The Jam – to remind someone of their youth and to tell newer fans how great this band are, adding to a lasting legacy that gets stronger with each year. To get so many old associates who worked with the band in some capacity and have never spoken openly (or been asked to) has been an absolute joy for us.

Everyone of us who lived through and grew up in the period between 1976–1982 has a tale to tell. Record buying was at a peak and was a passion shared by millions. The Jam, with the help of Paul Weller's family, became one of the best-loved and most vital groups to have ever come from these shores.

It was the importance and depth of meaning that The Jam had given so many people that made Stu and I confident that a new book on the band was worth doing. Only, we wanted this book to be mainly person-centred and from the fans point of view. The fact that in 2012 it was going to be 35 years since The Jam released *In the City* was just a fortunate bonus and another reason to celebrate.

So, Stu and I set about inviting people to contribute to the book and write accounts based on their own personal memoirs. We also set about interviewing others. Our intention was always to gather a diverse collection of people from all ages, locations and backgrounds. Quickly, it became apparent that the subject matter was something deeply important to many people. In many ways, it was if people lived their younger selves to the soundtrack of The Jam's music. It was as if their energetic, youthful days had been lived to the sound of Paul Weller's voice, Bruce Foxton's bass and Rick Buckler's drums.

Yet although it doesn't seem likely those same kids still exist, they do, albeit below the radar and not as mainstream as before. But the faces are still there. Take, for example, the scene in John King's and Nick Love's film, *The Football Factory*, where the Chelsea boys find themselves strutting through a typical tunnel common in the deep south bandit country and spray-painted on the inside of the tunnel are the words *The Jam*. The film even closes with the song 'Going Underground'. The story goes that when Weller was first approached about using the song he was against it because he didn't want the song or The Jam to be associated with football hooliganism. But once put into context, he agreed. After all, the football firms were, in a way, just another example of 1970's and 1980's 'Saturday Kids'.

The Jam had been squeezed out of an era when pop music was a hugely important part of young people's lives. Nowadays, new music is on tap and at the push of a button we can listen to an iPod full of albums. But growing up in the 1980s, that technology didn't exist. We eagerly waited for the next Jam release, we kept a keen eye on the charts and we continued to play our records for months, years even; whereas today, a latest album is easily and quickly replaced.

When I bought *Setting Sons* the album had already been out for two years, but it still had weight and it most certainly still sounded magnificent. It still does. Hopefully, this book will transport you to the times and places of the point of impact, contact and continued love of the three-piece that we still hold dear.

I believe *Thick As Thieves* to be up there with the best of them. It's real, it's passionate and it's evocative. It's of a time, but also, like the music, timeless.

The relevance of the songs written in that six-year period from 1976 onwards still ring true and are held dear. The lyrical content of a bloke wiser than his young frame belies, with his soulful voice and cutting guitars mixed with the precision bass and drum patterns of master technicians, still leaves the listener enthralled, excited and ever ready to turn the volume up!

Snowy

When you've lived with The Jam as the musical backdrop and main inspiration for most of your life, looking back really does seem like a dream mixed with nostalgia. The first time I can remember seeing the band was on the one TV programme my whole family would sit, watch and argue about: *Top Of The Pops*. Now this was 'The Modern World' I'd been looking for that autumn of 1977. The black and white suits, the controlled aggression and energy showed by Paul, Bruce and Rick was a bit different from the usual pop rubbish I watched most weeks. I subliminally stored the band for future reference and went back to obsessing over football and torturing my younger sister.

Forward to Christmas 1978 and music had started to have a bigger impact as I approached my teens. My family and myself were over to visit my auntie and uncle in Twickenham. My older cousin Claire was in the front room playing various New Wave and Punk 7" vinyl, which grabbed my attention and seemed to upset my even older disco-loving cousin, Karen.

Now in amongst The Stranglers, Sex Pistols and TRB was The Jam's 'Down in the Tube Station at Midnight'. It was rarely played on the radio and I'd only seen it on *Top Of The Pops* once, so I asked her to play it. She duly took the record out of the sleeve and put it on the record player; the initial crackle made way for the ticket inspector's lo-fi, gruff-voiced, barely audible shout for tickets and then the compelling intro of guitar, bass and drums took me to a place I've never actually returned from. The record has always had an aura. With its story of an innocent man trying to get home to his wife caught up with London's fear and loathing on the underground, the song takes on a life of its own. It stands almost unopposed not just in The Jam's catalogue, but from anything released before or since by any other artist for pure drama. The tension and the dark undertones of a snapshot, a BBC *Play For Today*, is brought to life by the magnificent craftsmanship of the song construction and the deeply affecting music.

After making Claire play the record another four times, she told me I could keep the 7". I took it home and immediately slung John and Olivia's 'You're the One That I Want' into the garden – even at the tender age of 12 I rejected my past.

To say I was obsessed with The Jam is an understatement. I loved plenty of other artists of the time, such as The Specials, The Clash and Madness, but nothing came near to the pant-wetting excitement I felt on the day before a new Jam release. I remember vividly the day The Jam went straight to Number One with the double A sided 'Going Underground'/'Dreams Of Children' (though the latter never got a look in): 20 Mods who were all a couple of years older than me, wearing US Army parkas, huddled round a radio on a Tuesday lunchtime to hear the charts in my school playground, all cheering as someone as unsexy as Peter Powell played the new chart topper.

For me it was a feeling akin to Didier Drogba's winning penalty in this year's Champions League Final for Chelsea, or the time my now wife agreed to go on a date with me after I'd given up hope of trying to convince her I wasn't a wrong 'un.

Everything The Jam did resonated. Whether it was a polka dot scarf from a gig photo in *Smash Hits* to a full page ad for 'Start!' featuring electricity pylons (!) in the *NME*, to trying to work out which park bandstand was used in shooting the 'When You're Young' video. It all meant something. Even the so-called 'orrible' year for songs, 1981, still produced the urgently cataclysmic 'Funeral Pyre'. The power of that song had me doing my best to put the downstairs ceiling through, as "the flames grew higher" came smashing out of the Sony hi-fi. 'Absolute Beginners' indeed.

That video having the band running round like lunatics was shot down my old road, in London's W14. I'd tell anyone who wanted to listen where that was with a big, smug grin on my face, thinking I was part of a secret Jam society and somehow linked to the band, however tenuously.

I loved every single second of listening, watching and reading about the band. I understood the sentiment of most Jam lyrics, even if not fully understanding the content. I back-tracked and bought all the previous singles in their original picture sleeves, and paid over the odds, as I was desperate to own everything they had released. I kept a scrapbook, made my mum tape the chart rundown off the radio on Tuesdays, even if they'd gone down the chart, and even wrote a letter to Paul telling him the band changed my life (he wrote back as well).

I never took on the look, but the attitude and the whole ethos of Modernism? I was a card-carrying member! Weller was/is the walking embodiment of MOD. Whether it was cropped hair or the Marriott cut, boating blazer or mohair jacket, bowling shoes or Penguin Gibsons, he looked the absolute bollocks (and still does). The obsession with clothes is something many of us shared, if not the dough to pay for a change of wardrobe every month or so.

As I started wearing expensive sportswear and became what is now commonly known as a 'Casual', The Gift album was massive to most of us who spent Saturday's at football matches wearing diamond Pringles, Lois cords and wedged hair. We'd much rather listen to American rhythms and Brit funk than the Mod revivalist sub-standard guff that came out in the previous couple of years (though I was in the minority of Jam fans with this, it has to be said).

As I became more and more disinterested with school, the more I became mobilised by The Jam's stance on CND, Margaret Thatcher and unemployment. I am not being over dramatic by saying that I learnt more from Paul Weller than any teacher. That may say as much about my own shortcomings as a pupil, and I'm sure Paul would visibly shudder at being thought of as a teacher, as he hated school as much as I did. But learning about the Franco-Prussian War or 'Just Who is the 5 O'Clock Hero'? No contest.

The Jam are a positive in so many ways. There might have been caution in the tale being told, but it was never downbeat or pessimistic (unless you believed the NME reviews). We all went through periods of being 'Thick as Thieves' with mates we thought would be around for ever; we've all found ourselves in a 'Strange Town' being betrayed by our accents and manners; or 'Dreaming of Monday' when we'll see our loved one once more.

Today, we now all identify with cutting down on beer or the kids' new gear, and 'Running on the Spot' as the powers that be put the squeeze on again and again. These words put belief and heart in our soul, as someone was singing about how we felt and how we lived.

For every knife-edged anthem, not far away was a tender and often melancholic number that would lay heavy on your heart. 'English Rose', 'Liza Radley' and 'The Bitterest Pill' spring to mind.

After a particularly horrible break up in my distant past, I attached to my work van's sun visor a written lyric from the hymn-like 'Ghosts', off The Gift album.

When you've got nothing, you've got nothing to lose, pick up your lonely heart and walk right on through.

If I ever felt myself wobbling whilst driving, I'd flick the visor down and temporarily release the pain.

The Jam and their audience always had a special bond. They always found time for their army of fans, replied to fan letters, let in people to watch them do soundchecks, sometimes just to get the kids out of the arctic winter conditions that their school blazers just weren't made for. Very few bands would let fans hear the newly-finished album in the recording studio. The Jam did.

The kindness (and sarcasm) of the road crew, led by Paul Weller's dad, John, is legendary. There was no 'us and them'. The fan club run by Paul's mum, Ann, and sister Nicky, made sure of that.

The stage shows were fraught with tension, excitement and explosive energy! Whether it was Bruce in mid-air, Paul rocking on his heels and then attacking the microphone with venom or Rick's effortless time keeping and tough drumming, the audience thrived on every second of the pressure-cooker atmosphere.

Direction/Creation/Reaction ... What you give is what you get!!

The Jam were vital, urgent, passionate and unique. We knew it, they knew it.

A lot of journalists who were born in the 1950s didn't get it at all, though, as they thought they'd seen it all before with The Who and The Kinks – they missed the point and importance of The Jam.

The Jam made sure they appeared on TV (TOTP was most people's point of entry to The Jam) whether it was late night (*Revolver*) or Saturday morning (*Get Set For Summer*). They didn't have a hang up about miming and worked their bollocks off on a six year constant of gigging and recording. It paid off, as 30 years on we're still finding new and fresh angles on the band that for some became not just a band to cherish, but an attitude that runs deep with an ability to touch their lives.

In these pages you will see the effect the band has had on a public's consciousness. The deep-rooted passion and memories that still hang large in the lockers of the original 'Saturday's Kids' are brought to the fore with touching insights that have never previously seen the light of day. Add some of the associates that still speak fondly of their time with the band, and the authors and musicians that took inspiration from The Jam, and we're left with a unique look into a band that near as dammit has a perfect story to tell.

So… from the humble beginnings of a commuter town in Surrey, The Jam serve a long apprenticeship round the pubs and clubs of their local environment. The singer's father hustling the boys' gigs, and making sure they got there even if it meant pulling strokes with his day job. After a couple of personnel change, the band gets signed by Polydor, and bit-by-bit, town-by-town, start to make waves across the UK. The third album, *All Mod Cons*, takes The Jam into the Top 10, and suddenly the outsiders are in the faces of the capital's media and country's youth. A Top Three single the following year, and in March 1980 – a moment that some can pinpoint exactly where they were – The Jam had got to Number One, JFK style, with 'Going Underground'.

On to changes in style and lyrics over the next two years, with a horn section and a Funk style for a UK battered by the rise of Maggie Thatcher and a Conservative government, followed by a world tour that left the frontman in no doubt about what he wanted to do next, leading to an eventual parting of the ways. The only difference with this band splitting compared to most others was that it wasn't drugs, dough or jealousy that smashed the comfort zone: in Weller's eyes, the youth explosion had grown up and out of its earlier habitat.

The band bowed out by touring and saying goodbye with dignity, honour and respect, and apart from a few who were unable to take in that their idols were nearly gone at the last gig in Brighton, it was beautifully reciprocated by the herds of fans, from St Austell to Glasgow.

One of the main reasons I decided to start the process of writing and compiling *Thick As Thieves* was after speaking to a 14-year-old from Stoke. Callum Tunnicliffe told me that The Jam are his favourite band.

I asked him why, as I was surprised that a 30-year-old band was still having an impact similar to what it had on me at the same age.

He replied: "They sing about me and my kind, they look cool and looked like they meant every word."

Stu

Bruce Foxton

Bruce, when did you first feel that The Jam had a loyal following?

I guess around the time we played a series of shows in London: The Nashville Rooms, the Hope & Anchor, the Red Cow, the Greyhound.

What would you say has been your strangest request from a Jam fan?

To sign the side panel of an immaculate scooter with a screwdriver!!

The Jam has meant and continues to mean so much to so many, and a lot of that had to do with the lack of barriers between the band and the fans. Was this a conscious thing or did it happen naturally?

It happened naturally. Soundchecks are essential but can be tedious: having fans in lifted everyone.

Can you think of the strangest thing a fan ever gave you?

A photo of himself!

Where was the most unlikely place that you ever bumped into a fan?

Checking in at a hospital.

Have you ever given a fan something and then regretted it? One of the book's contributors recounted a story when he knocked on your parent's door, you answered, chatted, then you ran upstairs and returned with a pair of Jam shoes that you then gave the young lad.

I'm proud of everything and anything to do with The Jam, so very reluctant to give anything away.

When The Jam split up, were you surprised at the fans response?

No. We all realised how much the band meant to them and, indeed, us.

Do you have a most memorable gig because of the fans response?

We were fortunate to have many great shows. The worst response was supporting Blue Oyster Cult in '78 and hearing 20,000 Blue Oyster Cult fans booing.

We have a section in the book on John Weller. Can you share any of your enduring/endearing memories of John?

John was a very passionate man. He believed in The Jam long before we were signed and gave us his all — he would beg borrow or stealing to get us transport, gear, etc. for shows. Thank you John. X

Rick Buckler

How would you describe the bond between the fans and The Jam?

When we were playing the social and working men's clubs the audiences weren't there to see us in particular, and we mostly played covers; so to move into the London pub rock scene and attract our own audience was very much valued by us, and to break down the 'them and us' attitude was also a poke at the dinosaur rock artists.

Did the fans ever get on your tits, to the point you felt it was out of control?

No, almost without exception everyone was respectful. Only when the numbers grew, did it become more difficult.

What would you say was The Jam's peak or most enjoyable period?

All of it.

What are your proudest memories?

The first offer of a major record deal with a single release and a chance of an album to follow — this meant we could be a full-time working band.

Did it feel like you were at the forefront of the country's working class youth and were giving them a voice that the bastards largely ignored?

Being in a band came first; playing live and having good songs and playing with a passion that meant something, the fact that whoever came to see us related in the same way, gave us common ground.

What were your favourite cities to play home and abroad?

The UK was always the top place for us. Abroad was always good, but people are people wherever you go.

Were there any special techniques to get your drum sound?

No real special techniques were used, just very good studio engineers and producers and the way the kit was tuned.

What was your favourite kit?

The kit I had on the Trans Global tour was the most comfortable kit to use and the best sounding.

Was the farewell tour surreal, enjoyable or hard work?

Paul had by this time already detached himself from the band. I always thought, and hoped, that he would change his mind, as The Jam was such a big part of our lives for the previous 10 years, and we had achieved so much to just disregard it. The reason Paul gave us as to why he wanted to leave didn't equate with what was really happening.

'Funeral Pyre' is possibly for my untrained ear your finest moment. What tracks are you particularly proud of?

'Absolute Beginners', 'Start!', 'Tales from the Riverbank' and 'Five O'Clock Hero' are amongst my top favourite recordings, but I love playing 'Strange Town' and 'The Gift' live.

Who were the other artists that you liked in late '70s/early '80s?

I didn't always get the chance to see other bands play as we were always working or in the wrong place, but I love the records of XTC, the Pistols and the Feelgoods.

Did you give Weller a hard time when he refused to get out of his seat to pick up the award for best single at the British Rock and Pop Awards?

No, we had no idea that he would freeze up like that, after receiving the invites and making the point of going to the event together. But it would have been twice as embarrassing if we had all sat glued to our seat like that.

Dennis Munday – Polydor A&R man

Had you ever seen or heard of a band that cared about its fans as much as The Jam did?

No, I can't think of another band that took so much time to be with their fans. Most bands after a show just want to party and get laid. The Jam were very different, as after every gig they went out front to sign autographs, which they didn't need to do. Also, they let fans in to hear the soundcheck, which I don't recall any other bands doing, either. A lot of their success is down to the way they treated their fans, who repaid them with a total dedication to their records and gigs.

Fans in the control rooms and studios – was it something you encouraged and what did the big-wigs at Polydor think?

I neither encouraged nor discouraged the fans from turning up at the recording studios. If The Jam wanted their fans in the studio, then it was their call. The big-wigs were never aware of this and even if they had of known, there was nothing they could have done about it. Having said that, it was unusual and I don't know many other bands that allowed their fans so close, at such an important time.

What was it like being in the middle between company and band?

Soddin' 'orrible at times, particularly when I started. Chris Parry turned down the demos for the third album and then did a bunk to set up Fiction [record label]. It was like walking into a lion's den and for quite a while, I was known as Jim Cook's (my boss) spy. There's no doubt that Chris was right, but he and the company could have handled the situation with a little more diplomacy. Once The Jam started selling records, the big-wigs had to keep quiet. There were also times when John and Paul pissed me off, but all of this goes with the job. It was worth it, just to be a tiny part of their success, though there were times when I could have cheerfully strangled everyone concerned!

What were your favourite venues and towns to go and see the band?

I never liked seeing the band in London, as the big-wigs attended and they were a royal pain in the arse. The Jam played London several times a year, which for my money, spoiled the London fans. I also felt that the fans from outside London were more enthusiastic, as they only got to see their fave band once a year and you could feel the difference out front. I tried not miss gigs in Liverpool, Glasgow, Birmingham, Brighton, Edinburgh and some of the remotes. The Winter Gardens at Malvern was a favourite of mine.

Are there any gigs that stick out, any Beatlemania type stuff?

Newcastle City Hall, 28 October 1980, which was recorded. I was lucky, as Malcolm Gerrie of The Tube was recording the show for TV, which meant I could watch from the mixing desk and not have to sit in the recording truck. The atmosphere was electric and when The Jam ran out, the hair on my neck was standing on end. It was the best gig I saw The Jam play.

There was one instance of Beatlemania that I recall, but as it was a long time ago, I can't remember the venue. We were all on the coach waiting for Paul to be smuggled out and there were a lot of fans hanging around outside. Kenny Wheeler asked me to go to the back of the coach and he opened the back door. Paul ran out and as there were no steps, he grabbed a hold of me and Kenny, and we started to pull him in. The fans noticed this, grabbed hold of Paul and it was like a tug-of-war match, with me and Kenny trying to pull Paul in, and the fans trying to pull Paul out. It felt like my arm was being pulled out of its socket, but we finally managed to get Paul on the bus, though I had large bruises on my arms from where Paul's fingers had gripped me so hard.

Which Jam songs did you relate to, and why?

It was fairly easy for me to relate to The Jam songs and the Punk era, having been a first generation Mod. When I was 15, I started to listen to modern jazz and by my late teens, I was into most music: Pop, R'n'B, Blues, Ska/Bluebeat, etc. when I started to work with The Jam I was in my late twenties, though I hadn't forgotten what it was like to be a teenager. Neither did I yearn for the past, as most of my generation did. At the time, most of my mates were listening to all that crap '70s rock stuff, which bored me to tears, so when Punk arrived, it was like a Dyson cleaner on speed. Working with The Jam and other young bands was like being a teenager again, although I

Ferry to Sweden 1980.
According to Dennis Munday the
true meaning of "booze cruise".

SNAP!

The Jam Christmas party 1980, at The Greyhound.

never went up the front for a pogo! If Punk hadn't have come along, I'm not sure what would have happened to me — I certainly wouldn't be writing books, that's for sure.

'Boy About Town' is one tune I can relate to directly, as it reminded me of Saturday afternoons in the 1960s, when me and my mates would shoot up to the West End of London for a breeze around the shops. I always liked live music and I could relate to the energy of their songs, particularly when The Jam played them live. Paul was an outstanding three-minute pop songwriter, and whilst it's easy to write a shitty pop song, it's extremely difficult to write a tune that is meaningful. Paul's exceptional talent put's him up there with the best songwriters of any generation.

Did you ever take any of the band shopping for clobber?

No, but I did go with them occasionally.

Was there much rivalry between other Polydor bands, such as Siouxsie and the Banshees, Sham 69 and The Jam?

Not so much rivalry, but they were all looking over their shoulders at each other, which was a pain for me, as I worked with all three bands. It didn't help when they released their singles and albums at the same time, which caused me a lot of aggro. Once The Jam took off, they left the others in their wake, though I have always felt that Siouxsie should have done better. If I did favour a band it was probably the Chords, but that's another story.

If push comes to shove, what's your fave single and album?

'When You're Young', though I got the message wrong. It was a turning point for me, as I thought the company had done a shit job on the single and it really motivated me. I gave everyone in the company a real hard time (wrongly) and I was glad 'The Eton Rifles' was a big hit. If it hadn't have been, I might have been picking up my UB40. As for my fave album, it has to be All Mod Cons. Sublime songs, great production values and it has my all-time favourite Jam song on it, 'It's Too Bad'.

Did the band ever thank you for the work you put in, or were they selfish bastards?!

I got a credit on every album I worked on and as thank you's go, they don't come much bigger than that.

Is that you in the 'Bitterest Pill' video?

Yep, that's the back of my head in the video. Bruce threw a wobbler and stormed off, so I deputised, though had he done it, you would have seen his face. It was a horrible two days: by the time shooting commenced, it had been announced that The Jam were going to split. Bruce was on edge and the director, whose name I forget, was very slow. The first day went ok, but on the Sunday, we started at 10am and finished the shot with me in it at 4am Monday morning. I don't blame Bruce for getting the hump — even Paul was getting pissed off, and it was his idea. The director had a flat in Leicester Square and kept disappearing from the various shoots (nose powder I expect). When we got to the last sequence I told them to get the shot ready and if he didn't return by the time they were ready to go, I would direct it myself. He returned just in time and I recall driving up the Old Kent Road as the sun was coming up. I think it was after this that Bruce announced he wasn't going to do the final Jam tour.

What was Polydor's reaction when they were told The Jam was splitting up?

Extremely pissed off, as it looked like The Jam were going to take the next step up and go on to greater things. They were also unsure as about Paul making it with TSC (The Style Council).

What was your reaction?

I wasn't surprised, as I saw everything unfurl from the inside. They'd moved apart as mates, and by the time The Gift was recorded, Paul had moved away from Rick and Bruce musically. I have always thought The Gift was half Jam, half Council, which I know some Jam fans hate to hear. History has now proved that the decision Paul took was the right one. And let's not forget, The Jam's legacy has stood the test time. Their music is as relevant today as it was on the 29 April 1977, when they released their debut single, 'In the City', which ain't too shabby for a band that ended over 30 years ago.

I had a great time working with The Jam and met a lot of nice fans. I have been asked often to sum that time up and I'll leave the last word on this to Tony Rounce. Tony DJ'd and announced the band on some of the last live dates. He came on stage and simply stated, "Put your hands together for the greatest thing on six legs — THE JAM." 'Nuff said!

Pete Wilson – Producer

When did you first become aware of The Jam?

I was working as a recording engineer for Polydor in their head office studio (off Oxford Street) from 1975, so I was there when Punk was happening. Polydor signed The Jam and Souixsie and the Banshees and were chasing The Clash and the Sex Pistols at around the same time. I recorded a bunch of Punk bands: Chelsea, The Cortinas and others for a 'Sniffing Glue' compilation, Sham 69, and demos with The Clash for Polydor (although they later signed to CBS).

The Jam frequently demoed new songs in the studio at Polydor. I recorded plenty of material with them or with Paul solo when he was working out new songs, such as 'That's Entertainment' and 'Pop Art Poem'. It was fascinating to see his brilliant songs in gestation. If he was in the studio but short of new songs we would record stuff just for fun – Beatles covers like 'And Your Bird Can Sing'.

Did you relate to Paul's lyrics?

Paul's lyrics were truly original – often combining deep social insight with a lyricism that he maybe got from some of his reading of poets like Shelley or the Liverpool poets – truly admirable and unique.

Did you have any particularly tough times in the studio trying to get sounds or vocals down?

Paul was self critical about his vocals – that's fine if he knows what he wants and wants to work to get it – the producer's job is to support that. I started working with The Jam as producer/engineer when they were allowed to have as long as it took in the studio.

Where did you prefer to record – Air, Solid Bond or Townhouse?

Air was great but a bit 'public' – it was stimulating as you would not know who you might bump into in the corridor, such as Paul McCartney! Solid Bond was cheaper and less time pressure! And more private. But both were good studios.

Kids in the studio – pain in the arse or not a problem?

By the time I was working with them ('Funeral Pyre', 'The Gift', etc) they had a handle on it so it was not intrusive.

Was the split a surprise?

Yes and no. Paul was getting interested in a wider variety of styles, and maybe wanted time out from the treadmill of album–tour–album–tour, so splitting The Jam was one way out of that.

As a producer of The Jam, what are you particularly proud of?

'Town Called Malice'.

Did you ever go on the road with the band?

Toured to Glasgow (Apollo) and Edinburgh (Playhouse) to record the gigs – amazing! The crowd knew all the lyrics – brilliant gigs.

What were Polydor like to be involved with?

Fine. They knew they had a winner so were fairly hands off.

Bill Smith – Sleeve designer

I was born in Elm Park/Hornchurch in 1951 and then we moved to Gravesend in 1960 and lived there until I was 22. I went to a Saturday art college in Rochester and then the LCP in the Elephant [and Castle]. When I was 15 I knew I wanted to be a designer and by 16/17 I was really into music, so I knew then I wanted to find a way of putting the two together. I count myself very lucky that I knew what I wanted to do at an early age and have been doing it ever since. I had some Mod tendencies, and owned a Lambretta and the tonic suits.

How did you get into designing sleeves?

I did the normal thing, went to the London College of Printing art college in the early 70s. I left in the middle of my second year to go and work for a small advertising agency and from there I went to Octopus books, which was run by Paul Hamlyn. I became the art director for their book covers and from there I went to Polydor in 1976 to become the art director.

Any inspirations?

I loved After the Goldrush by Neil Young. I also loved the band America and claim to be the first person in Gravesend to own those records. The Goldrush sleeve looks like it could have been shot anywhere with the bricks and iron fencing. The stencilled title looked nice and the slightly solarized cover made it very iconic. Fantastic record, fantastic sleeve – the perfect combination.

What do you remember about those early days?

Both Bernie Rhodes and Malcolm McLaren both came into the art department whilst trying to get Polydor to sign The Clash and the Sex Pistols and said hello. At Polydor, I did everyone from Peggy Lee to Rory Gallagher to Ella Fitzgerald to The Who – a huge spread that was a great education in commercial design within the music industry.

How many albums would you work on in a month?

We would generally be working on two or three albums a week and then with the explosion of 7" picture sleeves we were doing loads of picture bags as well.

The first Jam album, In the City, felt like it should be black and white and this meant that the Polydor logo had to be black and white as well – so that decision went all the way to the head office in Germany. The logo had always been red and had never been in black or white before. The record companies were kings back then; anything they said went, so it took quite a lot for the companies to start doing coloured picture bags, etc. Polydor was a very strictly run record company, it was very structured and hierarchical. I reported to my head of art, and then he had to report everything to marketing and it went up through various managerial levels. You very rarely saw anybody at directorial level. You worked not so much in isolation but you were the designer and you put the ideas together, then you had to try and sell them through the company system. For the first couple of years everything was done that way.

Could you believe some of the rubbish that got signed then?

At the time I can half understand why the Pistols and The Clash got touted around Polydor, as most record companies didn't know what to do with them or how to cope with Punk. Those two bands were deemed not right for the company. The Jam was the first band to be signed during that era. I still don't think they were ever as Punk as some believe: they wore suits and had a schooling in the working men's clubs and the pubs of Surrey, playing covers. Even then, to me their influences were Mod/Who/Beatles. Coming from Woking I can't imagine they'd have that sense of fashion, but I believe they had as much to do with the fashion side of that era as Vivienne Westwood and McLaren.

During the early months of Punk I went to see the Pistols at the Royal College of Art and The Clash early on, and it was a bit of a shambles! You could tell that the Pistols couldn't really play or Rotten couldn't sing. Possibly they would get through two or three numbers before it would fall to pieces. Fights would start in the crowd and chaos ensued.

When I first saw The Jam at, I think, the Hope & Anchor, you could tell they could play and sing. There was structure to their songs and this is why I think they stand outside Punk and were more the vanguard of New Wave, as it became to be known. They were fresh and weren't rebelling in the same way as other Punk acts. Even though they came from a very working class background I thought Paul was quite conservative – this came out in some of the things he said in interviews early on.

I bet he didn't think it would be haunting him 35 years later!

No, unfortunately once it's in print…. Nowadays, everyone would have known about that in three minutes! But they set a pretty high standard right from those early gigs.

Did you see them before they got signed?

I was told Polydor were thinking of signing this band, so I went with Chris Parry, the A&R guy. Polydor were looking at lots of Punk/New Wave bands around this time, so I went to plenty of gigs. Chris was the 'go to' guy if you had a Punk or New Wave band that you thought should be signed. Chris was a very nice guy, genuine and very instrumental in the sound, and we worked closely on the look and feel of the images and the way it was put together. He was a new A&R man rather than the old-fashioned fellas, who were record company men. Chris was definitely on the side of the bands. Polydor had its own recording studio at Stratford Place so he had them in straight away.

Right from the very beginning with Chris, The Jam had a champion within the record company who was on the same wavelength musically, and as the designer, I understood what they were trying to do with their image. It was great for me, as I'd done all those sleeves for the MOR artists, such as Bing Crosby and Peggy Lee, and I now had a fresh, vital young band to work with. It was a wonderful opportunity as a designer, to get a new band without any background or baggage to work with. With The Who and Rory Gallagher you had to work with the band to a certain extent, but this was completely new. I'm sure Chris felt the same.

This new approach led to a new way of thinking on photo sessions – they were very straightforward before and done in studios – but now we thought, let's take some photos on the fire escapes or the back of the building, on the street, etc. I had this idea on the first album that it should seem like we'd shot the band in a toilet. This was in a tube station and the guys had just run in there, they were either running away from someone or running to something, and had sat down against a wall, which they'd graffiti'd their name on.

From 1976–78 onwards, there were lots of young designers coming through, like Malcolm Garratt, Rob O'Connor and Peter Saville. Seventy-six through to the early 80s – for me, that was pretty much the golden era of music design. There was a backlash to the Hipgnosis-style design work for bands like Pink Floyd, etc. Very over the top, although some of it was brilliant stuff. But for The Jam it was quite simple: very graphic, stripped away design. Every session we did was pretty good, pretty straightforward, and they were always up for doing whatever I suggested.

I worked for Polydor until '78 then I set up my own studio. The Jam continued to work with me and it meant that I could work outside the confines of record company demands. I started doing more New Wave bands, such as The Cure and The Pretenders.

Is it pretty unheard of that a designer works with a band for most of their careers?

Most of the singles and five album covers is an awful lot to do with one band. I'm very proud of it and there's not much design in there that doesn't work – ok, there's a couple, but that's not unusual. Maybe 'Funeral Pyre' and Sound Affects, which was Paul's idea to do it as a BBC sound effects sleeve pastiche. The images all came from the lyrics on the album. I had the most input in the first three albums and most of the singles' bags. I'm not much of a collector myself, although I always loved the music. I have bought albums for the cover then listened and thought what a load of rubbish.

I think what I try to do with covers is get an essence of what is on the vinyl or the CD and have someone get an inkling of the point of the music from the image. That started probably before I was working with The Jam, but they definitely made me think hard about what a band is about with a particular sleeve, although, most of it is very obvious.

Being an original Mod, did you and Weller talk about the times you grew up in?

He definitely liked a lot of that stuff, especially The Small Faces, and he loved to talk about Stevie Marriott.

Side 1   1976   Side 2

GO—   SOUL DANCE   MY SONG JAN '80
    BACK IN MY   CHRIS WEST GARAGE
    ARMS AGAIN
    GOT BY IN TIME.
P. WELLER. B FOXTON
R. BUCKLER B. GRAY.

JAM

Manufactured in the United Kingdom by EMI Tape Limited.

EMITAPE X100

1   Mad

1976 – GET OFF YOUR ARSE!

1976 would be remembered by the British public as the year of the long hot summer and the start of a youth generation rejecting the music and groups that had grown bloated, fat and old (well, 25 was old back then). This Albion has seen nothing close to the impact of either since. By the end of summer the British public had been slowed to a sweaty existence as temperatures reached up to 96F degrees, and at the end of the year had been outraged by the foul-mouthed frothings of the Sex Pistols during the Bill Grundy show.

However, the year had already begun with the nation needing to defend itself against hurricane winds (which left behind it a shocking mess and 22 dead) and 12 IRA bombs in London alone, even before the Punk rockers exploded onto the unsuspecting British public.

Punk was already happening, but not for the majority of kids still wearing flares and long hair. Mainstream music was serving up the latest Eurovision Song Contest winning number from British act Brotherhood Of Man, who asked if you could 'Save Your Kisses for Me'. Comedy records by the likes of Radio 1's Hairy Cornflake (and universally loathed) DLT reached the Top Ten, and although there was a decent stream of soul and disco it seemed to be overridden by abject shit like Tina Charles and Pussycat.

The entire collection of Beatles singles (23 in total) had also been released all at the same time (another band did a similar thing in 1983 with much greater success!). Much of the nation was hooked on TV shows like *Space 1999*, *Multi-Coloured Swap Shop*, *The Sweeney*, *The Old Grey Whistle Test* and the *Rise and Fall of Reginald Perrin*. Liverpool Football Club marched on, winning another First Division title in their final game of the season and leaving tears to flow at Loftus Road as QPR came a close second. Riots broke out at the Notting Hill Carnival, providing a stark reminder that black British youth were pissed off, angry, unemployed, depressed and ready to explode.

In September, London's 100 Club responded and hosted a Punk festival that show-cased eight British Punk acts that included the Sex Pistols, The Clash, the Buzzcocks, The Damned and Stinky Toys. Kids stumbled out of the 100 gig signed up to Punk and carried away with them a new dance, called the Pogo, following its introduction to the crowd by Glen Matlock (or Sid Vicious according to Malcolm McLaren). The Damned released 'New Rose'. This would be credited as the first British Punk single and its urgency found many a home and pissed off many a parent.

Paul Weller's song writing changed overnight after seeing the Pistols at an all-nighter at The Lyceum and found the songwriter's untamed wit and repartee overriding previous slushy love songs…

What Punk offered, shook up and made a statement about was arguably the greatest thing that had happened to Britain's youth and its relationship with music. And whilst many today say Albion waits for the return of King Arthur Pendragon, maybe what British youth culture really needs is King Punk Pogo and his revolution to shake things up, refocus and inject some pride back into the UK music scene and its conscribers [sic].

story about walking around bare footed only happened once. The story behind that is that it was too hot to sleep and we got up really early one morning and went out. But we weren't a couple of barefooted hippies, that just wasn't the case. It certainly wasn't an attempt to be different, or anything like that.

Later, after I left The Jam, I opened up a guitar shop in Brookwood. The band came down for the opening. I laid on some cans of beer and so on, and what I got was a bunch of Mod kids who came and drank all the beer and never even looked at the guitars. This was in 1979. I started bringing guitars in from the States in 1980, but it never really paid. I remember Ricky Parfitt [of Status Quo] coming in one day. He took a fancy to a Les Paul Junior, stuck it in the back of his Porsche, and off he went. No money ever changed hands. Funny really.

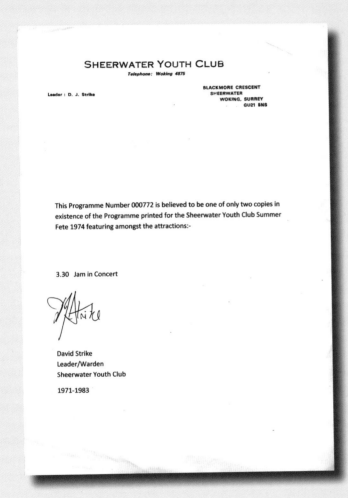

'Jam and Jerusalem' – an early Jam performance.

The following photographs are from the Winning Post Twickenham gig (December 1974).

Not your typical Saturday's Kids!

I grew up with Bruce on Sheerwater Estate, Woking. He lived on Albert Drive, I lived on Devonshire Avenue, just up the hill from me, and we both went to the same school, Sheerwater Secondary, but he was a year below me. Bruce and I were mates as kids. He took up the guitar about the same time I took up the organ – that just sounds so wrong!

We played in a couple bands growing up; one I remember being called Rita. I had ditched the Vox organ for an electric piano.

I moved to Canada when I was 20 and over the next few years I had to come back and forth from Canada to the UK to get my papers. In '76 while I was back in the UK I met up with Bruce. He said he was in a band and they needed a keyboard player, and that they were called The Jam. I never answered an ad in a newspaper – Bruce asked me to sit in on a rehearsal. I said ok as I was over for a while and had nothing better to do.

The first rehearsal was in a back room at the Sheerwater Youth Club – that's where I first met Paul and Rick. I recognised Paul as a guy I had seen a long time ago outside the Birch and Pines, the local pub on Sheerwater, with a scooter and dressed like a Mod. Now my time line may be a little skewed as to when I actually saw him or whether he actually owned the scooter (he probably did) – the only reason I mention this, is that at the time (and this was probably well before I first left for Canada in '74) I remember thinking, wow this guy is a decade late with the parka and scooter. My older brother was an original Mod from the 60s and here's this guy, years later, dressed the same. He probably was responsible for the whole Mod revival, who knows?

Anyway, Paul had an amp that he said he 'borrowed' from Rick Parfitt of Status Quo – Rick Parfitt's parents also lived on Devonshire Avenue, a few doors down from me. Rick lived off the estate in a big house but we would often see a Range Rover parked outside his parents' house. I played on an old piece-of-crap upright piano. I don't recall what we played but I guess I passed the audition. I remember talking to Paul about who we liked musically and Steve Marriott was a common link. After the audition I remember Paul's dad showing me a poster of The Jam playing at The Greyhound and I remember thinking that the logo of The Jam was a straight rip off of The Who's logo. But I was also impressed that they had already played The Greyhound, because when I told John that, he said, "And you can have your face on there too."

My first gig with the band was at the Dunstable Civic Hall, opening for the Pistols. We travelled up in an old Bedford van, Paul's dad driving, and all of us in the back with the equipment. Paul read the *Melody Maker* most of the way there and was pretty quiet. I'm pretty sure that the Sex Pistols were on the cover of that *Melody Maker* and someone telling me that we were opening for them. I was impressed that we were actually opening for a band that's on the cover of *Melody Maker*, far bigger than anything Bruce and I had ever done when we played together years before. But none of it made any sense when the audience ended up being no more than a hundred strong.

I remember the Pistols coming in for a soundcheck and they had all this expensive equipment and I was thinking, what the fuck do they have all that gear for when they don't even know how to use it? Not sure if they had just ripped off EMI, but that would have explained it. Only the bass player, Glenn Matlock (pre Sid V) seemed to have any clue. Anyway, remembering that I had been away in Canada and didn't know what was happening in the UK, my impression of the Sex Pistols was 'what a load of shit'... really out of tune, some tosser shouting the odds with the microphone and loads of gobbing – what the fuck was that all about? Everyone spitting all the time – anyway, I wasn't very impressed. I do know we performed 'In The City', had a burger afterwards and drove home.

I played two other gigs before I jacked it in, at the 100 Club, which I believe was with The Vibrators, and upstairs at Ronnie Scotts. Before I left we went into an 8-track studio to record the following three songs: 'Soul Dance', 'Back In My Arms Again' and 'I Got by in Time', which I still have on an old Emitape X1000 60-minute cassette tape from 1976.

contd.

I didn't follow The Jam after I left for Canada. Bruce invited me to a recording session in London a few years later. I sat in the booth and remember Paul throwing his guitar across the room and spitting on the floor and shouting the odds, just like Lydon, obviously pissed off at something, and I truly remember thinking, like I did of Lydon, "a bit of a wanker".

I was back in the UK a couple of years back and was in Brighton, where my wife's parents lived, and went to the last From The Jam gig, apparently at the same venue The Jam had played their final gig 25 years before, and had a couple beers before and after the show with Bruce. Bruce has always been a nice guy (I never knew Paul or Rick from my brief stint with the band). Had a nice conversation with Rick, too, and he also came across as a stand up guy, no pretentiousness. Can't say I know anything about Paul: I love some of his music and some I can do without... probably go far if he keeps his head screwed on.

Bob Gray

I went to school with Paul. I recently found a copy of Maybury Junior School's punishment book from 7 February 1969. Paul's name was at the top of the list: there was also Charlie Barrow, Dave Spencer, Dave Bennett and myself (I was 10 years old). We all got a single stroke of the cane that day. We went on to get many more at Sheerwater Comprehensive.

We used to get our records from a shop called Maxwells, which was just by Stanley Road. We got our clothes from a shop called Squires. That's where the band took its name from. There were two shops next to each other. One sold Looms and cheesecloth shirts and the other Crombies and Ben Shermans.

There were a lot of skinheads and suedeheads around Woking at the time. Paul was already wearing a parka by then. This was around 1972. I recall going to Michaels where The Jam played loads. It was a very small venue in Woking. It was the kind of place where the older men played cards for money upstairs and you had to be 21 to get in, while downstairs there was the more traditional disco with live band. Even by this time John (Weller) was getting them gigs up in London. Around this time we were just interested in going to the pub. People like Enzo Esposito and Paolo Hewitt were perhaps more into going to see bands.

Vic Falsetta

Every Sunday we use to go over to a pub called The Swan in Croydon. It was just opposite the Fairfield Halls. Upstairs was this room where they had bands. I remember seeing Thin Lizzy, Motorhead and I did see The Jam there. This was in 1976. The place was not even half full. It was the only time I ever got to see The Jam because I was probably out gigging, too. The Jam were one of the best Punk bands.

Max Splodge – Splodgenessabounds

It all happened so fast. Paul and his family moved into the house that backed onto our garden. "I went to school with that bloke", said my brother Pete. A couple of days later I met Paul in the Princess of Wales. Within the first hour the Sex Pistols had been mentioned. "Have you seen 'em yet?" asked Paul. I hadn't, but had been following their progress in the *NME*. "We are going to see 'em on Monday, why don't you join us?"

So I found myself in the back of a Transit van with my new mates Paul, Tony and Dave. John Weller drove us to London. On the way I learned that Paul was in a band. That night changed my life forever. The Sex Pistols were what I had been waiting for. Before that day I had been spending my money on David Bowie and Alice Cooper. That evening at the 100 Club made me see everything differently.

Within days I had been to see The Jam (coincidentally, the bassist Bruce Foxton had been in my year at school). I was knocked out, they were brilliant. What's more, I could see they fitted completely into what was happening in London. We became a proper gang. We even wrote our own fanzine, though we didn't bother to get it printed.

Every weekend we would end up at one of the growing number of Punk rock clubs that were springing up in the city (sorry). Paul's dad would often be with us, hustling for gigs. Within weeks it was obvious that The Jam, along with the Pistols and The Clash, were the only three groups with any real talent. (I didn't like the Stranglers.) I remember thinking: the black-and-white suits, shirts and shoes should be dropped (but what did I know?). It marked the Jam out as 'different' – not just ANOTHER punk band. Genius. A bonus of this style was that soon, girl Jam fans would turn up in school ties, their dads' white shirts, stocking and suspenders, without bothering to wear a skirt....

Every time I saw the Jam play, and it was like twice a week now, Paul had written another song. I would watch the soundcheck and think, they just get better and better. I distinctly remember the first time I heard 'Away From the Numbers'! ...I was blown away, Paul was coming up with fantastic stuff; I was still singing it when we went for a pre-gig drink round the corner from the 100 Club. When they played 'Numbers' that night it sounded perfect. As the gigs became more frequent the set got longer and 'Art School', 'Time For Truth' and 'Bricks and Mortar' were added.

My mates were in a group that I thought was the best band I had ever seen! At each gig the crowd got bigger and bigger, and residencies at the Red Cow, 100 Club and the Marquee followed. People were queuing round the block by the third week. I can remember the Red Cow emptying of pogoing fans, the dance floor being covered with enough small change to buy a round of drinks.

Word of mouth was also spreading fast.... Polydor soon spotted what I had known for months. The Jam had a recording contract. Everything shifted up a gear the day of the first *Top of the Pops*. I was in the boozer celebrating. Paul arrived later, saying "Why didn't you come round for me?" (How was I to know it was recorded the day before?). "Sorry mate... How was it?" I asked. "Yeah, ok", mumbled Paul (he was never one for getting too excited: maybe he just had total belief in his own ability).

I recall seeing him within hours of landing back in the UK following the first US tour. "How was the USA?" I asked. "IT SUCKS!" he laughed. That was the first time I had heard anyone use that phrase (it was 1978), but it summed up Paul's sense of humour....

We were all around 20 years old and would spend afternoons sitting around in Polydor Records, drinking their beer and watching videos of The Who. Within a year all our lives had changed forever....

Steve Carver

I first saw The Jam play live at The Hope & Anchor Pub in Islington in the summer of 1976. I remember '76 for two major reasons. One: it was the hottest summer ever recorded; and two, I was a Punk rocker! The Hope & Anchor was an hour's walk away from the college where I was studying music and drama, and was my regular hang-out. It was an exciting time for teenagers like me, who were bored shitless with the pomp and false grandeur of bands like Pink Floyd, Jethro Tull and Yes. The Hope was a tiny basement with ceilings so low that you risked concussion if you pogo'd, but it was definitely the place to see first hand the emergence of the new music genre that was being called New Wave.

The Jam were a lot smarter than the bands I was used to seeing at that time and I don't remember anyone 'gobbing' at them. I also vaguely remember Weller playing bass that night, or maybe I was just pissed?! I can't say that I was an 'instant fan'. But they were definitely more polished than some of the other bands I was seeing. My record collection at that time was mainly imported reggae and dub music, since the British music scene was littered with Glam rock and The Bay City Rollers – which unless you were a female, Tartan-wearing pierrot clown, didn't make it past my little sister's bedroom door!

The next time I saw The Jam play live was at London's 100 Club on the 9 November 1976. I remember the date well as it was the day before my 18th birthday, and my girlfriend at the time had acquired tickets as a treat. I seem to remember them having a keyboard player for that gig, or maybe I was just pissed again! The 100 Club was a bit more 'up-market' and was more used to a 'jazzy groovy' kind of cliental, with goatee bearded dudes and women called Clarissa, but the 100 Club would go on to become just as important as The Hope for breaking New Wave acts. Between 1976 and 1979, I saw some bands that would change the way we listened to music forever, including 999, the Sex Pistols, Siouxsie and the Banshees and The Dammed.

I didn't see The Jam play again until 1978, when they headlined at Wembley for The Great British Music Festival. My mum worked in the bar at Wembley and got me tickets for the whole three-day event. Making *Quadrophenia* was a bit strange as far as the collective music listening experience was concerned. I remember that The Who (unsurprisingly) were rarely off the turntable, also Sting and the boys [The Police] had just released 'Can't Stand Losing You' to critical acclaim, which was very exciting for us all. I was just starting to get serious about music at this point, and although Dire Straits were the hot new thing, I was more interested in virtuosos like the bass player Stanley Clarke. His album, *School Daze*, redefined for me how the bass guitar could be played and recorded.

I don't think I actually realized just how musically proficient The Jam were until I bought my first Jam album, *All Mod Cons*, at the end of '78. I must have worn out three styluses playing that record, and even to this day I find playing Foxton's incredible bass line on "A' Bomb in Wardour Street' really tricky!

My favourite albums are *In The City* for its pure raw energy, and *All Mod Cons*, 'cos it was my first Jam album. Plus it has one of the coolest sleeve covers ever! I still have a pair of those shoes that Bruce is wearing and will make sure I am cremated in them! Years later, whilst dating a future wife who was a session singer, I went to pick her up from a London recording studio one evening and was very excited to learn that she had been working on one of Bruce Foxton's solo projects. My fiancé introduced us and I was totally flabbergasted that he knew who I was! A truly magic moment indeed!

Gary Shail

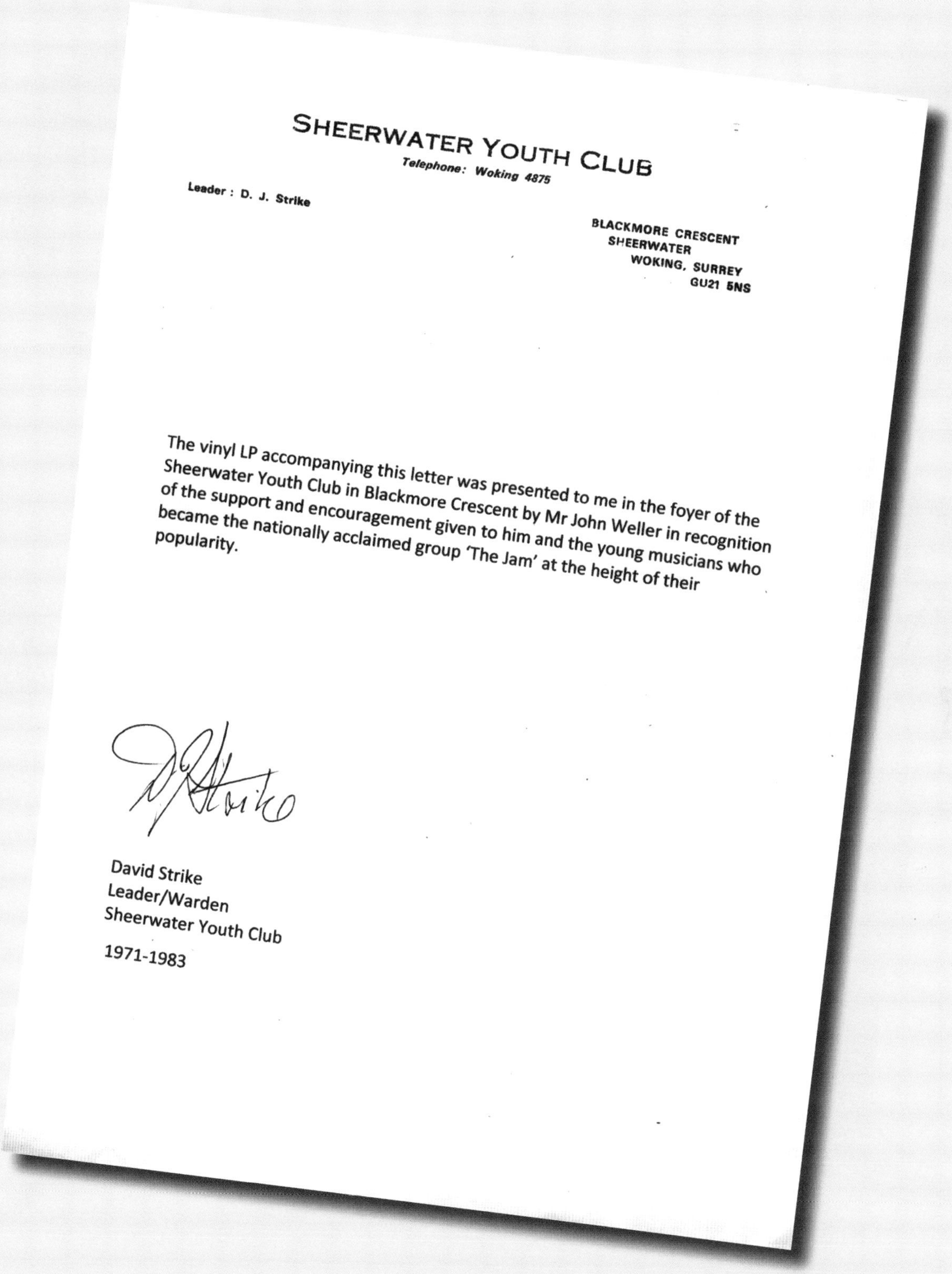

SHEERWATER YOUTH CLUB
Telephone: Woking 4875

Leader : D. J. Strike

BLACKMORE CRESCENT
SHEERWATER
WOKING, SURREY
GU21 5NS

The vinyl LP accompanying this letter was presented to me in the foyer of the Sheerwater Youth Club in Blackmore Crescent by Mr John Weller in recognition of the support and encouragement given to him and the young musicians who became the nationally acclaimed group 'The Jam' at the height of their popularity.

David Strike
Leader/Warden
Sheerwater Youth Club

1971-1983

1977 - ABOUT THE YOUNG IDEA

So what else was going on when The Jam were grabbing people's attention with their first release, *In the City*, in 1977? Having some understanding of that year helps give a sense of the context and public reaction to the band.

January was the month where the Sex Pistols found themselves dropped by their record label, EMI, as the Bill Grundy interview had the nation enthralled or outraged, and the moral majority scared for their children. It wouldn't be until 10th March that the band would sign to a new label, A&M. However, this contract was terminated six days later as a result of the band playing up to their Public Image.

Musically, the first half of 1977 saw The Clash release *The Clash* on CBS, Keith Richards was fined £750 for cocaine possession and Peter Green of Fleetwood Mac was committed to a mental hospital.

The Jam released their debut single 'In the City'/'Takin' My Love' in April. It wasn't until May that the debut album, *In the City*, would be released (the same month as *One of the Boys* – Roger Daltrey, *Love for Sale* – Boney M and *Sneakin' Suspicion* – Dr Feelgood) and November when their second album, *This is the Modern World*, also released. Alongside the two albums and debut single came two more singles: 'All around the World'/'Carnaby Street' and 'The Modern World'/'Sweet Soul Music'/'Back in My Arms'.

Other significant events of 1977 included the death of the King, Elvis, at his Gracelands home and Marc Bolan dying in a car crash in Barnes. The Sex Pistols also celebrated the Queen's Silver Jubilee in their own way and performed 'God Save the Queen' from a boat on the River Thames before the 'old bill' decided to nick everyone for being a threat to national security. The Queen just got on with things though, and continued her jubilee tour visiting places like New Zealand, Fiji and Tonga; working class communities rallied around, had street parties and waved flags for what seemed to be months (whilst the old man got pissed on Double Diamond and Mum got lively on Harvey's Bristol Cream).

On the flipside amongst the frivolity, the fire service went on strike, alongside London's undertakers (which meant 800 corpses were left unburied) and thousands of workers at British Leyland. The city also witnessed several clashes between the National Front (NF) and Anti-Fascists.

While the angst, aggression and desperation of the British public dominated the Nine O'Clock News, the IRA continued to make their presence known and the 'Yorkshire Ripper' continued to spread his evil. The M5 was opened and racehorse Red Rum won the Grand National for the third time. The same year, Liverpool won the league for the tenth time and their first European Cup but missed the treble as their bitter rivals Manchester United turned them over 2-1 in the FA Cup final. *Star Wars* burst onto the cinema screens and by the end of '77 every kid was clutching small plastic toys of the characters and space ships and some pathetic white, faintly-lit, plastic tubes called light sabres. (They were rubbish and you couldn't even hit anything or anyone with them because they would break too easily.) On the square box were comedy classics like *Porridge* and *Rising Damp*, weirdo kids' programme *Rent-a-Ghost*, and the one programme guaranteed to show talking dogs, children with obscure talent and penis-shaped vegetables, *That's Life*.

By the end of 1977, The Jam had made an impact on the young kids of the day and the music industry was taking notice of the best-sounding three-piece on the scene. But The Jam still had a long way to go if they were going to compete with the biggest UK selling single of the year: 'Mull of Kintyre' by Wings.

Chris Parry – Original Polydor A & R man

The signing of the band to demoing was done quite quickly – did they take to recording or was it hard work to start with?

The signing of The Jam was fast as I did not want to lose another group, having missed out on the Pistols, then The Clash. I wanted to quickly see how much of their then live set would work for an album. The fact was most of it did, so I could plan accordingly. Once I got Rick to simplify his drumming and understand that the first rule in the studio is time keeping, things went well. They all learnt quickly and were rightly excited.

Was Polydor a good company to work for?

Polydor were good to work for as far as I was concerned. Their structure gave the A&R man a big role in marketing and that, along with a special budget I was given to create a groundswell for The Jam (gig posters, etc), helped to accelerate things.

Were The Jam all 'heads down, work to do', or were there plenty of nights on the piss and having it large?

The Jam lived at home and I only saw them on the road or in the studio. They were normal with their alcohol and women. I remember Paul's favourite LP at the time was Exodus, by Bob Marley, for some reason. He also liked a lot of Soul and enjoyed the attention of the girls, as did Bruce. There was competition between him and Paul in having a 'Hampton' the night before. 'Hampton' came from an early hotel they stayed at.

Did you think even then, whilst doing 'In the City', that The Jam might end up being the biggest band in Britain?

It took Vic and I ages to get the excitement and energy into the mix for 'In the City'. So much so that I began to hate the song! Paul was in no doubt that he was going to be very famous in the UK. He told me so before the record came out in Polydor's local, The Lamb and Flag.

Were the gigs back then as violent as they're sometimes portrayed?

In those times violence was common at gigs. The scariest time I had was at the Newcastle Mayfair on a Friday night. The violence was palpable, inside and outside the hall. Kris Needs (a journalist) got his nose broken as we tried to get into the hall. We eventually got in via a police escort in riot gear. It didn't seem to bother The Jam nor John Weller. It bothered me, however. Some of the most violent were the bouncers themselves.

The Jam getting on TOTP with their first single, was that a stroke of luck or clever marketing?

Clever marketing. I worked out with the distribution manager at head office that the presale orders were unlikely to provide a Top 50 entry. We decided to put a block on the shipment and wait another week, sighting production problems to the retailers. The resulting retail inquiries pushed the presales up and the demand up, so the later shipment had the desired effect.

Were you happy with the outcome of *This is the Modern World* LP? (It got a kicking at the time, but most Jam fans actually love that album more than *In the City*.)

I really enjoyed the progress of the second album in a creative sense. Things were being written in the studio. I didn't know it had become popular over time, but that pleases me as it was a lot of hard work for all and I really encouraged Paul to try different things and allow different influences, say like the Beatles. I didn't like the time pressure I was up against to get an LP finished. Paul's Rickys [Rickenbacker guitars] were forever losing their tuning and a couple were smashed in the middle of a take by a very frustrated and angry Paul. We had to track the last remaining guitars around the UK. I told John we would not be doing it this way again. He had to lay off touring and allow time for Paul to write and reflect. I finished the last mix at around 7am and was on a flight to LA the same day with the band for their first US shows. I read a book on the flight. Paul and Bruce got hammered. They were close to being sent back by the immigration people.

Was being around the band like a whirlwind, as everything happened so quickly? Did being involved at Polydor and The Jam play havoc with your home life?

Before The Jam arrived I was out most nights. My home life was always a bit stressed. Weekends were more settled, but with The Jam exploding and my role as a proxy manager, time was tight.

What are your fave tracks off the first two albums and do you ever play the albums now?

Will come back to you on that. I have not listened since the time they were made. I will reacquaint and see if I still feel the same as then…

What was a typical day like, whilst working with the band? Where they a 9 to 5 or in the studio all night?

The Jam were a day time group when it came to laying tracks. Overruns and vocals were usually done in the night after a few drinks. They were not night hounds. A studio day would start around 10am and finish around midnight.

The story of *All Mod Cons* and the rejection of the first batch of songs is well documented, but when you actually told Paul 'it's shit', were you nervous, or was it an instant reaction to a playback?

I was very annoyed when I heard those demos as it was clear that John and the band had not learnt the lesson of being rushed into making Modern World. Worse still, there was little input from Paul. I suppose I could have been a little more diplomatic but I was not going to go down the same road again. I knew from Rick and Bruce's reaction that my days with the band in the studio were numbered, but it didn't bother me as I knew I couldn't possibly keep up all my responsibilities with the band as they became more famous.

'I Want to Paint' was a supposed track for *All Mod Cons* that has acheived mythical status now: can you remember any part of that song and what could you compare it to (if it existed)?

Is that Paul's contribution? Nothing on the original demo pleased me. Nothing is remembered. I do believe, however, that Paul's contribution was the best of a bad bunch. To this day I think Paul knew that he needed to allow the others to write but knew also that he was the real talent in that department, so he pulled back and allowed me to do his bidding. Whether he thought it out beforehand, it did work out like that. In the end, as we now all know.

Was it a relief to hand over to Vic Coppersmith and crack on with Fiction?

To be fair, I wanted to move on before I heard the demos and got Paul to concentrate on All Mod Cons. It was an exciting time for me, as I knew there was more I could do and now was the time to do it. I loved a lot about The Jam but I hated their Little Englander view of the world. I wanted to see more and work with bands that shared my sense of adventure and excitement of changing musical tastes in foreign countries. When it was decided for me to leave the band, I knew it would work out better for them and I also knew my time to move on had arrived. It was a sense of excitement I felt, not relief.

The JAM

Most Rock & Roll
Maximum Rhythm & Blues

Rick Buckler
Drums
Backing vocals

Bruce Foxton
Bass Guitar
Backing vocals

Paul Weller
Rhythm & lead guitar
Vocals

John Weller
Manager
Woking 64717

The JAM

Photographs taken at
The Greyhound,
Fulham Palace Rd.
Courtesy of Bill Axe

Rick Buckler   Paul Weller   Bruce Foxton

'In the City'/'Takin' My Love'

That was based on the album cover, with the same background as the tiles and the shots we did at the time. The live shots were to get some action into the cover. I used the Punk/fanzine approach of torn corners and sticky tape to get away from flat studio photography. It was all about establishing the band and the logo from the first single. The live pictures are taken by Walt Davidson, who was an old-school photographer that had shot a lot of 60s blues artists.

In the City LP

I had this feeling that the band would be down in the subway, maybe in a toilet. In the studio I built a wall, put the tiles on and then I sprayed The Jam logo onto the tiles, immediately before taking the picture – as if they'd just done it themselves and they'd sat down against it. I very much wanted it to be a statement, very graphic, black-and-white, like a newspaper cutting. And the idea on the back cover was 'let's smash it up a bit' to give it a slightly different graphic quality. That's how The Jam logo came about.

The spray paint idea was slightly Punkish, but the fact that they wore suits and it was black-and-white took it somewhere else. I had prepared the logo in my head, if it had gone wrong I would have been in trouble. That was the first time I sprayed the logo. I think we did this in the photographer Martyn Goddard's studio.

Looking at this now, I loved the attitudes and how young do they look? Rick looks fantastic! On the back Weller is on tip-toes 'windmill' swinging on the guitar – very Townshend. I loved the shade of blue against the black and white. Also, the signatures look great. I still think it's a great sleeve, but I'm biased.

My favourite tracks off it are 'In the City', 'Away from the Numbers' and 'Sounds from the Streets'. "In the city there's a thousand things I want to say to you." Brilliant.

It seemed like they always had problems with their live sound, every gig I went to! Even in places like The Rainbow on the 'White Riot' tour. I particularly remember that gig as the seats were ripped up once The Clash came on stage. From the moment The Jam got on stage Weller got the hump, and the band were very aggressive. The way he played his guitar and sang had an air of menace, and that channelled itself to the audience.

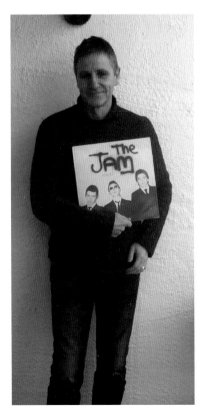

I bet you wish you had a penny for every time you've seen that logo?!
I wish I had a penny for every one of those pin badges that sold! They sold thousands upon thousands.

Early memories of Rick and Bruce?
They were a band in the beginning, all new to the game, but once Paul started to establish himself as the leader and the main songwriter, they became sidekicks, I suppose. Because John was managing it was hard for him not to favour his son, naturally.

Bill Smith

IN THE CITY [Review by John Reed]

A New Zealand-born A&R man with a nose for what was happening in London, Polydor's Chris Parry had already missed out on the Sex Pistols and The Clash. When Shane McGowan recommended that he see The Jam, he wasn't about to let it happen a third time.

On 24 February 1977, Polydor announced they had signed The Jam. Parry rushed the band into Polydor's Stratford Place Studios to work on their debut album. "I was keen on production but I needed an experienced engineer and brought in Vic Smith," Parry explained. Smith was one of Polydor's in-house engineers, a veteran of the recording industry who'd worked with the Rolling Stones. "Like many new bands, they had an album's worth of songs and were already playing them," Chris continued. "We just wanted to capture the feel of what The Jam were about, not polish it. Paul wanted it rough and ready. He liked Rickenbacker guitars, but they're difficult to tune, so he ended up throwing them across the studio!"

Eleven days later the LP was completed, to be fan-fared by a single. On 29 April, The Jam's first single reached the shops. 'In the City' began with an angry, stabbing three-chord guitar riff, then Foxton's pounding, descending bass-line kicked in, before Buckler's snare-drum roll signalled the start of the song proper. It mirrored the live Jam sound — harsh and energetic, but still rooted in melody, Weller's voice blustering and hoarse but still tuneful. A middle-eight began with the sound of plectrum scraping against strings to create an atonal burst reminiscent of the second half of The Who's 'Anyway, Anyhow, Anywhere'. The lyrics owed more to 'My Generation', although proclamations like "I wanna tell you, About the young idea" and "But you'd better listen man, Because the kids know where it's at" were clumsier than Townshend's more considered prose.

Weller was keen to emphasise the line about "a thousand men in uniforms", suggesting the song was about an innocent victim of police brutality, about the police beating up and killing for no reason. It wasn't — or, at least, that wasn't the main thrust of the lyric — but this is a poignant example of Weller's desire to take the political initiative offered by The Clash's Joe Strummer. The single's B-side needed less explaining: 'Takin' My Love' was a more aggressive version of the band's earliest-known recording, Punked-up with perhaps Paul's most blatant debt to that tense, staccato R&B guitar style popularised by Wilko Johnson.

In the City followed in mid May. "Just the stage act we were playing at the time, which we just put down on vinyl," was how Weller accurately summed it up. Clocking in at just over half-an-hour, the 12 songs were played at a furious pace — attracting such adjectives as "hurried", "bleak", "chaotic", "intense" and "highly-charged". Vic Smith and Chris Parry created an incredibly 'live' production — the sound isn't dissimilar, for example, to the best-known early live bootleg of the band, from an August '77 100 Club gig. But buried beneath this dense, sometimes impenetrable sound were some definite peaks and troughs in Weller's songwriting.

Older compositions like 'I Got By in Time' (which included a verse about the passing of Paul's close friendship with Steve Brookes) and 'Non-Stop Dancing' (inspired by Weller's visits to those Bisley Pavilion Northern Soul all-nighters) had a tuneful Motown feel; while cover versions of Larry Williams' 'Slow Down' (no doubt discovered via The Beatles' Long Tall Sally EP) and 'Batman Theme' (beefed up by The Who on their 1966 EP, Ready Steady Who) were pedestrian. 'Art School' was punchy three-chord Punk, which Weller probably named after the education of Townshend/Ray Davies/John Lennon — Punk = '60s beat. And 'I've Changed My Address' echoed the message of The Who's 'Much Too Much', of giving a girlfriend the shove when marriage beckons.

Inspired by what Weller described as "urban politics", those lyrics which seemed to be plundered from The Clash's political agenda have rightly been criticised for being trite — but they are no more so than those of most of The Jam's contemporaries. The 'Bricks And Mortar' lament about the faceless urban development was inspired by a series of upheavals endured by Woking town centre. 'Time For Truth' launched a direct attack on the Labour government of the day, its jibes at "Uncle Jimmy" prompted by Prime Minister James Callaghan's visit to Woking in December '76. The song also latched onto the death in police custody of suspect Liddle Towers in late 1976, after the coroner's verdict of 'misadventure' led the news media to demand a full enquiry. Towers became something of a cause celèbré, although Weller's calls to "Bring forward them six pigs/We wanna see them swing so high — Liddle Towers!", lacked political finesse, to say the least.

One of the album's highlights was 'Sounds from the Street'. Influenced by the vocal harmonies that had crept into some of The Who's mid-60s music courtesy of surf fan Keith Moon, it was a celebration of British youth which, like 'In the City', centred on London's nascent Punk scene — of "young bands playing, young kids diggin'". When Weller sang, "I know I come from Woking, and you say I'm a fraud/But my heart is in the city, where it belongs," it was difficult not to believe him.

In the City harboured one true masterpiece. From its opening power chords, the claustrophobic 'Away from the Numbers' was compelling. There was none of the unifying message heard elsewhere on the LP; instead, Weller vowed that "this link's breaking away from the chain". Too much could be made of lines like "I'm gonna break away and find what life is" — after all, Paul had never left the security blanket of his parents' support — but there does seem to be a grim determination to look beyond existing boundaries, onwards and upwards, and away from the 'numbers', Sixties Mod slang for the throng. Together with 'Sounds From The Street', the medium pace of 'Away from the Numbers', helped by a dreamy middle-eight, perfectly contrasted with the rest of the LP's breakneck delivery.

(Adapted from the Paul Weller biography *My Ever Changing Moods*, by John Reed, courtesy of Omnibus Press)

'In the City'

To start this story I first have to explain that in around 1975 I became obsessed with The Who, chiefly due to hearing 'My Generation' on the soundtrack to a film – *That'll Be The Day* – or its follow-up, *Stardust*. But I was always acutely aware that it belonged to another generation – not mine – and yearned for something to call out to me in the same way. My Who obsession grew with the purchase of *Quadrophenia*. Not just the music, but that book that came with it, showing all those cool-looking kids in smart gear – at a time when everyone was wearing flares and big collars and big hair, it looked like pictures from another planet. One I wanted to be part of. I just didn't know how.

Fortunately for me (and thousands of others, as it transpired) a kid in Woking, just a couple of years older than me, knew exactly how. On a Saturday morning in 1977 I was to finally experience the seismic moment I'd yearned for.

People of a certain generation always say they knew where they were when Kennedy was assassinated, or when England won the World Cup. For other generations it might be where they first heard The Smiths or the Stone Roses, or where they were when the Twin Towers were hit. I remember exactly where I was the first time I heard 'In The City'.

I'm 16 and I've run myself a bath and switched on Alan 'Fluff' Freeman's *Saturday Morning Show* on Radio One. I've just eased myself in when it happens. The most electrifying intro to a song I've heard since that moment when I heard 'My Generation' for the first time. It was as close as you could get to an epiphany without the bright light shining down from heaven and the main man smiling down from the cross. THIS was what I'd been dreaming of hearing, for MY generation.

It had such an effect on me that when 'Fluff' said it was available in the shops today, I just had to have it there and then. I jump out of the bath, barely drying myself, dressed quickly, grabbed some money and was out the door shouting, "See you in a bit" to my Mum's question, "Where are you going in a rush?" I then legged it down to the nearest record shop as quick as I could and breathlessly asked, "Have you... got... 'In the City' ...by a group called... The Jam... please?"

I got the record home and put the arm up on the record player so that it just repeat played over and over until I knew the words off by heart. Then I flipped it over and checked out the B-side, 'Takin' My Love', which I was pleased to find sounded like Dr Feelgood – another band I liked.

I was aware of the Pistols, of course, and loved them, but this was the song and the band that made me really believe. At last I felt I had a band I could proudly call my own, who looked cool as fuck – the picture sleeve cover blew me away. They looked like the Mods in those *Quadrophenia* shots – they had the energy, the attitude, everything. I'd finally found what I was looking for; all the pieces of the jigsaw.

Incredibly, I discovered that I had more in common with the leader of the band, Paul Weller, than I first thought. I read in an interview in the *NME* or *Sounds* that he too made that same 'My Generation' discovery. Being a hell of a lot cooler than me, he also knew what to do with it: form a band.

The greatest band in the world as it happens.

Diz

'All Around the World'/'Carnaby Street'

Again another studio shot, with me spraying the logo onto the plastic orange background. The footwear came from Carnaby Street, I think, along with the suits. If I remember rightly some old guy used to make the suits for them in one of the tailor's shops nearby. I went to quite a few of the gigs on the first tour. I liked the band from the first time I saw them, and immersed myself in their music. These days, I would have done shots of them every night and put them up on Facebook with a daily blog. From 'In the City' onwards they had a following. It didn't take long for it to gain momentum either – hence 'All Around The World' reaching number 13. *Direction, Reaction, Creation* at the bottom under the band works well – very post-modern.

This is the Modern World LP

This sleeve was heavily influenced by Situationism (a late '60s early '70s political movement) and I see as very post-modern. We shot it underneath the Westway roundabout down by the five-a-side pitches near the old White City. Obviously the Pete Townshend/Who influence is high and Paul had this idea to put the arrows on his jumper, so we cut them out of gaffa tape. This was taken using flash lighting and daylight, shot in late summer. I liked the idea of a flash shot in daylight: this gave it rather strong shadows, which was very important.

The reason we went there was for the graphic quality of the angles, the post they are leaning against, the overhead road, the tower blocks. They're as important as the band for me. Trying to put them into an environment and a situation hopefully summed up what the title was about. I definitely wanted to use that location, as I drove round there quite a lot. My friend, photographer Gered Mankowitz – famous for Jimi Hendrix and Rolling Stones shots – took the pictures. As soon as I knew the title I wanted to find "the modern world". The idea is to show an underlying aggression, which I liked – the flash and the shadows make the band look tough.

On the flip, again I did the logo and Bruce really is jumping high. I love that shot – it really represents the band at that time. The inner sleeve illustrations were done by an illustrator called Conny Jude – I gave her the titles and some of the lyrics and she matched them up.

'London Girl' and 'This is the Modern World' were the stand out tracks. I couldn't see why it got the slagging it did. Maybe it was 'second album syndrome', maybe it came out too quickly and maybe not enough time was spent on it, but I thought it was a good record.

Again, it still stands up and I'm proud of it.

'The Modern World'/'Sweet Soul Music'/'Back in My Arms Again'

This would have been taken around the same time as the previous single and I'd add a bit of a Warhol influence to keep a whole graphic quality around it.

Again, a photo by Martyn Goddard, who did a lot of the early photos in and around Carnaby Street. The band styled themselves completely. Great track. Paul thought The Jam was the best band ever and couldn't understand if people didn't like them.

Bill Smith

THIS IS THE MODERN WORLD LP [Review by Joey Saunders]

The age old tradition known as the 'difficult' second album, when all the songs that have been prepared for a while go into the great debut LP and what's left over (and also made on the hurry up) sometimes send a band either sideways or backwards. Most thought the band had gone truly sideways at the time, in the six months between *In the City* and *This is the Modern World*. The album only spent five weeks in the charts and in hindsight things didn't look as rosy for the band as Polydor first thought. Especially as John had negotiated a better deal for the band and the record company must have hoped to capitalise on the blistering live shows and growing audiences.

It's only really in the last few years that most Jam fans have gone, "Oi, you soppy journalists. Although not perfect, it's got some fantastic songs, some truly great insights into Weller falling in love for the first time, the influence of the pop art poets of the 1960s in the lyrics and the band pushing the sound, vision and power chords up a gear. So do one…"

Side 1 opens up with the title track, fucks and all. That unmistakeable intro, where in seconds Weller has already inferred that what's gone before is now irrelevant, then bursts into life on a Rickenbacker-fuelled two minutes of power pop. You sense it's the opportunity Weller had long been yearning for; to stick it to anybody that ever doubted him. Like a lively session on the psychiatrist's couch, he unburdens himself with a real sense of joy in his voice: "That one day I would be on top, and I'd look down upon the map". Musically, it shows a degree more control from the first album, suggesting that months of gigging had tightened the band's playing even further.

Next up is the Foxton penned 'London Traffic', which manages to douse the flames of momentum instantly. A ridiculously rudimentary observation of the capital's issue with… traffic. "No one knows the answer" states Foxton, and neatly forgets to offer a solution, apart from "taking the traffic elsewhere". It's not exactly Nietzsche. Onwards and upwards to the Weller penned 'Standards', which is the first showing of his literary influences. Taking its lead from George Orwell's *Nineteen Eighty-Four*, Weller playfully takes the part of the government and barks out the warnings from those up on high to him and his generation.

It's at the point that we reach 'Life From a Window' that things start to get really interesting. A plaintive stab at a piano ushers in a beautiful piece of reflective Who-esque pop: "Looking from a hilltop, watching from a lighthouse, just dreaming". In the space of the opening line, the sound and outlook of the band have taken a quantum leap forward. Played with great skill and restraint, it was probably the first clear sign that the band was a cut above from many of the other bands of that era.

'The Combine' comes back to the theme touched on in 'Away From the Numbers', the sense of not wanting to be a part of the machinery, wanting something more from life. In fact, 2011's riots had me thinking of 'The Combine', as social network sites were alive with — shock horror — status updates from the safety of their homes. Lyrically it's basic, with references to Wetherfield's finest, Ena Sharples, *News at Ten* and Page 3 girls. The first half of the record winds up with possibly Foxton's most bizarre offering to the Jam catalogue in 'Don't Tell Them You're Sane', a tale of a young boy wrongfully put in an asylum. This and 'London Traffic' made it abundantly clear as to where the songwriting skills of the band lay and were the fruits of having to put out two albums in the space of half a year.

Side 2 opens with the Weller/Waller colaboration, 'In the Street Today', with Rick's tribal drumming and Weller's "GO!" pushing the pogo level up a notch as the Rickenbacker's get urban in the track's simplistic but effective message of bored kids, murders at football matches, fools in high places and the same old 'no one wants to pick up the reins and push people to a higher plane'. "It's all so sickening and we're so satisfied"… Indeed.

Not one of Weller's best, 'London Girl' tells of a girl arriving in London town who thought the streets were paved with gold and fame and fortune, but ends up on the streets, not washing for three weeks and begging for cigs and beer. The Who influence looms large with the power chords and crashing cymbals being brought home by Bruce's sympathetic final verse, "I don't condemn what you've done, I know what it is to be young".

'I Need You (For Someone)' is a marvellous unsung hero in The Jam's repertoire. The bass opens up the track and the single strum through the opening verse with the lyrics pointing at the writer needing his girlfriend by his side, even though he can be a right moody sod. The Woking harmonies carry the song through in similar fashion to 'Sounds From the Street', off the earlier album, *In The City*.

'Here Comes the Weekend' is one of the classic stick work/school up your pipe — the weekend's here and we're gonna 'ave it! Do something constructive with your weekend, paint on the smell of soap (ever wondered if Rick wore Brut 33 back then?) and go pick a girl up. The statement of intent and uplift always inspires when you're driving home, knowing your local boozer has got a 2-for-1 offer for the ladies and the chances of getting amongst it are in your favour.

'Tonight At Noon' is based on the Adrian Henri poem, which appeared in the *Mersey Collection* poetry book in 1967. Weller finds a subtlety, sensitivity and a subject matter away from the numbers, away from the bile that surrounded London streets as the tribes fought each other because of different tastes in haircuts, music and clobber. The acoustic-led track again showed a maturity and intelligence that you didn't get with other bands of the period, like The Boomtown Rats, Sham 69 and Generation X.

'In the Midnight Hour' is a straight cover sung at breakneck speed, featuring a sexy bit of harmonica playing. It got largely ignored by most casual listeners, but what most people failed to recognise when The Jam did a cover was the knock-on effect it had on the young fans. Most will check out who the strangely named Wilson Pickett is, buy a single or album by said guy, and then discover the beautiful world of Stax Records and its immense back catalogue.

Love, life, lunacy, bored violent teenage kicks and homelessness all packed into 32 minutes of vinyl, with a cracking front sleeve of a young band looking cool, clean and hard. Love it.

'All Around the World'

The cover shot: three blokes, black suits, white shirts, black ties and dirty, stage-worn Gibson shoes. Weller bored, Buckler in his square sunglasses and Foxton indifferent. The yellow plastic with the spray-painted logo is stark and bold, like the band, and exactly like the songs contained on this piece of plastic.

This, the second single from The Jam, crashes in to your consciousness like a steam roller versus a pack of Smiths salt 'n' shake crisps. That drum roll, the Rickenbacker strummed in abject anger, the shout of "Oi!" This is a song not to be messed with. Paul and Bruce take turns in spitting out triumphant lines – "What's the point in saying destroy?", "We wanna direction" and "Youth explosion" among many others.

Guitar crashing in angular passion, bass thumping along indignantly and drums scoring out that brutal back beat: this is not a single, this is a fucking revelation, a call to arms, a challenge to see the world from a differing viewpoint than the average Punk fan was being told to at the time by the nihilist peers of The Jam. At just under two-and-a-half minutes this song leaves an indelible mark on the listener's mind; it's no throwaway tune, there's a message to be heard, The Jam "want a new life for everyone". All around the World they've been looking for you!

Flip the cover over and what do we have? Same yellow plastic but a head shot of the band, different clothes but the same faces and the legend, in typeset, cut and pasted (quite literally) to the bottom: 'DIRECTION – REACTION – CREATION'.

This is 'Carnaby Street', a nod to the famous street's fabulous past, an ode to a finer time in its history as by '77 the street had seen better days, was in decline and just full of shops selling tat. Bruce does vocal duties here, his finest vocal for The Jam, if you ask me. The same sound is going on here – a little more laid back, maybe, but Weller's same cutting guitar strikes are balanced by the rhythmic brilliance of Rick and Bruce working hard together to produce that sound that we all know and love so well. Weller lays some backing vocals here and there, some echoes giving it an air of being sung in an empty street, vocals bouncing off shop windows. This is 'just' a B-side, but as with all Jam B-sides it eclipses many contemporaries by the bucket load.

This single 'only' reached Number 13 in the charts, back in a time when reaching Number 13 with your second single was a huge achievement. It's one of my favourite Jam singles, certainly of those up to (but not including) 'Tube Station', and still makes the hairs on the back of my neck stand up when I hear it. Everything about it just screams MY FAVOURITE BAND!

Youth explosion!

A new direction

We want a reaction

Inflate creation

Looking for new!

Indeed!

Col Baker

Hastings, 1977

…Didn't we have a nice time….

"Have guitar, will travel", was John Weller's motto. So when the group was offered a gig as a last-minute replacement for Johnny Thunders and the Heartbreakers, he snatched at it. In the van we jumped, off for an away day in sunny Hastings by the sea. I think it was a Saturday, and I remember buying water pistols and generally mucking about on the pier – these were the times of our lives.

We set up for the gig and went for a beer and a bite to eat. At 7 o'clock the doors opened and punters started to file in: the usual mix of Punks, Mods and local kids. AND A BUNCH OF HELLS ANGELS! Shit! The feeling was tense, but what did I know, maybe it was like this every week?

Weller senior strode on stage and gave his usual, "Let's hear it for the greatest rock and roll group in the fuckin' world …… THE JAM!!" Paul, Bruce and Rick bounded on stage, looking sharp in their black-and-white suits. They started with 'This is the Modern World', and the audience went nuts, except for the motorcycle gang. The Jam are nothing like Johnny Thunders and the Heartbreakers (thank fuck!).

By the second number the 'Rockers' had positioned themselves at the front, sat on the edge of the stage, with their backs to the group, staring at the audience, daring anyone to dance…. Now I'm not a big bloke (or particularly brave), but I had come a long way, and The Jam were my favourite band, so as we did at every gig, myself, Tony Pilott and Dave Waller started to jig about. Remember this was 1977: Punk rock was in its infancy, and the way to go was pogo!

"You some sort of kangaroo?" sneered a hairy-arsed hells angel, who had clearly never been to a London Punk rock club. I decided to ignore him and just moved back a few feet to enjoy the greatest rock and roll band in the fucking world. 'Art School', 'Changed My Address', 'Batman' and of course, 'In the City' for the encore, and they were gone….

After the show, we were having the usual post-gig debate, when suddenly Bruce hurled a beer bottle at the wall. IT STUCK! The bottle went straight into the plaster wall and stayed put. We all picked up whatever was close and threw it – bottles, glasses and a chair hit the wall with varying degrees of success. I must admit it was a bit messy.

Eventually the promoter arrived with the money. "Jesus, what happened in here?" he asked. "It was them blokes in black leather jackets," we said, thinking on our feet. "I wouldn't muck about with them." Amazingly he seemed happy with that explanation and coughed up the readies. Another great gig and a brilliant day out. And a bit of luck: Chris Parry turned up to check out his new signings and gave me a lift all the way back to sunny Woking. It had been a busy day, I slept all the way home (sorry Chris).

Steve Carver

'The Modern World'

Following the relative success of 'All Around the World', The Jam's third single was 'The Modern World'. Although at this time, still regarded by many as a Punk band, despite their clean-cut image and traditional suits, Weller used this track both to make a strong statement of his Mod roots and to dismiss the old guard that had come before. The use of the term 'Modern' referenced both the Modernist (Mod) culture of the '60s, with which Weller was fascinated, and the here-and-now modern generation to which he belonged. This reference to Mod culture would again be emphasized when the song was subsequently performed live, as the words, "This is the modern world" were often abbreviated to "This is the *Mod* world"!

Lasting just 2 minutes 30 seconds, the song packs in a powerful message. It begins with a full-on drum and guitar assault, and Weller delivering the title lyrics in such a way as to emphasize that all that had gone before was irrelevant to him, particularly those who had had so little impact on his education. It moves forward with a fast tempo, intensity, and with screeching guitar chords. The lyrics reflect an arrogance: as Weller claims, "I've learnt more than you'll ever know", and sticks two metaphorical fingers up to the teachers "Who said he'd be nothing". It also demonstrates his contempt for those who had questioned the band's position in the music industry. Through the song Weller, affected by early criticism of the band's Mod image, offers a retort to the critics and invites them to "Say what you like 'cause I don't care". However his proclamation, "I don't give two fucks about your review" was slightly changed on the single's release, and replaced with "I don't give a damn about your review".

Although the message may have been heard, many critics did not appreciate the track and it came to be regarded as a disappointment. With the main riff having been copied from The Who's 'Pictures of Lily', some labeled the track as merely ordinary, and not representing any development from the band's initial material.

The single was backed by three tracks. Cover versions of Arthur Conley's 'Sweet Soul Music' and The Supremes' 'Back in My Arms Again' both reflect Weller's early Motown and Soul influences, whilst 'Bricks and Mortar' was a track the band had been playing for some time. These tracks were recorded live at London's 100 Club earlier that year, initially with the intention (by Polydor) of releasing a live album. But the use of these 'old' songs led some to ask: is Weller's creativity already drying up?

All of the criticism now seems well placed as the single failed to capitalise on the success of 'All Around the World', reaching only Number 36 in the UK singles chart. Weller may have been affected by this, as it was a Foxton penned track that was released next.

Andy Winter

I arrived at the University in Kent, Canterbury, in October 1976 aged 19, just as Punk was stirring in London – the *NME* and *Sounds* were full of the Pistols, The Damned and The Clash, and a Punk scene was clearly coming together. I'd avidly read about the bands but not seen any of them. I assumed that loads of new students would be into this exciting new musical world, and keen to see off the pomp rock and disco that was everywhere in 1976. I was wrong. Our fresher's ball was headlined by Shakin' Stevens & The Sunsets, and a load of 30-plus Margate Teds turned up, unwanted and threatening. Our college had a weekly soul disco and most of the 'big' bands were tired old has-been acts like Renaissance, Steeleye Span and Larry Coryell.

Partly driven by a determination to get some better bands at our university, and partly because DJing was allegedly a good way to meet drunk women, I ended up on our college entertainments committee and was soon offered a string of small bands, some of whom had had a music press review. One I'd read a couple of excellent reviews about, a Punk/Mod hybrid called The Jam, were offered to me by their agent Pete Hawkins for £50 (about the going rate for unknown bands midweek) and so I booked them for Monday 14th March 1977. Some websites say the gig was on Friday 11th, but they are wrong, it was definitely Mon 14th.

Hawkins rang me a week later to push the price up to £60, after "pressure from the band's manager" because of the positive press they had been getting. Somewhere in the loft I have the signed contract between myself and John Weller. In the weeks between the booking and the show, The Jam signed a record contract, had just gone in the recording studio and were getting lots of music press coverage.

The Jam turned up late at the college having driven from Woking (pre M25) in a battered old van containing the band and the burly middle-aged guy – Paul Weller's dad, John, their manager and driver. Paul Weller's first comment on seeing the tiny bar they were playing in was, "another shitty Pete Hawkins gig". They were clearly unhappy about the money they were getting, and also the size of the venue. They were staying the night in our college committee room, I suspect so John Weller could have a drink.

I do remember they seemed very young and Paul Weller was very hyped up before going on stage – nothing was right. His dad got the £60 cash straight away – John Weller apparently kept up this preference for payment as quickly as possible, and in cash, through the many years he managed his son's various musical line-ups. Rick Buckler and Bruce Foxton were pretty offhand and withdrawn before the show, though I guess looking back that was probably nerves.

There was no support, just a disco. I was the hapless DJ. There were almost no Punk records out, so I guess those that were (The Damned, The Stranglers) were played. I know I also played most of the first Who LP (*My Generation*), which I had got on import, and a bit of Motown, having read about Weller's interest in all things Mod. Not that it made any difference, as nobody danced. It wasn't till the band came on that people wandered round the corner from the bar to see what was happening.

The Jam came on, filling the tiny stage, followed by a quick introduction and into the first number (probably 'In the City'?). Within a couple of minutes their PA, which was extremely rickety, promptly blew. They didn't have a 'proper' roadie and for a while it looked like the show might be cancelled – if it had been, I didn't fancy my chances of getting £60 back from Weller senior. Fortunately a fellow student (ironically a heavy metal fan) wired up the sound through the very rudimentary disco speakers and the band came back on stage.

Given the band were still very inexperienced, and the PA was extremely basic, the next 45 minutes were truly astonishing. Weller channelled his anger, energy and frustration into his guitar work and singing in an archetypal front-man performance, and Foxton and Buckler showed similar anger. The only numbers I distinctly remember are 'Sweet Soul Music' and 'Batman', but I'm pretty sure they played the whole *In the City* LP, which was released only two months later. Bizarrely, some people left after a couple of numbers, but I think it was clear to most people present that we were witnessing something very special.

They were pouring with sweat and completely knackered when they came off stage. We got talking about The Who and Motown and in the common room we played the first Who LP again. My lasting impression was that Paul Weller's commitment to the band, and to music in general, was overwhelming. Little did I realise how overwhelming. We sat up chatting with the band and a few locals for ages, until John Weller said time for bed (bed being settees or the floor in a room stinking of stale fags and beer). They drove off back to Woking at 6am, and I'm pretty sure Weller senior then went straight to work.

Looking back, we hosted the band at exactly the right time, because their breakthrough was absolutely meteoric. Within two months they had recorded and released their first single and before the end of May that was followed by the *In the City* LP. Also within two months they were second on the bill to The Clash (and ahead of The Buzzcocks and Subway Sect) on the 'White Riot' tour, and I was lucky enough to see the second of two Rainbow shows in early May. The rest is history.

Tim Rolls

I first heard and saw The Jam on *Top of The Pops* in May 1977. I was 10 at the time and back then, TOTPs was for many the weekly fix of all that was new (or not so new) in the all important 'pop' charts. I say 'all important' because, not unlike the football league tables, the 'pop' charts were a measure of the progress of your favourite acts and tracks.

Whilst there were only three of them, I distinctly remember thinking as they played 'In The City' that May evening that their black suits and Rickenbacker guitars reminded me of The Beatles. However, unlike The Beatles, they jumped around and were clearly aggressive – like some of the new Punk stuff my elder brother had been playing at that time.

It was all good, not least because since discovering the Fab Four a few years earlier I'd become obsessed, pouring over every album, sleeve, lyric, etc. However, the arrival of The Jam couldn't have been better timed as my first musical love affair was waning simply because the Fab Four were no more. The Jam's appeal was cemented when, having made it home in time from school to catch *Marc* (the Marc Bolan show) that July, I witnessed another incendiary performance, this time of the new single, 'All Around The World'.

By now I was beginning to soak up every detail: the length of their trousers, their hair (credited to someone called Schumi), the black-and-white shoes and button down shirts. With the arrival of 'The Modern World' single in October, I'd added Holland–Dozier–Holland to my list of people to search out, a list which already boasted Hefti and Williams, who'd all penned songs they'd covered. It would be the former that would lead me to discover Motown – a love that endures to this day.

And so it was that like many I came to follow the band. In interviews they always seemed to recommend the music, books and art of others – which just added to the experience – and trust was quickly established between fan and band. Singles were ordered in advance, saved for and collected on the day of release, to then be played and flipped and played and flipped and played and flipped… whilst the sleeve design, pictures and info were studied.

And then you'd wonder how they'd do. The charts were watched, music paper reviews read, the knocks and the plaudits logged. *Sounds*, then *Melody Maker* and the *NME*, of course! 'Down in the Tube Station At Midnight' going straight to Number 15 still amazes me, 'Strange Town' matching it a delight, but 'When You're Young' stalling at Number 17! It was 'The Eton Rifles' the following autumn/winter that changed everything. Eton Rifles, eating fucking trifles, so many were singing it. The same was true of the next salvo, arriving four months later. 'Going Underground' getting straight in at Number 1 brought elation, vindication, and most of all, pride; something akin to a Premiership title win.

Albums were a big spend, and when I play *All Mod Cons*, *Setting Sons* or *Sound Effects* now, for a split second I can taste Christmas Day '78, '79 or '80.

It was in November 1980 that I finally saw my first live Jam gig, at Bracknell Sports Centre. Gigs were violent then, but unlike Sham 69 before and The Specials afterwards, the show went off without incident. Perhaps support act The Piranhas, whose fun single 'Tom Hark' had just hit the charts, was the critical factor in this brittle *détente*.

In terms of achievement there was still much to come and to be shared. They inspired great loyalty and in return you got great inspiration and entertainment. Yet by the time the split was announced I felt a sense of relief. The music was still great but I was 17 and needed something new. I'd grown up with them but needed to fly, to 'leave home'.

Back then (as with youth now, I guess), you defined yourself by the team you supported, the music you liked and (increasingly) the clothes you wore. And so it was that the fortunes of your team and favourite band and the cut of your hair and clothes came to have great significance. The Jam were hugely significant and consequently 30 years after they split their legacy still resonates.

Johnny Chandler

Battersea Town Hall, 27.6.77

Battersea Town Hall was sold out, too many people trying to get in. A bunch of us managed to force open a window that led into the kitchens downstairs, the security guys ran down and tried grabbing bods but the tidal wave of peeps meant that they just got shoved out of the way. We ran up into the main hall, where the sweat was dripping off the walls, high octane buzz and the band stormed it.

Ray Gange

The Jam were a people's band. They were one of those bands you bought into hook, line and sinker. You were into the records, the clothes, the whole lifestyle, really.

I went to school just off the Edgware Road near Lisson Grove. The Beatles were the big band for me – then I devoured the Stones and The Who, around the age of 14 or 15. I read anything I could about them from the local library. I then saw the Pistols doing the Bill Grundy interview on telly; and truth be told, I was actually a little bit frightened of them. I started buying the music papers at the start of '77. I read about The Jam and thought, this is the band I've been waiting for! They looked great and Paul stood out with what he was into – and it was what I was looking for. Being in the centre of town was perfect for getting to gigs. We hijacked our school fanzine and called it *The Modern World*. I used it as a blag to meet my favourite bands.

I saw the band first, before I actually met Paul, at Battersea Town Hall. Seven or eight of my mates got the 16 bus to Victoria and then a 77 to Battersea. I've got the poster up on my front room wall. This was around the time of the Jubilee. We got there really early at 6pm. We were at the front of the queue and there was a big rumour going round that some Teds were coming down to kick off, which made it even more exciting!

I remember walking into the venue and it had big drape curtains. My dad told me to put cotton wool in my ears as it was going to be so loud. I thought the support band, The Boys, were great and then the atmosphere built up and then The Jam coming on – it was like, 'Oh Yes!!' and in my mind's eye I can still picture it now: I remember them doing pretty much the whole of *In the City* (including the single, twice), plus 'Carnaby Street', 'The Modern World' and 'All Around the World'. It was love at first sight, just the best.

I remember coming out of that gig and reliving it on the bus home and the next day thinking we should do a fanzine. Anyway, one of my old *Melody Makers* included a fact file on the Jam. Written on it was John Weller's telephone number and I can still recite the number today: Maybury 64717. So I rung up the next day and Paul's sister, Nicky, answered and I said, "Hi my name's Gary Crowley and I'm starting a fanzine called *The Modern World*", and Nicky saying, "Calm down, calm down, he's here, have a word with him!" I was talking 20 to the dozen! Paul came on the phone and told me he was up in London tomorrow and to come and meet him at Polydor.

Me and my mate Chris Club turned up, me with my flares on, as I was still at school and had no dough, and we interviewed Paul. It would have been along the lines of what coloured teeth have you got, what did you drink for breakfast aged 15! Pretty limited stuff, but Paul was very encouraging, as were they all (John used to frighten me a little bit!)

At school lunchtimes I used to commandeer the phone box out on Bell Street, armed with a stack of 2p pieces, and ring up record companies to try and blag tickets and records. It was a very exciting time.

My first interview was with Paul Weller, my second with Joe Strummer. I met Strummer as I was going up to Micky's Fish Bar for my lunchtime chips and Joe was coming out of the Metropole Café. "You're Joe Strummer! Can we interview you for our fanzine *The Modern World*?" "Yep, come down to rehearsals tomorrow."

I told a couple of people and then word got round and eight turned up! I was thinking, we can't turn up with eight people?! I was pushed to the front as always, and in a squeaky voice said: "Joe said it'll be alright!" Their roadie roadent, who was very intimidating, said, "What's this, a fucking school outing?" Joe, like Paul, was very accommodating and we all trotted off down to George's Café by the lock in Camden. I was the worst in a way, as the thing I was most concerned about was having my picture taken with the band, ha, ha.

I never missed a London show afterwards. Hammersmith Odeon, 100 Club, Nashville, Marquee, etc....

Fast forward a couple of years and I'd left school and got a job as an office boy in Decca Records and then a job at the *NME* as a receptionist, taking over from Danny Baker. Paul would come in every now and then and Dennis Munday, who'd become The Jam's A&R, knew I was about to go and work for Clive Banks, the record plugger. The week before I left, Dennis said, why don't you come down and listen to *Setting Sons* at Stratford Place? The first Jam single both myself and Clive worked on was 'Eton Rifles', which gave The Jam their first Top 10 record.

I met people at those early gigs who are still friends now. You'd see someone and ask, where did you get that jumper from? "My Nan knitted it" – like mine did – was sometimes the reply. Then the Mod thing

contd.

happened and it drew some of us even closer together, like Tony Lourdan, who was a postman up at Wembley, or Vaughn Toulouse and Bethnal Bob. Piller I met at Bogart's.

The first *Top of the Pops* I went to was when The Jam did 'Eton Rifles' and I was also there when they did 'Precious' and 'Town Called Malice'. Very exciting times.

There was something very real about The Jam and what attracted me to them in the first place was how passionate and intense they were. They evolved, mutated, brought in different styles. Stuff like Joy Division, Dub or Funk, mixed with influences from 1965. It was always interesting and within those kinds of parameters it was great thinking, where's he going to take us now? That's why it was great then, and why it's dated so well and kids are still interested now.

The sense of anticipation around the release of a new record was phenomenal: the pre-ordering, the physical attachment to the album, the sleeve, the vinyl. *This Is the Modern World* wasn't as good as *In the City* but hold on, I'll give it a go; and you play it and play it and fucking hell, 'Life from a Window' has just blown my head off and 'Tonight at Noon', he hasn't written anything like that before....

The gigs, the records, the TV shows were events. I had to bribe my brother and sister pocket money to be quiet as I recorded them on my cassette player from TOTP! Even though it was all mimed!! "Sue, Steve please be quiet I'm going to record it."

Gary Crowley

I don't think I had any idea what Punk or New Wave was. I had heard all about it and the clothes the Punks wore, but I wasn't interested in that. It was the music that mattered. I was watching the Marc Bolan show and on comes this band called The Jam, playing a song called 'All Around the World'. They weren't like the other Punk and New Wave bands. They were smart, wore suits and played guitars like the ones The Beatles played, which I later learned were called Rickenbackers.

So, why The Jam more than anyone else? Well, apart from the fact that the band looked better and cooler than any other band at the time, it was the songs and most of all the lyrics. Funnily enough, it was a biker who said to me one day, "Have you read the guy's lyrics? They are amazing. I tell ya now, mate, that guy is the new Ray Davies." From that day on I read every word on the album sleeves. I read all of Weller's interviews and found myself agreeing with him about almost everything. Some kids may have worn CND badges because it was trendy or because Weller did, but I was already wearing one because I believed in it.

So, that was it, the band was perfect. They really were the best band in the world, who wrote brilliant songs that we could all relate to. The Jam had strong beliefs and stood by their principles. Most of all, there appeared to be nothing fake about them.

Gordon Waring

They were an immense band, The Jam, back in 1977. Aged 15, I was primed, waiting and ready for their arrival. Almost exactly two years before the April 1977 release of The Jam's debut single, 'In the City', my elder brother, Paul James Martin, aged 19, had died. The fraternal embrace of rock & roll stepped into the breach.

Life-changing bands – the Pistols, The Clash, Talking Heads – were coming my way at a rate of knots. Even so, a livewire, kick-ass rock & roll trio, boasting tense, terse, soul-screaming songs alive with fire and magic? Fronted by a guy called Paul? Are you kidding? OF COURSE, they held a pretty special place in my mind and heart. My thing now, son of a Commie and Occupy supporter that I am, is Talking Musical Revolutions and I was always brought up to loathe capitalist Conservativism.

I knew this, in spite of the interview quote, because of something FAR more reliable – the music. Even in extraordinary times, The Jam were extraordinary: suited and booted for action, sounding 'n' looking there, at the start, like a keen contemporary spin on The Feelgoods? I was IN, like Flynn Jim!

Jam records, especially the singles, were mind blowers: 'Going Underground', 'Town Called Malice', 'Tube Station', and "'A' Bomb in Wardour Street' ("HATE BOMB HATE BOMB"). 'In the City', the classic first single, which was also the title of their first album. That single was like a UK version of 'Born to Run', to me, two years on, but set in London. Claustrophobic and relentless, where Bruce's US song suggested a wild ride beyond the city limits, but both boiling with a similar excitement-anger.

'In the City'? Whooah, yes, I will have some of that! I always knew I'd leave my Northern Irish No Future home and head to London, and this was the song that prepared me for the trip.

A few weeks after the single was on its way to grazing the Top 40, in my class at Bangor Grammar School, Timothy, the impossibly tall, blue-eyed, blonde-haired, posh Malone Road-voiced, rugby-playing, fascist fuck, addressed the googly-eyed, prematurely balding, rugby-playing, history teacher. Timothy went through the entire time I spent at this same-sex shithole with the words 'National Front' emblazoned on his ruck sack. (Years later, the school was found to have been sheltering, for upwards of 25 years, a teacher whose paedophiliac crimes included spreading jam, and sometimes talcum powder, on young boy's behinds.)

Back in the classroom he asked if, in the class's hip 'n' swinging, current affairs slot, anyone would like to address a particular topic. Timothy (officer class) puts Martin (Punky cannon fodder) over the parapet.

"M-m-m-m-mm Martin," he says, because Tim isn't just a tall, blue-eyed, blonde-haired, posh Malone Road-voiced, rugby-playing, fascist fuck. Oh, no: he is a blue-eyed, blonde-haired, posh Malone Road-voiced, rugby-playing, fascist fuck with a stutter.

"Martin," he continued triumphantly, "wants to tell us about" (cue big input of disdain and ridicule in his plummy tone) "PUNK ROCK, Sir."

In truth I had no wish to tell Timmy or the gormless grinning teacher, or anyone else, about Punk Rock. I wanted to be down the town seeing if Carol Brown and her friends were at the chippy. I wanted to be... as far away from this hell hole as possible. And I would be, as soon as this term was over. So, I held my nerve. I accepted Timothy's challenge and talked about the music and the words of Punk, and picked out The Jam's 'In the City' as a prime example of why it's important to me and the world. I got the impression half the class thought it was funny ridiculous. But in a year's time loads of them would be die-hard Jam fans. I said something about how the death of Liddle Towers at the hands of the police is referenced in The Jam's 'In the City' in the line, "In the city they have the right to kill a man". I added a bit about it being a warning of a future where the police are a private security force working at the behest of municipal governments and big corporations – I got laughed at, shouted down and ridiculed.

And I think, what the fuck is the point?

Rudi, the band I came from Belfast to London with, to live in a Clapham squat for three weeks in the summer of 1978, ended up signing with Paul's Jamming! label. I moved to London in 1980 and first met Paul in 1981, backstage at one of his label's showcase gigs. I had just reviewed the single 'Funeral Pyre', unfavourably, and Paul was not happy.

"Are you Gavin Martin," he asked, in a style best described as confrontational.

I could hardly deny it.

contd.

"You're a fucking spunker mate, a waste of fucking spunk."

It wasn't a great start and we've had a few ups and downs over the years, evened-out when I came to my senses and realized Paul is among the best we have got.

I remember stopping his dad, John, after a show at Glastonbury in 1994. Paul was magnificent that day and I told him so; John seemed to appreciate my effusions. I had a drink with Paul and his wife Hannah after the Albert Hall show last year [in 2010]. I really like his company and I love the way he's stayed true to all the things that turned me onto The Jam in the first place. He appreciates compliments and always holds his corner when slights come his way. He reminded me that at certain points I'd written him off. I told him about the first time we'd met, the review of 'Funeral Pyre' and he was right back on it – lippy, combative, telling me that I was wrong.

I loved that, loved the way he still gets worked up about it. That sort of passion – it's probably why he still makes great records, why The Jam remain pure and unsullied, a band that stand as an example to many that came after them – well, shame many that came after them if the truth be told. And there's The Dad Rock thing too, meant to be a derogatory putdown but Paul has that approachability to appear like family. To me he'll always be a blood brother from the sacred church of rock & roll. Long may he thrive.

Gavin Martin

We gigged with The Jam in 1977 at the Red Cow. We had an every other Wednesday slot for about six or eight weeks. The admission was 20p. We did other venues like the Nashville and Roxy. The turnouts at these gigs during this period of early Punk were always heaving with a young crowd.

The Lurkers were a bit different to a lot of other Punk bands at the time. We formed in '76 and played as a band until 1980. We were very influenced by the US trash rock & roll from The Ramones, Iggy Pop and the New York Dolls. We came from the suburbs and although giving it our best, we did like a drink and maybe valued a laugh over the business side of things. The Jam were professional, they would turn up in their everyday clothes clutching bags that contained their suits and ties. Then they would come on stage in their outfits – it was an act, and they were good at it.

As I say, they were professional, knowing you had to plan ahead. I remember Paul Weller giving guitar strings to our guitarist, Pete, because he was always breaking them and John Weller, Paul's father, would say, "Don't you guys think of these things?" John Weller was a pleasant man. He would buy us a beer at the bar. What was obvious was that he was looking out for his boy, supporting his son and the band.

The other thing about The Jam was that they could play their instruments. They were very good at what they did. They would play the gig but I don't remember them hanging about in the crowd before or after gigs, whereas we did. There was no stand-offishness or conflict, they were just very professional. They were all very friendly, though, and down to earth.

Pete 'Esso' Haynes – The Lurkers

My first Jam gig was at the Hope & Anchor on 28th April 1977. I was 14 years old. In those days the crowds were probably a couple of hundred. There would be a lot of Punks, all the bondage stuff. We were still at school, so we wore our black blazers and trousers whilst trying to mimic The Jam – the school uniform came in handy – complete with velcro school badge. The Jam had been on my radar because of John Peel. I remember that I first heard 'In the City' on his show – you had all the Punk stuff, which I was really into – The Clash and the Pistols, Lurkers, 999, Chelsea. It really was like a youth explosion but The Jam had something more. They came across as more professional. I had no idea what a Mod was until later, after Weller started to mention bands like The Who and The Small Faces.

As '77 went on they were still playing the Punk circuit really: the Greyhound, the Roxy, the 100 Club. The biggest venue that they played would have been the Rainbow during the 'White Riot' tour. The thing about The Jam was that they managed to produce such a powerful sound on stage, even in those early days. Bands like The Clash were also powerful but The Jam still had that R'n'B, soulful edge, Weller was energetic and Foxton would be leaping about – and of course they were wearing the black suits, white shirts, ties and so on. By now, the band had a mainly original setlist, unlike the previous three or so years, where they relied mainly on cover versions.

So I saw The Jam on the 28th and *In the City* was released on the 29th. Then the first John Peel sessions were in May. I know it's been said that after Weller saw the Sex Pistols that he wanted The Jam to be like them, but musically they were miles apart. You have to remember that Chris Parry had missed out on the Pistols and The Clash but he did manage to sign The Jam for a snip at £6000, for a one single and one album deal. That was in February '77. In August they got £20,000 for *This is the Modern World*. By then Polydor knew they had something of a cash-making machine on their label.

It was around this time that the venues stepped up a gear, with places like the Top Rank in Birmingham and Reading and the Apollo in Glasgow – what's more, they were filling those venues.

October saw The Jam's first US tour – within months of just being signed, The Jam were trying to break into America. They never really did break America, and I understand that was a major regret.

In December '77 they played the Hammersmith Odeon, and they managed to sell that out – in less than eight months they had gone from playing the Hope & Anchor to a US tour to selling out the 'Hammy' Odeon. One of my favourite gigs of that year was at the Canterbury Odeon, home turf for me.

One of the first TV appearances was on the Marc Bolan show, where they performed "All Around the World'. Despite Bolan's obvious lack of info on the band when he introduced them, by all accounts he went onto say that he really liked them. The Jam used a cover version of 'Desdomona' in early setlists.

Back in those early days Shane MacGowan [later of the Pogues] was at all the London gigs. I remember that he used to wear a Union Jack jacket. He would always be at the front. He was really into them. Then The Nips came about anyway and Paul went onto to produce their first single.

Jon Abnett

Growing up in a small village in the Kent countryside, there wasn't a big music scene of any description. A couple of mates were into Bowie and Queen, but for me and my mates, the biggest interest was football and we'd be found kicking a ball about practically every evening down on the recreation ground, dreaming of scoring the winner at Wembley for what ever team we supported.

With an older sister, music at home consisted of Deep Purple, T-Rex or Bowie spinning on the music centre in the corner of the front room. I can't remember the radio being on much, but as a family, we'd all sit down and watch TOTP on a Thursday evening. Up to that point I hadn't been a big record buyer, a few Slade singles but not a lot else, but as the Punk/New Wave thing happened I started to take more of an interest in music. I watched The Jam playing 'In the City' on TOTP and liking what I saw and heard, I had to get a copy. After I'd saved enough pocket money, the single was followed by the album of the same name, and then the arguments started about who was going to play what on the music centre at home. It was also at about this time that I started picking up *NME* on the way to school on a Wednesday morning, something that continued for many years, always scouring the pages for any information, tour and release dates, interviews and gig reviews.

Towards the end of '77, there was an opportunity to see the band live when they played at one of the cinemas, the Odeon, just up the road in Canterbury. I can't remember much about the gig but I do remember the energy and sound from a three-piece was out of this world. At this stage the thought of going to see the band elsewhere never crossed my mind: I'm not sure if this was down to my young age or lack of finances, but the next opportunity to see them came almost exactly a year later when they played in the sports hall at the University of Kent, just after the release of *All Mod Cons*.

Singles and albums continued to be purchased, together with a few other artists – The Clash, Elvis Costello and Blondie spring to mind – but it was always The Jam on the turntable at home. By the time of the last single release of '79, 'The Eton Rifles', I'd left school and had started work, so this was the first new single that I pre-ordered from the Longplayer record shop in Canterbury and picked up on the day of release, a ritual that was repeated for all future new releases. Back then, there wasn't the promo plays on the radio that happen today (at ever ridiculous lengths!) before release day. As a result it was always exciting to pick up the new release, rush home and play the disc to death!

Towards the end of '79 rumours started to circulate that The Jam were down for a return appearance at the University's sports hall, so most Saturday's resulted in a trip to the Longplayer to see when tickets were going on sale. Week after week the answer was always, "No idea what you're talking about", and I wondered if it was ever going to happen. So you can imagine the excitement when the date was confirmed as part of a four-date, warm-up tour before the band went to the States in March 1980. My only memory of the gig was how small the crowd was for a band that was reaching the height of its powers, which was demonstrated by their next single, 'Going Underground'. This release coincided with me going out with my new girlfriend, Yvonne, for the first time – a great memory as we are still together, happily married with two fantastic boys, Nick and Phil.

Another first in 1980 was getting a few mates together to see The Jam at the legendary Hammersmith Odeon in London. We could only get standing tickets at the back of the circle so the view was poor, but that was certainly compensated for by the atmosphere: I'm sure that at times the circle was actually moving!! Having seen Paul Weller as a solo artist at some of the other great European venues, such as the Paradiso in Amsterdam and Ancienne Belgique in Brussels, I can only imagine what the atmosphere would have been like when The Jam played. The 'Bucket and Spade' tour also happened in 1981, which I managed to catch at the Granby Halls in that well-known seaside town of Leicester, courtesy of a cousin that was based at nearby RAF North Luffenham.

And so to '82 and the split. When I first heard the news, like many others I couldn't get my head round it: why? It just didn't make sense. But when the tour was announced I had to see the band one last time: off went the cheque and self-addressed envelope for a date at Wembley Arena, then an anxious wait before the tickets came back. How things have changed today with the internet, when you're only a couple of clicks away from booking tickets to see your favourite band. The details of the gig itself, like all the others, is long forgotten, although I can remember being both on a high and deflated on the journey home. I'd just seen the "Best f*****g band in the World" for the last time.

Paul Thompson

One of the important things about The Jam was that they came across as a very down-to-earth band. What with John Weller being so involved too, it had that sort of family thing about it. I always felt that was in their music and maybe that was partly why so many latched onto them. I mean the sound was quite warm by around the *Setting Sons* period.

There is something in the music that people could relate to. Take 'Saturday's Kids'. I can imagine a scene down Slough shopping centre on a Saturday summing up the meaning of the song. The song is something for all generations and all types of people. It was about that very middle class sort of thing where you hate your parents or rebel against them. I don't think most kids did. I think most kids liked their parents. I never really understood all that thing about youth rebellion within a family setting. In a way, I think The Jam stood for something about that family connection, and put it into their music.

To me personally, I have always thought of The Jam as being a Punk band. I mean, in 1977 I was 16 years old and had been really into Bowie. I use to have the feather crop hair-cut and all the albums: *Hunky Dory*, *Diamond Dogs* and so on. There were other bands around, like Slade and Sweet. I was also really into Dr Feelgood, who kind of played a speeded up R'n'B, and then Punk just sort of arrived.

So Punk came along. I think the first Punk record I heard was 'Sheena is a Punk Rocker' by The Ramones. I was at a disco one Friday somewhere in Slough. I can remember that my skin just started to tingle. It was a feeling, just like when I first went to Chelsea and heard 'Liquidator', which was at my first game in 1970.

One of the things I liked about Bowie was that he sang in an English accent and at the time a lot of people didn't. Most just mimicked American. Paul Weller did the English thing. Then at school someone brought in *The Clash* album and it just sounded totally right, it sounded so English. It was around this time that I first heard The Jam, and from then on just got into Punk.

Punk suited me also because I have never been one for style. I mean really the only people that dressed up were those in the bands. The rest of us were just scruffy. Mostly average kids then were just herberts, really, in denim jackets or PVC fake leather jackets. I mean, in the late '70s I was still wearing flares. Even around this time there were still groups of Teds and the Soul patrols (with their permed-hair, dungarees and Hawaiian shirts).

The early Jam stuff was great but I also really liked *All Mod Cons* and *Setting Sons* (which is my favourite Jam album). But I still considered them to be a Punk band. I know they dressed like Mods, but it was something in their sound: I think they developed their sound quite quickly from the first two albums and they added something to their sound. The Jam grew as they went on, whereas a lot of the Punk bands did one album and then broke up or something.

There was also the lyrical aspect. The Jam wrote songs with very socially aware lyrics. I was always really into lyrics. I don't think Punk had any – or many – good lyrics before The Jam. And there was generally nothing in the lyrics of the other music around that related to your life. I think it was the same in literature as well. I mean, when I was young I use to read all the Richard Allen books – you know, skinheads and suedeheads and so on – but there was nothing else that seemed to relate to your life.

As a kid I wasn't a big reader, but I do remember picking up a copy of one of Alan Sillitoe's books, and even though it was set in the Midlands in the 1950s, I thought, fucking hell this book strikes a chord with me. I just really got it. It was about ordinary people with ordinary lives. I then got all of Alan Sillitoe's books, and then I got into George Orwell's works. I found it all very honest.

So when Paul Weller and Joe Strummer came about I sort of saw them as writers, really. I think Johnny Rotten said something to the effect of him writing literature. I think Weller and Strummer were just normal boys that wouldn't have usually thought about writing a book, so they did it through their songs and they put their feelings and their culture into their songs, and I think that was quite unique at the time. It was as if The Jam's lyrics told you about your life. Social realism or whatever you want to call it.

The London Classics series that we have been doing through London books has a load of writers that were coming through in the 1930s, who were writing about Soho and places like the old East End of London. They had a period when they were getting published and then the war came and they didn't get published anymore

contd.

and they faded away. Then you had to wait until the '50s for writers like Alan Sillitoe, who just wrote about their own lives. But it's as if they are treated as a novelty, given a bit of time and then pushed back into the shadows, and I think Punk was treated a bit like this. Punk came around but was quickly marginalised.

You had the first wave of bands like the Pistols, The Jam and The Clash, and then the next wave of bands like The Lurkers, The Ruts and X-Ray Specs. And then Two Tone came along, which in its way was quite Punky, and then that was it. Nothing. I mean, when you think about who was the last big London band? The Jam! It's amazing and it was 30 years ago. And you have to think what are the reasons for that. I think it's a prejudice. I think there is no interest in local culture. It's all public school boys and northerners. So I think The Jam, for many, were considered to be ignorant southerners. The Jam were a great suburban working-class band, who just blew everything away; and even though they developed they never lost sight of their roots. The Jam was a very honest band.

The Jam are a band that the kids should be listening to today. It helps with an education. The Jam and The Ruts should be taught in school – ha, ha! Going to gigs in the '70s was also an education. We use to go and see The Ruts, The Clash and The Jam at places like Dingwalls and/or the Lyceum on a Sunday night, where you could see five bands for £2.50. One of my most memorable Jam gigs was at the Rainbow. It was the same night that The Exploited were playing around the corner. I think there was a big punch-up, or something like that, between the parka-clad lads and the Punks. I remember thinking at the time, this is madness because The Jam are also a Punk band.

By the early '80s we were doing a lot of Chelsea away games. The Jam was our soundtrack for the car journeys. We always played Jam tapes in the car and sang along. I can remember moments when the passengers in the car would erupt, when we would all sing "And a kick in the balls" [from 'That's Entertainment']. That was another thing about Jam songs, and I mean this in the best way: Jam songs were sing-alongs. It's that English thing again that probably goes back to the music halls and then found its way onto the football terraces and then into songs by bands like The Jam. Even now I'll play a Jam CD in the car if I know I'm going on a long trip and I'll still be singing along to it. It just makes you feel good.

John King

The night I was with Sid at the Speakeasy, Nancy was in hospital and I was keeping Sid company. We were in the restaurant and someone said Paul Weller had just come in. I was pleased as my good friend Gill was going out with him and it meant I would be able to catch up with her. Sid said he would be back in a minute and went off into the club. Ages passed and I decided to leave the table and go into the club, too. I asked a friend where Sid had gone and he said that Paul and Sid had got into a fight and that Sid had gone to the hospital. I'm not sure what had happened exactly, but apparently Weller had put a glass over Sid's head. About an hour after that Sid came back into the club for another drink and we hooked up again. I found out years later that it was a row over a guitar riff.

Vanessa Jayne Lindley-Blunt

My overwhelming memory of seeing The Jam at Liverpool's Erics in '77 was one of GREAT EXCITEMENT! I had bought the *In the City* picture sleeve and was BLOWN AWAY by this power trio playing what were great pop songs at the end of the day… Not Punk at all!!

Steve Proctor

It all started with the Marc Bolan show in the late summer of 1977. I had been a bit of fan of Marc through playing my older brother's records and would belt home from school to catch the new ITV series that Marc was presenting. I was impressed by the new bands on there – Generation X, the Boomtown Rats and the Radio Stars – and this would lead me to a future Punk and New Wave obsession. But, more than any of these bands, it was a three-piece, black-suit wearing combo led by an angry young man with a cool, short haircut that really grabbed my attention. Performing their latest single 'All Around the World' on the Marc Bolan show, I was mesmerised and hooked from there on. Along with The Clash, The Jam meant more to me than any other band before or since, and in my head, like all fellow Jam fans, I became their number one fan!

While I was just getting to know the sound of The Jam, unbeknown to me, some of my older mates were going to see them just a short bus ride away at the Sheffield Top Rank, while they were on their *In The City* tour. The day after that gig, The Jam even arranged to go and meet their fans and sign record sleeves and chat with them the next day at Sheffield's Punk record shop, Revolution, a shop I would frequent regularly. Christ, if only I had known!

The next year saw me reach heights of true obsession, buying every one of their records on the release date and trying to keep track of every music weekly that they appeared in. Even the August '77 *Look In* pull-out poster was spread across my school jotter for backing, and the lasses at school would turn up almost every day with torn out posters of the band from their *Jackie* and *My Guy* mags. Badges, patches, mirrors, posters... you name it, I fell for them all and whilst my record buying gradually included just about every Punk, New Wave, power pop and short-haired band in the land, The Jam were always at the top of the playing list.

If they were on *Top of the Pops* with a new single, I would make sure I caught the performance, be it on the youth club's portable telly, where kids would congregate every Thursday at 7.30pm, or at a mates house or my own. By the age of fourteen, I was also at the point of aping Paul Weller, copying his hair style (often badly), look and arrogant expressions. Such is the impressionable exuberance of youth. The only thing left to do was see the band live on stage.

I had to endure a stream of Jam gigs over in Sheffield being played out without my attendance. Older mates would go and catch them perform at the Top Rank again (*Modern World* tour, supported by a band called New Hearts, soon to be Secret Affair), then two nights at the University, where Garry Bushell was in on the act and covered it in *Sounds* music weekly. For the *All Mod Cons* tour, me and my mate tried to buy tickets for their upcoming 'Apocalypse' tour date at the student-based polytechnic, only to be turned down because of our age and their no non-student policy. Of course, non-students did get into the gig, but had to have a student sign them in, a common occurrence at gigs back in the day. Paul Weller himself made sure that some of his fans made it into this gig. He was in the bar having a drink and got chatting to some fans who didn't have tickets and took them up to the hall where they were playing as part of his guest list. Again, if only I had bloody known.

You know, it's hard to convey how much The Jam meant to me back then (and still do). For me, they were just about perfect. They really meant it too, unlike a lot of the bandwagon jumpers of the time. Part of the appeal of Weller was that we all wanted to be like him. I suppose he was our very own David Watts! He had the right kind of Punk attitude, too, but wouldn't toe the Punk party line and conform, which appealed to me. Yes he was a Mod, and always will be, but for me The Jam, along with The Clash, were the most idealistic and committed of all the New Wave bands. They truly were the real thing.

The Jam could do no wrong by mid '79. They had really discovered their muse with *All Mod Cons* and were attracting fans by the day. Classic singles followed: 'Strange Town', 'When You're Young' (one of my personal faves) and 'Eton Rifles', and when they finally hit the number one spot in March 1980 [with 'Going Underground'], me and my mate leapt into the air with joy! Not long afterwards, a new tour was announced and I finally managed to get hold of tickets for their Sheffield Top Rank gig on the *Sound Affects* tour. I was now a seasoned gig-goer, so nothing was gonna stand in my way of getting to see them play live.

It was a Sunday night and pissing it down with rain. The support band were The Piranhas, who were just riding high with their newly released 'Tom Hark'. They were quite good that night, but it was clear that everyone was here to see Woking's finest. The place was packed with a mix of Mods, Two-Tone kids, Punks

contd.

and Rock fans. When Weller came on stage he tripped up on a guitar lead; his face not very happy at that. A new song from the new LP was introduced, 'Monday', and I can remember thinking, shit, its school in the morning, don't bloody remind me, Paul. There followed a set of all the classics: 'It's Too Bad', 'The Place I Love', 'Modern World', "A' Bomb in Wardour Street', 'Eton Rifles' and the immortal 'Tube Station'. The atmosphere was truly electric and my excitement levels were on overdrive. Life just couldn't get any better than this, surely!

Towards the end of the gig, me and my mate had to go to the back of the venue for a drink – we were so hot and exhausted from our hour-and-a-half involvement in the massive pogoing crowd. We stood at the bar drinking a pint of cola, watching the band go into their extended live rendition of 'David Watts' – it was gig heaven!

Afterwards, the band came out to meet us all and I got my ticket signed. As a smashed, bottle-wielding skinhead broke into the venue chased by two coppers, Paul just looked up, the cool cat, and carried on signing autographs. We watched the band get onto their tour coach and a kid who looked just like Bruce Foxton was waved onto the bus by Bruce himself, obviously a friend of the band. I wish that was me, I thought. I had school in the morning. The comedown after a gig like that on a dreary Monday morning was something I used to dread and of course, I skipped school and spent the day playing through all of my Jam LPs instead. I had seen my favourite band. How could I put up with RE by a boring old teacher with smelly breath the next day!

I saw The Jam twice more after the *Sound Affects* gig. Two nights in a row at the very same Sheffield venue. They were amazing on both nights and supported by a great Irish Punk band that I loved called Rudi. On the second night The Jam came on with 'Strange Town' and the whole place totally erupted!

By that time (March '82) The Jam were simply massive and little did we fans realise, but the end was drawing near for our band. When the end did arrive, I strangely felt a sense of relief. I truly believed what Paul was saying about them not wanting to be like the Stones and go on forever: they wanted to leave a real legacy for their fans, which they did. The Jam were far too special to just go on and on, year after year: tour, LP, single, tour, etc. They meant much more than that. The Jam's music and words were the soundtrack to our growing up, the late '70s to early '80s youth, and no band since has come close to being as great as them. They finished at their peak and because of that brave decision made back in 1982, they mean just as much now to a generation of fans (old and new) as they did back then.

Tony Beesley

1978 – DIDN'T WE HAVE A NICE TIME

By the time 1978 kicked in, The Jam were seasoned musicians pushing their songs around the industry and the towns of the UK. The timing was right and there were gaps appearing in the musical market as the record companies started looking for all things spiky. January saw the Sex Pistols perform their last gig at the Winterland Ballrooms in San Francisco. For many, this marked the end of Punk. For others, this heralded something new. Well, for Rotten anyway, as he got Public Image Ltd out of the traps by producing one of the greatest debut singles of the era, if not ever, with 'Public Image'.

Things were far from content on the streets, either. By April, thousands had responded to the increasing support that right-wing groups like the National Front were getting. The Anti-Nazi league organised a march through London that also included a concert where The Clash played their biggest gig to date in Victoria Park in support of the anti-Nazi cause. The same month was also shared by the release of the Bee Gee's massive album, *Night Fever*, which became a staple of most house parties and medallion men reeking of Brut 33, trying to pull to 'More Than A Woman'.

Things were definitely changing. Anna Ford became the first female newsreader. May saw the introduction of May Day as an official bank holiday and later that month Ipswich Town beat Arsenal in a shock FA Cup win and gave Sir Bobby Robson his first trophy as manager. Keith Moon died a few months later, on 7th September. The Jam's response was to include The Who song, 'So Sad About Us', on the B-side to 'Down in the Tube Station at Midnight', one of the bands three single releases in 1978.

A bulk of the nation remained cheery, however: after all, they had the movie *Grease* to digest, and with it all the singles that spilled out from the film. By the close of 1978, virtually everyone had at some point found themselves humming along to 'You're the One That I Want'! But then, if it wasn't a *Grease* song that grabbed your attention, then surely the sixth best-selling single of the year did: 'The Smurf Song' by Father Abraham and The Smurfs. Other musical masterpieces of the year included 'Rasputin' by Boney M, 'Figaro' from Brotherhood of Man and 'Oh, What a Circus' by David Essex.

The Jam's 'David Watts', 'Down in the Tube Station at Midnight' and 'News of the World' were sounds of salvation to many angry, scruffy and spotty young people, as New Wave started to take a foothold and classic singles' bands like The Undertones and Buzzcocks made inroads with kids bored of listening to their older sister's disco classics.

TV provided us with the first ever episode of *Top Gear*, which if you like driving fast in faded jeans, cowboy boots and hair that looks better on a donkey, it changed your outlook on life… dude! *Cheggers Plays Pop* and *Butterflies* also made their debuts, and *The Muppet Show* was a big hit for kids of a certain age and strange men with fixations about Miss Piggy.

The working public were still restless for a multitude of reasons. November bought with it the inconvenient bakers' strike, and with it panic buying of bread from the masses, who were certainly not going to forsake their baked beans on toast or Marmite soldiers for any bugger.

1978 was the year that The Jam played the four gigs with the Blue Oyster Cult and bombed every night in front of a 20,000 US audience – it was a total mis-match from the promoter.

All Mod Cons came out in the spring of '78. This is my all-time favourite album, and like all my Jam LPs I played this one to death. 'David Watts' had been released ('Billy Hunt' was the original choice). *All Mod Cons* was a Mod album, in every sense of the definition. By this time, you had the London and Essex Mods following the band, people like Bob Morris, Grant Fleming and Eddie Piller. (Fleming went on to play bass with a band called Kids Next Door and they supported The Jam at Kent University in Canterbury in 1980 – Jimmy Pursey's brother was the lead singer). Fleming has been credited with kick-starting the Mod thing at that time and he was a big fan – a large group of them followed the band to Paris and were featured in 'The Jam Pact' tour programme. He also played bass for The Chords when they reformed for a short tour about 15 years ago.

Personally, hearing tracks like 'David Watts' and 'Tube Station' live for the first time was just awesome. Buckler's drumming and Foxton's bass playing on the likes of ''A' Bomb' and 'The Place I Love' showed how tight a rhythm section they had gelled into. I still hadn't met the band by this time but I had met John Weller and Kenny Wheeler.

They made two TV appearances, on *The Old Grey Whistle Test* and *Revolver*. In the summer they also made an appearance headlining at the Reading Festival and considering the make-up and the crowd (mainly 'Hippy' types), they went down well.

By the autumn of 1978, you could tell that the fan base was taking off; tickets were harder to come by.

Jon Abnett

'News of the World'

Again, the photography was done around the time of the previous two sleeves. Rick being contrary, with the leather jacket and Mod target T-shirt.

'David Watts'/''A' Bomb in Wardour Street'

That's the most 'desingnery' of the sleeves that I got away with. Didn't use the logo. I just took the arrows from Paul's jumper on the 'Modern World' sleeve and played about with it. I'm wondering why I split mine and Martyn's name on the back — pop art, I suppose. The lettering being so small for the title probably got me told off by Polydor, and I'm sure John Weller would have hated it. He wanted his band to be the main focus and would have wanted everyone to know what they were buying. I think this was the last record I did for Polydor before I went on my own, so I probably didn't care too much what the record company thought. I was definitely in the band camp back then. The band seemed to be pretty happy with everything I suggested, Chris Parry the same.

'Down in the Tube Station at Midnight'

I said we've got to go down to the tube station, so the nearest to Polydor was Bond Street. I got them at the end of the platform. I wanted a train just coming in. Didn't take long to get — we were on our toes as the guards were trying to move us on. I seem to remember I told the band to go down then I'd come down with the photographer and get the shot. Done on a tripod, no flash and using the available light. The tribute to Keith [Moon] on the back was poignant for me, as I did the *Who Are You* LP sleeve that year as well. Keith was sitting on a chair with the words, 'Not to be taken away', and died two days later. This single was released in October 1978 and reached number 15.

Bill Smith

'News of the World'

It was early March 1978, and the eagerly awaited new single from The Jam was out, 'News of the World'. In a tradition going back to bands from the 1960s, none of the tracks on this single featured on the original's album.

As with the two earlier singles, the word 'World' was in the title, but this was a bit different, as it had been penned by bassist Bruce Foxton, who took the main vocal slot, with Paul Weller doing backing vocals.

The sound was very different, almost rock, with a great riff from Weller playing big power chords and one of his best guitar solos. Bruce came up with great lyrics about the gutter press, now even more poignant with recent events. I loved it and it was great to see live, though at the time it just made Number 27 in the charts.

The B-side featured two tracks: the first by Weller, 'Aunties and Uncles (Impulsive Youths)', and the second by Foxton, 'Innocent Man'. We were, as always, treated to a quality B-side, with Weller's familiar choppy, rhythmic style of playing ringing true on his Rickenbacker.

Foxton's 'Innocent Man' starts off with a familiar riff on an acoustic guitar and heartfelt lyrics from Bruce about the downside of capital punishment when a mistake is made and an Innocent man is killed. It wasn't perhaps one of Bruce's finest songs, but not a bad effort, bearing in mind this was only the fourth single and the band were still finding their way.

'News of the World' has stood the test of time, with Bruce earning some royalties from it: it is used as a theme song for the satirical BBC show *Mock the Week*. It still sounds as fresh as it did in 1978. "READ ALL ABOUT IT!!"

Tim Filor

'David Watts'/"A' Bomb in Wardour Street'

I have to confess that I hadn't heard the original Kinks version when I first heard The Jam's take on 'David Watts'. I'm not sure when I finally got round to it, back in the day when there was no YouTube to instantly check it out, but when I did I remember thinking it was a bit weedy in comparison. I love it now but to me the definitive version is still The Jam's. It's not often I say that about a cover; and although I realise the first one you hear is often the one that sticks with you, I really feel that The Jam's version of 'David Watts' is one of the great covers. They did what all bands/artists should do when covering a song: they put their own stamp upon it. It has that bite and urgency that marks it down as a Jam record. It was the second successive single to feature lead vocals from bassist Bruce Foxton, showing that The Jam were never solely about Paul Weller. That said...

The real diamond on this 7" single is on the flip side. Something that was to become a recurring theme of Jam singles: the great B-side (although technically I think this was classed as a 'double-A side', but I'm sure you get my drift). "A' Bomb in Wardour Street' is simply magnificent. It's a song that perfectly summed up the sometimes hostile environment that existed during those times. Inspired by Weller's visit to a Punk club in London with his girlfriend and witnessing first hand, "The fear and hate linger in the air", it perfectly articulates the story of a young couple getting caught up in the melee.

> I'm stranded on The Vortex floor
> My head's been kicked in
> And blood's started to pour
> Through the haze I can see my girl
> Fifteen geezers got her pinned to the wall.

It wasn't something restricted to Punk clubs in London. A Friday or Saturday night out in Southsea would often bear witness to the same sort of carnage.

This was evidence of Weller's growing maturity as a writer. "A' Bomb' wasn't simply a pop song, it was art reflecting life. It is said that Weller also took inspiration from an actual unexploded Word War II bomb found near Polydor's offices near Wardour Street. Of course, the lyrics would not have the same force without the accompanying music, which punches the air with the same intensity.

I remember at the time wondering why "A' Bomb' hadn't been chosen as the A-side. The songs were recorded at RAK Studios, where music mogul Mickie Most (a Simon Cowell of his day, with Mud and writers/producers 'Chinnichap' both part of his pop empire) ruled the roost. Apparently, John Weller asked Mickie's opinion, and he said 'David Watts' should be the A-side. He was undoubtedly right. "A' Bomb' would never have got the airplay.

Both songs were live favourites. I was lucky enough to see The Jam six times (I wish it had been 60). Two of those gigs were in 1978, the year this single came out. My memories of those gigs are now frustratingly dim but a good mate, Kev Griggs, tells me that at the second of those gigs, at Pompey Guildhall, the crowd were calling for 'David Watts', to which my retort was, "Wankers! They should be calling for "A' Bomb', not a Kinks cover!" Well they treated us to both, but it was definitely "A' Bomb' that brought the house down – the perfect ending to a perfect gig, with that "A-P-O-C-A-L-Y-P-S-E... Apocalypse!" ending and Weller throwing his guitar to the ground in a wail of feedback, as though signalling the end of not just the concert, but everything. In reality, it was the start of something: a golden age of The Jam's best work.

Diz

'Down in the Tube Station at Midnight'

First, there is the faded-in roar of the sound of the train. It's a familiar sound to anyone that has ever travelled on a tube train. It's not hard to imagine the gush of wind that rips through a tube station after the train has departed. Then there is the faint sound of a young female child's voice yelling "the skins are coming", at least that's what all my mates thought anyway, whilst we played it over and over again on the youth club juke box.

Then the song slips in with the aid of Foxton's memorable bass line, backed up by the rapid sixteenths that Buckler plays on the hi-hats, emulating the pace of a train racing down the tracks. The song is already driving along by this point, and Weller has begun to introduce the concept of the song. The first words tell a story of a lone man who is down in a tube station, it is late at night and all he wants to do is go home to his wife.

The story and the song build, there is a real momentum unfolding and the listener is captivated by the story of the man. Then the lyrics introduce the attackers. They have pub breath and carry the presence of Wormwood Scrubs prison. The story tells us that the man falls prey to the attackers. He is a victim and no one helps him. The victim is alone in his ordeal. Weller forces us to empathise with the man – after all, there appears to be no real reason for the attack. There is a sense of injustice. There is a sense of what could, would and did happen in tube ways in 1970's Britain.

Then comes the middle-eight section and it is a drummer's delight. There is a sound of a train rolling along and Buckler mirrors the sound with rolls on the tom-toms. At least that is what it sounds like. Then the cymbals crash away and the song calms a little as it leads to the outro. The song is a masterpiece. At the time of its release, it was considered to have been one of Weller's finest songs. Four decades later, it still is.

'So Sad About Us'

This is one of my favourite Jam covers, and it is also one of my favourite Who songs. There is a wonderful bit of footage on YouTube of The Who performing the song at The Marquee Club in 1967. The band look and sound great, and Keith Moon grins his way through the song whilst bashing away on his drums and cymbals.

The Jam included their version on the B-side to 'Tube Station' in homage to Keith Moon, who had died the month before the single was released. The single's rear cover shows the face of Moon from his early Who days.

The Jam had once included the song in their live set and their recorded version is not that far away from The Who's version. The song is basically a love song about a boy and girl who have split up. The boy is singing about the loss and how they are still in love. He tells us that they cannot switch off their love, and compares it to not being able to switch off the sun. Both Weller and Foxton share the harmonies of ooohs and lah-lahs. The song is typical early Who: simple and to the point. The Jam were always going to do the song justice.

'The Night'

This was a Foxton composition. The song crashes in and is reminiscent of a song with its roots firmly placed in Punk. The guitars screech and the drums bash out a typical upbeat, to the point, tempo. The arrangement is similar to a host of Punk tunes that bands like The Clash used in their early days.

This is also one of a few songs that include a harmonica. The harmonica only happens in the introduction. The lyrics are sung by Foxton and tell a story about having a Friday night out with mates. The mates are blowing off steam after having worked hard all week. There is a sense of binge drinking. They go to the amusement arcade. There is an urgency to have fun, get drunk and be a little wild. The song has a sense of familiarity and something that probably most of us can relate to. This is what is on offer in the night, Foxton implores, and he concludes the song by shouting "The night!" and trots off for a light and bitter. Probably.

Snowy

All Mod Cons

It's my favourite cover. I wanted to find an enclosed space but with an urban-type feel to it. Also, I had the idea of the instruments and tape recorder on the back representing each band member and the music they played. Paul was obviously very influential on the inner sleeve and we had to scour round to get certain pictures and the idea of the scooter, but I decided it would look great as if taken from a Haynes manual. To me it's the strongest Jam album cover. No Polydor logo, but a target label on the vinyl, which I was personally quite pleased about.

Paul was really keen on the lettering, which came from his love of the Small Faces when they were with Immediate records. The old Jam logo wouldn't have worked on this record. There is a definite Mod feel to both the imagery and the music on this album. 'English Rose' is such an iconic folk song and so different from everything else they were doing. I still think it's one of Paul's best-ever songs. I think you can hear The Beatles influence as well on this album.

I used to go to the studio a lot, I really enjoyed it. Way back from the first demos I would love to hear the start of something special being built. I used to work this way with many musicians to get a better 'feel' of the music, and it was a real pleasure to be around the making of this album.

Bill Smith

First time I saw The Jam was at Sheffield poly in November 1978. I was a big Jam fan at that time, and after seeing them I came out an even bigger fan! Next time round was May 1979 – The Jam were doing a tour that took in Sheffield for two dates. The previous time I saw them the crowd was a mix of mostly Punks, students and maybe a few Mods, which at the time I didn't know much about. But with the release of the *All Mod Cons* album it opened up a whole new way of life for myself and thousands of other teenagers.

One of the things I remembered about this gig was how it was 95 percent young Mods such as myself; it was the start of something big and new, something that us 15-year-olds could call ours. We were there at the start, or probably just before the start, as myself and my friends at the time had got the basics of the Weller/Jam look, with the Harrington jackets and the Doc Marten shoes and the suede boots plus the Shermans and the Perrys!

At the gig the lager was 29p. I bought a tour badge, which I still have, and I think I bought a 'Strange Town' T-shirt. I remember being stood near the front-middle or stage-right front and a hippy roadie moving stuff about on stage; a Mod shouted out something about his trousers and the roadie replied, "Do you want your teeth kicking down your throat?", to which a great roar went up and loads of stuff got thrown at the roadie!

When I've chatted to lads from Sheffield about The Jam and this gig it was a major turning point in the scene in Sheffield. Loads of now mid to late 40 year olds state how these two gigs changed their lives and decided which musical road they would go down. Me and my mates were never the same again, we made it well-known that we had been there at this gig; we were part of a new exciting scene, The Jam were our band.

Pete Skidmore

ALL MOD CONS [Review by Jon Abnett]

Between 3rd July and 17th August 1978, The Jam refocused and entered RAK and Eden studios to record their third album, *All Mod Cons*. It was released on 22nd November and reached number six in the UK album chart. Within the space of five months, The Jam would become one of the most revered bands in the history of UK music. After *This is the Modern World* (probably my least favourite LP and panned by music critics), most songwriters would have thrown in the towel, especially after the first batch of songs were infamously rejected by Chris Parry as sub-standard. But not Weller. Although he was disillusioned, he managed to write one of the best Jam LPs ever!

Two important demos were rejected during the fatal *All Mod Cons* sessions: 'She's Got Everything' and 'I Want to Paint'. The former is not as most people would expect: it's NOT a cover of the Kink's song by the same name, but a very 'Jam sounding' song. Having been lucky enough to hear the song, personally I feel that with more work this could have easily appeared as a B-side to 'David Watts'.

Although Parry co-produced with Vic Coppersmith-Heaven, this was to be Parry's last involvement with a Jam album. He moved onto pasture's new and set up his own record label, Fiction.

This was the album that saw Paul Weller become a 'Mod' in every sense of the word, even down to the title name. Ok, prior to that he wore the clothes but AMC was a Mod album – he left Chuck Berry behind and became Ray Davies. It has always bugged me why 'David Watts' appeared on the album and was even released as a single. Weller was more than capable of penning his own 'David Watts'-type song. Maybe it was a nod of approval to his idol? The sleeve art designed by Bill Smith contained a schematic diagram of a scooter and various Mod paraphernalia dotted about.

From the one minute 20 second opening title track to 'Tube Station' (which, incidentally, was the highest-charting single for the band at that time, reaching number 15), every song tells a real-life story: from the ageing rock star who had everything but lost it all ('To Be Someone') via a creepy businessman who came on strong to Weller's girlfriend in a hotel one night ('Mr. Clean'); to the violent scenarios of the Punk scene that was dead on it's arse ("A' Bomb In Wardour Street'); and, of course, the innocent husband getting his head kicked in after a night out. As with much of Paul Weller's songwriting, most people can relate to the songs on this album in some shape or form.

All Mod Cons also saw Weller pen his first proper love song with 'English Rose', a beautifully haunting acoustic riff with a classical connotation, which over 30 years on experienced a make-over to celebrate 40 years of *The Old Grey Whistle Test*. Weller deemed the lyrics of this song too personal, so they were not reproduced on the original release. Apparently, The Stone Roses took their original name from the song title.

In *Q* magazine's top 100 albums of all time, *All Mod Cons* was voted number 50 – not bad for a band signed by Polydor for one LP, especially after the second LP was panned and Weller had (supposedly) lost his direction. A year later, the album was released in the US, with the song 'The Butterfly Collector' replacing 'Billy Hunt', as it was thought that Americans would not understand the gist of the song! It had moderate success Stateside, but mainly because this was an 'Englishman's' album, first and foremost. After all, who else outside of London would have got the meaning of 'Billy Hunt'?

To sum up: this album saw Weller becoming one of the UK's best songwriters, and shows what excellent musicians Foxton and Buckler were. It also cemented The Jam fan base that was to become so loyal over the next four years, and indeed, continues today. Ask most fans and they'll probably quote *All Mod Cons* as their favourite Jam LP.

As a teenager growing up in the '70s, I always felt like I was out of time with my musical surroundings. Then the Pistols happened! And from them came this glorious explosion of Punk, with The Clash, Buzzcocks, The Stranglers and more. But best of all, a young band with an enigmatic lead singer/guitarist only a little bit older than me, talking about his love of My Generation-era Who and wearing 1960's style suits. The Jam were everything I ever dreamed of. They were my band, making songs and creating a scene for *my* generation. As everyone who is familiar with their music history knows, they went on to become the biggest band in Britain. But in 1978 it could have worked out so differently.

All Mod Cons was the pivotal third album in The Jam's career. The second album, *This is the Modern World*, though not exactly a flop, had failed to pick up sales-wise on the momentum of their debut, *In the City*, and rumours circulated in the press that a third album had been scrapped by Polydor. Paul Weller was struggling as a songwriter and evidence of this could be seen in Bruce Foxton taking over A-side duties for the 'News Of The World' single and also lead vocals on the Kinks cover, 'David Watts'.

But tucked away on the B-side of that was a clue that Weller was about to find his muse again. "A' Bomb In Wardor Street' was a searing slab of Punk power that *NME* darlings The Clash would have been proud of. It gave us hope. The follow-up would obliterate all remaining fears. 'Down in the Tube Station at Midnight' was the song that Weller always promised. A *Play For Today* condensed down to four minutes that perfectly captured the violent, threatening mood of the times. Listening to it you felt you were taking every step down into the tube station with the song's main character; feeling his trepidation, carried along by that incredible bass-line and with the words ringing in your ears: "They smelt of pubs, and wormwood scrubs, and too many right wing meetings." You didn't need to have been in a tube station to know that feeling.

I remember clearly getting *All Mod Cons* home and pulling out the inner sleeve. Before even putting the record on I just sat in my room for ages gazing at the artwork, taking in all those beautiful Mod images. Then the crackle of the needle hitting the vinyl and we're in to the title track. What a way to start an album and the way it segued straight into 'Too Be Someone' – Wow! I was totally hooked. Weller sang about the dreams of all working class kids, but he also knew the pitfalls – the snarling, threatening louts on the street, yet set to a gorgeous melody and harmonies. But two songs on and hidden away is the tender love song, 'English Rose', before Side One comes to a close with the psychedelic feedback of 'In The Crowd'.

Side Two introduces us to the character, 'Billy Hunt', 'It's Too Bad' gives us Beatles harmonies, before leading into two absolute gems, 'Fly' and 'The Place I Love' – the former being an incredibly delicate number that would have been unheard of a year before at the height of Punk. Here, more than anything, was proof that Weller had outgrown his humble Punk beginnings and had now blossomed into a mature, fully-rounded songwriter.

The album finishes of course on "A' Bomb' and 'Tube Station'. I remember sitting there tingling at the end of it, like I'd just witnessed history in the making. When The Jam first burst onto the scene just over a year before they dared to be my generation's The Who. After I'd listened to *All Mod Cons* that first time I knew they had become our Beatles.

Diz

Paul Weller once set fire to a copy of the Punk fanzine *Sniffing Glue* on stage and told the audience, "This is your fucking bible!" in response to the elitism of a certain section of the Punk movement, who viewed The Jam with unbounded scepticism and distrust – mostly because they could write, play and sing.

Well actually the above statement was seen another way…

A story started that what Weller really did was set fire to the flag of Ireland on stage and rant about 'Irish murdering bastards' in response to the IRA bombing campaign in London and other parts of England. Allied to the fact that The Jam wore Union Jack suits and sported the UK flag on their drums, guitars and amps, it was more than apparent to many in Belfast that they were in fact 'National Front' and that they would never play in Ireland for fear of assassination.

It became clear very quickly that The Jam stood firmly against fascism or racism of any kind and promoted the idea of working class unity and pride. The rumour faded away but still they never played Belfast and it has long been one of my great regrets that I never got to see them live. I guess that back in those days Belfast simply wasn't an attractive venue for most bands. A large part of it was down to the Troubles as there was always the chance of the gig being cancelled due to some incident or other, but I would imagine that there would also have been logistics and financial drawbacks to putting on a gig in the Ulster Hall, with its limited capacity.

Every time The Jam released tour dates I ran my eye frantically over the list to find out when the Belfast gig was. We were never on the list. I always held out hope for the "Further dates to be confirmed", but they never were.

In 1982 two of my mates decided that they would travel to Wembley Arena for one of the farewell dates. Firstly, I had no way of affording the fare or the spending money and secondly, I didn't actually believe they would go. But go they did and caught The Jam on 2nd December 1982, a gig I have heard many times since on bootleg tapes and CDs. I was extremely annoyed that I didn't have the money or the push to get there and the following week they played their last gig and that was that.

However, despite all that I actually have been to see The Jam live in concert and at Wembley Arena as well. My mate who went to the gig brought me a souvenir programme and obviously told me all about it and how they waited outside to see Weller in a Rover and Buckler in his Mk III Cortina Estate, complete with roof rack, drive past and wave at them before and after the gig. He told me about the atmosphere, the venue and the people they met, and all about the trip.

And so we made a deal. If anyone ever asked, then I was there with him, providing that he could claim to have been at The Clash gig in the Ulster Hall in 1978 (which I most definitely was at). And that's what we did, for years and years. I was there, I have memories of The Jam being driven in, I know the running order and how they played all the songs (we particularly went mental at that fantastic guitar intro to 'Going Underground') and although I lost my ticket stub in the push to get out of the arena, I have a souvenir programme of the event.

Tony Spence

It was the summer of 1978 and I was 16. My musical tastes at that time ran from the Beatles to the Carpenters, Elton John to a bit of chart shit! Little did I know what was round the corner! What was waiting for me a few short months away? From a fashion point of view it was drainpipe Levis, baseball boots and lumberjack shirts – Happy 'fuckin' days. The Fonz, Richie and Ralph, "Malph".

In November of that year I walked into Our Price records in town and the song blasting out caught my ear in an instant. The track ultimately changed the way I looked at life, the way I approached life. The way I played it out. The track was 'Down in the Tube Station at Midnight'.

Over the next few years I discovered what real music was all about. Not my mum and dad's music… but my own. I immersed myself in this whole new scene. The Jam, The Who, the Small Faces, Northern Soul… everything I could get my hands on. The Sony music centre was "red hot"! During 1979 I also discovered girls, who until that point had been an elusive dream! I discovered amazing love songs like 'Fly' and 'Tonight at Noon'. Songs that when played in the company of my first real girlfriend, seemed to have an amazing effect!

I remember missing out on tickets for a gig once. The recorded message said "SOLD OUT". Only one course of action… get down to London on the train to get some. We arrived at the Rainbow in Finsbury Park to, well, I don't know what we had planned – we just thought we might be lucky. We rocked up at the front box office and asked the lady for three tickets to that night's gig. She said, "SOLD OUT", to which a gruff voice in the doorway behind her responded, "I've got three you can 'ave". John Weller to the rescue! Made us pay, though – but what would you expect from the great negotiator!

From there we went straight to Shelley's Shoes in Carnaby Street to get new shoes. Once inside the shop we started chatting-up the lady manager. She showed us the new Jam shoe: black suede, white leather stripe up the back and down the front, with two down each side. We had to have them! We arrived at the front entrance at 7pm – the foyer was chocker. We walked in and I swear we were the only ones in the place with those shoes on… well, until Paul Weller walked on stage.

James Tindley

From seeing The Jam I had checked out artists like Lee Dorsey and Wilson Pickett to hear the originals of some of the covers they were doing, and got into Soul music proper from that.

Bob Manton – The Purple Hearts

The first music I really loved was Bowie, Genesis and Pink Floyd, but then Punk happened and amongst the brilliant music to come out of '77 was The Jam. I first heard them on John Peel's show, though I can't remember which song it was. My favourite has always been 'Down in the Tube Station at Midnight'. I didn't get to see The Jam until the Glasgow Apollo gig on the farewell tour, but the feeling was of being at something very, very special. The place was mental and the band were perfect – they seemed particularly up for it. I think they also played every song I wanted them to. Fantastic night.

Pat Nevin

START Buying the *In the City* album the week it was released. There was something different here: not Punk, not Rock.

TIME FOR TRUTH Weller's statement that he would probably vote Tory, awakening my own political consciousness. I didn't know what I was, but I knew I wasn't a Tory.

THAT'S ENTERTAINMENT My first Jam gig, bizarrely enough at Wembley Arena. With Generation X, The Pirates and, err, Slade. Some geezer got knifed, Noddy got hit on the head with a plastic bottle thrown from the front row.

STANDARDS After a difficult second album, Weller & Co now shook up the music biz with *All Mod Cons*. From now on, Punk would have to change.

IN THE CROWD The Music Machine, Camden, December 1979. My favourite Jam gig. Camaraderie, Solidarity and Civility. The Jam audience were different. This would soon change with their popularity.

SET THE HOUSE ABLAZE Paris '81. Long coach trip, arrogant fans, stupefied French, too much alcohol and drugs. Something had to give. A mid-gig ruck between the homes and the aways pulls a reaction from Weller. Tying a Union Jack to the mic stand does not help matters. Afterwards, I get my ticket signed by Paul and Bruce. No Rick. Still a regret that I don't have a full house.

IT'S TOO BAD Weller announces the split. Much shock, but the timing is right. Last tour. Catch 'em at Wembley. I do not have tickets for Brighton.

HERE COMES THE WEEKEND Brighton, Saturday, 11th December 1982. Grey day, in all senses. Still no ticket. Original cost – five English pounds. My friend Keith sells me two tickets for an enormous mark up. Some friend ("business is business", etc). Yeah, and bullfrogs are bullfrogs. Tense gig. Both band and fans know what's coming. At the end, my wife cries. So do I, thinking of how much I was fleeced by Keith.

DIG THE NEW BREED It would be a long time before another white English rock band would generate this sort of devotion (The Smiths were too niche), and what did we get? Oasis!? A bunch who would take us right back to the days of The Quo. Same turgid tune, different lyrics. The game is up, my friends, and The Jam were the last of their kind.

Neil Pearce

Buddy Ascott – The Chords

How and when did The Chords start up? What music/clobber were you into on the approach to The Chords?

The Chords were started by the cousins Billy and Martin in 1978, and then they recruited Chris Pope on lead guitar, who turned out to be quite a good songwriter! I was the last to join, in response to an advert in Melody Maker for a "Keith Moon-type drummer"! That was early in 1979. We were gigging within a month or so. Chris and I were massive Who fans, Martin was a Beatles fanatic, and Billy was into Hendrix, Buzzcocks, John Lennon, etc. We were all Clash followers, too. Clothes-wise, I think Martin was always the smartest, most fashion-conscious among us… I was very much a jeans and make-my-own T-shirts bloke. Billy was the frontman and always took care how he looked. Popey – not so much!

How did you get to know The Jam?

Weller came along to a very early gig at the Wellington pub in Waterloo. I don't remember him speaking with us, but we were aware he was there. This alerted Jimmy Pursey [of Sham 69], and it was him who tried to sign us to Polydor, via his nascent JP label. I don't think we met Rick or Bruce until we supported them at the Rainbow in May 1979.

Can you recall your first gig with The Jam? Where was it?

We had (literally) a five-minute soundcheck! There was another band on the bill – The Records – and between them and The Jam we were left with seconds to get our sound right. That mad rush only added to the nerves on the night – we had only been playing for a couple of months and here we were, at the Rainbow! We knew nothing about working a stage, projecting into a huge auditorium, or pacing ourselves… we were pretty manic that night. Well… every night!

Can you recall any atmospheres at gigs – the crowd, outstanding moments?

Well, at the Rainbow we were so new, nobody really knew us apart from a handful of fans – but we were brilliantly received, and sure we'd have got an encore if we hadn't been swept away with our drums and amps as we finished the last note! It was a fantastic experience. At Loch Lomond it was an all-day festival, and that was a crazy day – Punks had come to see SLF, skinheads to see Bad Manners, Mods to see us and The Jam…. Every time a band came on there was a surge in the crowd as the warring factions swapped places. There was so much violence that day, it was distressing. And The Tourists – they could drive anyone to violence! We're still mates with some people we met that day, though. Scotland was always a great area for The Chords – lovely people.

Are there fave Jam songs and albums for you?

'Away from the Numbers' and 'Got By In Time' from the first album. Later, 'When You're Young', 'Man in the Corner Shop' and 'Ghosts'. Fave album is still probably Sound Affects.

Did you ever meet John Weller? Do you have any memories of him?

Many times. He offered to manage The Chords – we said no because we felt just being on the same label was already too strong a connection. John was a very straight bloke, very tough-talking, too. We respected The Jam, but they weren't a huge influence, no matter how many times we have to say it! I was a fan of The Jam before we signed to Polydor, but then I felt we became rivals somewhat, and the press just wanted to call us copyists… that was very hard for Chris especially to take. His songwriting was never influenced by Weller, nor my drumming by Rick's – great drummer though he is! Fortunately, I got to know Rick a lot better in 2006–8, when Pope supported From The Jam many times. He's a great bloke, very down-to-earth. The one band we were all influenced by was The Who – they were, and always will be, gods!

In the '60s it was the Beatles v the Stones; in the '90s it was Blur v Oasis. The media has always tried to play groups off against each other. When Punk came along they were at it again: The Clash v The Jam.

I have to admit that at first, it was The Clash for me. At 11 years old in 1977 I thought I was a Punk. Clash T-shirt, army greens and monkey boots. A mug probably. A Punk never. To be honest, the way my old dear was, there was never a chance of me being able to embrace Punk properly. I would have to find something more socially acceptable.

Anyway, The Clash came to Edinburgh in 1978 on the 'Give 'Em Enough Rope' Tour, and without my parents knowing (I knew there was no way I would be allowed to go, so I was going to see school mates who lived on the other side of Edinburgh as far as they were concerned!), I went along to the gig. So, The Clash at the Edinburgh Odeon was my first gig. What can I say? It was a benchmark for every other gig that I have been to. They were superb. A night of complete chaos and well worth the battering I got when I got home over an hour late.

At that time I was aware of The Jam. I had bought the singles 'In The City' and 'All Around The World' when they were released, and I thought they were cracking songs. But what confused me was that the band didn't look like Punks. Too much for my young mind to take in. Anyway, when *Sounds* told me that it was one or the other – The Jam or The Clash – The Jam were kicked into touch and The Clash it was.

I think it was when 'Strange Town' came out that I got interested again. The song summed up city living, and it was something that I related to immediately. I loved the "BREAK IT UP, BREAK IT UP" outro as well, of course. I think this was the first song where I actually started listening properly to the lyrics – something that I have done ever since with anything written by Weller.

Back in the day the only music paper that was worth reading was *Sounds*. The *NME* was for posh wannabe mugs. Your 'Bromley Contingent' – that sort of person. Middle-class suburban rebels. They had journos like Caroline Coon, who epitomised everything that was wrong with the Punk scene. As for *Melody Maker*? Who actually bought it? Nope. As hard as it will be for younger people to believe now, but Garry Bushell was the only music journalist that mattered back then. I read everything that he wrote and was beginning to get interested in his promotion of all things Mod in late '78/early '79. He educated me to the fact that rather than looking like a bunch of idiots in suits, The Jam were actually the most sussed band out. Then, as I said, they released 'Strange Town', and the rest is history.

I don't know about everyone else but I think it's when you listen to The Jam albums that you really appreciate how good they are. Yes, the singles were awesome, but so were a lot of singles from a lot of bands. The Jam's albums, however, were something else.

Due to money constraints – the paper-round money had to fund *Sounds*, singles, youth club discos and running riot across Scotland in the name of Heart of Midlothian Football Club – I hadn't been able to afford albums. However, I got *All Mod Cons* when the old man surprisingly gave me some pocket money, and that was that. My life changed. Everything about the album fascinated me: the cover photo with the band looking spot on; Weller looking the business with the suedehead and Sta-Prest; the inset sleeve with the diagram of the scooter; and the record itself with every song an anthem.

I had to find out more and for my 13th birthday in June 1979 I got *In the City* and *This is the Modern World*. Everyone slags off *Modern World*, but I always thought it was a decent record. Not as good as the ones before or after, but an essential filler between the Punk sound of *In the City* and the 1960s/Kinks-sounding *All Mod Cons*. It also gave me 'Here Comes the Weekend', which was a regular tune for me to play on a Friday night as I was dressing to impress at the weekly youth club disco. However, it was *In the City* that contained the best of all The Jam tracks, 'Away from the Numbers'. It was always a bit of a Mod anthem but even in those pre-Mod days I thought it was probably the best song that I had heard up until then.

By the time the Merton Parkas appeared on *Top of the Pops* to bring the Mod revival into the nation's living rooms, I was already on the road to becoming a fully-fledged Mod. So, 13 years old in 1979 and I was

contd.

trying my best to dress like Paul Weller. It set me in good stead. You know how it is in high school? You have to have something about you, especially when you are at a shit secondary modern. I wasn't the best sportsman in the world, which was one way to get some status, and I have never been the hardest of blokes, but I always got away with it because I knew a lot about music. Becoming the first Mod in my year was natural for me and about a year later, when everyone else was getting into it, that was always remembered.

I had another advantage: my dad was a British Rail employee, which meant that we got free rail travel. Therefore, most of my clothes were bought in London's Carnaby Street or Johnsons in the King's Road. As such, I always got a bit of respect from the hard lads in my school, who were mostly Mods. As the Beach Boys sung: "...the bad guys know us and they leave us alone..."

The Jam came to Edinburgh in December 1979 but much to my disgust I was grounded after a neighbour had grassed me up for getting involved in trouble at a Hearts away game. So, my first Jam gig was almost a year later, in October 1980, at the Edinburgh Playhouse. This gig came about a month after Secret Affair had played the Edinburgh Odeon and I didn't think I would ever see so many Mods in one place again; however I was proved wrong at this gig.

The excitement of the occasion still lives with me. Approaching the Playhouse about an hour before the doors opened, there were gangs of young Mods all over the city. Too young to go to the pubs, we ruled the streets that night. Walking down to the venue was a sea of parkas. In all honesty I had actually been a bit nervous about the gig, as I thought there may still be a sizable Punk presence, but on that night in Edinburgh it really was a Mod world.

The main problem with the Playhouse is that it is a seated theatre and initially, the bouncers were on top, making sure that everyone stayed in their rows. Then Paul's dad came on stage with his famous, "...best fuckin' band in the world... The Jam!!" and the place erupted. A youth explosion, as Weller himself might even say! Everyone piled down the front and steamed into the bouncers who were soon on the back foot. The Jam looked immaculate and they were straight into the tracks from the forthcoming *Sound Affects* album. As well as getting into the music all of us lot were trying to clock the gear that Weller was wearing so that we could try and keep one step ahead. Looking around the venue that night, I can remember it being wall-to-wall boating blazers, tonic suits and parkas. Hardly a Punk in sight. My concerns were allayed.

It was over all too quickly and then it was out into the Edinburgh night. There were a group of about 50 skinheads hanging around. In Edinburgh, the "skins" usually had the upper hand on the streets, but not that night, as they were scattered all the way from the venue into Princes Street. A great end to a first-class night.

After that I saw The Jam on another three occasions. Twice in Edinburgh and once in Glasgow. On 6/4/82 they came to the Playhouse again on the 'Trans Global Unity Express' tour, then later, in '82, they played at Ingliston on the 'Solid Bond In Your Heart' tour. The Ingliston gig was all standing and a bigger venue – maybe about 6000 or so. Again it was a sea of parkas, and as it was just outside of the city I can remember rows and rows of immaculate scooters parked up in the car park.

Just before the band came on stage there were two Punks in the crowd near us. One of them wore a *I Hate Mods* badge. You have to admire his bottle but he must have had a death wish. I just remember the two guys disappearing in the flurry of punches that were being thrown and then getting stretchered out of the venue. All in all a great prelude to get the adrenaline running before the band came on.

The last time I saw The Jam was at the Apollo in Glasgow on the 'Beat Surrender' tour. Weller always liked playing the Apollo for the Glasgow crowd and it was very emotional that night. Glasgow always had a huge number of what would be considered "gang Mods", and they were out in force. However, because of the significance of the gig I remember feeling sad. It was like being present at the end of an era. While The Jam probably played a better gig that night, my favourite was probably the first Jam gig back in 1980.

The Jam influenced my life! There, I have said it. I know it sounds muggy to say, but it's true. I was a

contd.

working-class guy from a council estate. The Jam taught me to take pride in that. To have pride in myself and care about my appearance. I think back on what a gang of teenagers looked like then to what they look like now. There is no pride now. Nothing.

The Jam influenced the whole Mod thing. Lazy journalists look back on the Mod revival now and deride it as being an offshoot fad of the release of the movie *Quadrophenia*. Of course that doesn't take into account that young Jam fans were adopting the Mod look as early as 1977 and that by late '78–early '79, the Mod revival was spreading out of London – and all this at least six months before *Quadrophenia* was released.

Even the transition into football Casual in 1983 was a continuation of the Mod ideals for me. Even now, in my mid 40s, the Mod ideals are there. New suit for work: needs to be single breasted, three buttons, tonic or mohair, preferably; new shirt: Brooks Brothers button-down, please. All that stems from a band from Woking!

As a parting shot: in the late '70s, when I got into The Jam, the group that all the "lads" followed was Sham 69. I admit that I was a bit of a Sham Army lad myself. However, to put things into perspective, when Jimmy was writing about going down the pub with some geezer called Harry, Paul Weller was writing 'The Butterfly Collector'. Says it all, really. Sham were a decent Punk band. The Jam are a lot more than that.

Gavin Anderson

Getting older makes you more cynical, I think – less tolerant of crap music, maybe. I often find myself thinking, if I was 15 years old today, in 2012, what would I be listening to? It's hard to imagine myself being caught up in TV talent shows, the dross and drivel that production companies are feeding the youth of today. How lucky was I, with thousands of other teenagers, to be born when we were, hitting our teenage years in the late '70s when The Jam were on the road to greatness. *The Old Grey Whistle Test* on a Monday night in 1978 was the first time I had seen The Jam on TV; they played two or three songs, I can't remember, but it was the black suits and the energy that stood out for me.

I was into the Punk and New Wave stuff around at the time: The Clash, the Buzzcocks and The Jam all done it for me, but it wasn't until *All Mod Cons*, in 1978, that my obsession really started. I got the album with my birthday money in November '78, in an old Co-Op Department Store in Belfast, and I was fascinated by the album's cover, and more importantly, the lyrics of the songs.

This guy Weller could really write great songs. The title track, 'All Mod Cons', criticising the fickleness of people, social climbers and bandwagon jumpers; 'In the Crowd' was captivating; the melodic 'It's Too Bad' regrets lost love, with no going back. 'To Be Someone' – not even a rock star, or a famous footballer – but just in life in general, to get yourself out of the mire and be better in everything you do (also the title of my Mods in Ireland book); to my favourite Jam song ever, 'Down In The Tube Station at Midnight'. I still listen to this today. If you close your eyes, its eerie, but you are there – it's amazing how the lyrics make you believe that you are actually experiencing the fear and terror of the victim. The poster on the wall advertising British Rail breaks, you can almost see it. It's an amazing song, timeless.

What that album did for me, and I'm sure thousands other kids, was give a wake-up call. It set the standard for The Jam. *All Mod Cons* was the one that done it for me, especially at an age when you are very impressionable and your whole life's in front of you.

Marty McAllister

1979 – WE WERE SO CLOSE

The last two months of 1978 were labelled the "Winter of Discontent". Following on from the bakers' strike there were more strikes from rail workers, lorry drivers and public workers. Money was getting tighter for most but Nottingham Forest fans didn't complain when their club signed Trevor Francis for £1 million and led the club to the most unlikely of European Cup wins. He was the UK's first million-pound signing. The public did, however, have 'YMCA' from the Village People to dance along to, alongside the sisterhood anthem, 'I Will Survive', by Gloria Gayner.

February marked the untimely death of an unlikely poster boy, Sid Vicious. He was only 21 years old. That same month Eric Clapton married Patti Boyd, the ex-girlfriend of George Harrison, and still walked about with a face like a slapped arse.

March was all about 'Strange Town' and The Jam were proving to be one of THE great singles bands, with classic B-sides like 'The Butterfly Collector' bringing in even more new fans.

April saw the release of the year's biggest-selling single with Art Garfunkel's 'Bright Eyes', which was taken from the blockbuster cartoon movie about rabbits. The Yorkshire ripper also claimed his eleventh victim. The country was devastated, nervous and suspicious. A pint of milk rose to 15 pence, while Arsenal won the FA Cup in dramatic style by beating Manchester United 3–2, with Alan Sunderland grabbing a late winner (helped by his aero-dynamic barnet).

On 4th May, the brutal evil genius that was Margaret Thatcher took the helm of the country and started her assault on the working class, changing the country forever over the next decade.

The summer arrived and with it the official opening of a nudist beach in Brighton. Which was nice. August saw the arrival of Two Tone with The Special AKA's 'Gangsters', who alongside The Jam and The Clash changed kid's lives with a mix of social comment and killer grooves.

September saw the release of the brilliant 7", 'When You're Young', B-sided with Bruce's finest composition, 'Smithers-Jones'. The Jam was sharing the airwaves with the 'Rappers' Delight' from the Sugar Hill Gang, 'War of the Worlds' from Jeff Wayne and 'Message in a Bottle' by The Police (and some old shit by The Dooleys).

November gave birth to a TV series that had the nation enthralled. Arthur Daley, ably assisted by Terry McCann, in *Minder* proved to be some of the most inspired writing and comical situations that television has ever seen. The year ended with threats of more strikes, imminent job losses, the Thatcher government announcing its 'Right to Buy' scheme and the opening of the first J.D. Wetherspoons pub (to house future generations of the dole culture). Eddie Kidd completed an 80-foot jump on his motorcycle to become the British Evel Knievel (and had to fight the women off with a shitty stick until he proper hurt himself a few years later).

'Strange Town' / 'The Butterfly Collector'

Martyn Goddard and I went to Norfolk to do this shoot. That's me in the picture. Paul loved the idea about someone standing at a crossroads with a signpost in a strange town, wondering where to go next. I didn't want the person to be recognised, so that's why it's soft focus. The butterfly on the back makes me think that the band wanted a double A-side. The Weller poem added to it.

Bill Smith

'Strange Town' was recorded on 9th January 1979 at RAK Studios, along with the B-side 'The Butterfly Collector'* and another unreleased demo 'Simon'. The song was released on 17th March and reached Number 15 in the UK singles chart.

Like so many singles, 'Strange Town' never appeared on a studio album, but appeared in later "best of" collections. The promo video uses the entrance to Victoria Underground station and features the band on stage at the Rainbow – apparently the neon sign was too delicate and only lasted a couple of nights!

Coming a year after the release of *All Mod Cons*, this shows the band developing The Jam sound: the trademark Rickenbacker guitar, driving bass riff and drums, plenty of reverb and feedback and overdubs, along with the trademark production of Vic Coppersmith-Heaven.

The song tells the story of a person finding himself in London, but could easily apply to any big city, with all the hustle and bustle, busy streets and tall buildings. A year previously, Weller found himself living in London for the first time, so these lyrics are a poignant reflection of how he probably felt, living in the capital as opposed to the suburbs of Woking. (Some of the lyrics first appeared in another song, 'World's Apart').

Original demos are at a faster tempo than the final cut. (The song got a rare airing at a Teenage Cancer Trust gig in 2007 with Noel Gallagher, although it was played in Japan and subsequently dropped on a 2008 tour. It is now back in favour and a firm crowd pleaser, although the latest live version is even slower than original demos). The single was released in the US, two months later, in May 1979. However, for this release 'The Butterfly Collector' was catalogued as the A-side. As such the single never charted in the States.

Jon Abnett

* Incidentally the acetate for this is incorrectly named "Collecting Butterflies".

Coach travelling back after the Bath Pavillion gig, 22nd December 1979.

'Strange Town'

'Strange Town' is one of the bands toughest songs and is almost like a three-part mini opera. The tune is full of bravado, excitement and anticipation, so naturally it would appeal to young people travelling to a gig or to a footy match. The song provides observations and feelings for someone, or something, newly arriving in Britain.

For a group of young males the thrill of turning up on the door step of some unfamiliar town and claiming it as their own for the duration of their visit promised much. There may be the opportunity to try it on with the local girls, go on the piss and throw up on somebody's garden path, or to take a piss against a wall before scratching The Jam or some football team onto a lamp post. All gone now, thanks to CCTV.

The song begins with all three band members coming in together. Weller strums his guitar in a stab-like fashion often found on Motown songs, as does parts of Buckler's stomping drum beat. Only, there is a more Punky edge to their technique. Then there are the hand claps, which we all join in.

If the song is about an alien turning up in Britain, he or she (or it I suppose) finds themselves trudging around London's Oxford Street. During their exploring they stop passers-by, but are shook off with responses of "don't care" and "gotta go mate". Weller is backed-up on the chorus by Foxton's harmonies and Buckler keeps the momentum of the song driving along whilst he switches from his hi-hats to the ride cymbal.

Weller continues to sing about the importance of having the right clothes. I remember when a young lad from Bangor arrived in the town where I lived. We couldn't understand a word that he said, but we accepted him into our fold for the short time he stayed because he was wearing a pair of red, white and blue Jam stage shoes. If this lad hadn't been dressed in such a Modish way, he may have got the smash on the nose that Weller sings about. The truth is, people are territorial and feel the need to defend the place where they live, whether they slag the place off or not.

'The Butterfly Collector'

I wait, I wait and I wait some more and then I get my cue and I'm joining in with the drum roll around the high tom-toms. I'm now into the song, I'm nodding my head in time to the beat, 1-2-3-4, again 1-2-3-4. I've done it, phew, rest, relax, I've got through the first part. Gather myself, concentrate, the song hasn't finished yet. Wait for it, wait for it. Now, more tom-tom rolls and I'm off again. Bollocks, shit, I've lost time, shit, I'm lost, I'm confused. Bollocks, I'll have to try it again. And this is how I learnt to play drums. The first song I tried to learn to play with the drums was 'The Butterfly Collector' and it wasn't the only Jam song that I attempted.

The song begins with an effected guitar sound strumming a gentle arpeggio. There is only a short intro but it's enough to usher in the atmosphere of the song. Foxton opts for the 'less is more' bass line that does the job in supporting Weller's words. Then Buckler arrives with a six drum beat fill and he is now into the song, pushing it along with a steady 4-4 rhythm.

Weller continues to sing about a groupie of the day (he mentions her second rate perfume) and her hobby or involvement in capturing minds more than their bodies at the expense of not learning to cook or sew. On the surface it's as if Weller is having a dig at the woman but this doesn't appear to be the whole story. Weller also mentions morals and an insane world and how we should all share the blame because we have all done something to contribute to the insanity. The song is haunting and captivating and Weller has the last word by stating that he feels no sorrow for the kings and queens of this self-created world of the butterfly collectors.

Snowy

'When You're Young' / 'Smithers-Jones'

I've got very little recollection of this, I'm afraid. I don't know why I've got everything covered in white sheeting. The shot of the crowd coming out of Piccadilly Circus on the back would have tied up with Smithers-Jones going to work.

'The Eton Rifles' / 'See-Saw'

The photo was from the Imperial War Museum and I'm pretty sure that they are Eton School Cadets in the 1950s. I like the lettering on this as well.

Setting Sons

That was almost a concept album for Paul, and the key idea was the army along with Britishness. I found the tiny statue of army medics carrying a wounded soldier in the Imperial War Museum, which was about a foot high, so we shot that and cut it out and put it against the sky background, and also embossed it so it had a bass-relief feel to it. At that time Paul had some new designers who he wanted to get involved in doing bits and pieces with the sleeves. They did the back cover with the bulldog and I said, let's do this statue for the front. On the inside I worked with the same guys to put that together. This was around the time Paul started to have more say in the design of their artwork.

Bill Smith

Pete Carver on lights, Bath Pavillion, 22nd December 1979.

Girl on the phone …

SETTING SONS [Review by Erland Johnson]

Setting Sons: the most important album of The Jam's career. Now before you start shouting, *All Mod Cons, Sound Affects* and all the others at me, let me explain why. *Setting Sons* will always be the band's defining moment, where they clearly showed that they were here for the duration. Any talk of AMC being some kind of fluke was completely squashed in half an hour's worth of vinyl, and it was the momentum that propelled the band to producing number one singles and being the number one in the charts of all our hearts. It also had the intelligence to steer a wide berth around the '79 [Mod] revival, whilst just throwing enough red, white and blue target-shaped carrots to those who yearned for it. It was that good, it could even allow 'Strange Town' and 'When You're Young' to sit this one out. Right then, now we're all agreed, let's crack on....

The St John's Ambulance bearers, cast by Benjamin Clemens in 1919, provide the cover material, and I fell in love with it instantly. Adverts for the new album were in the music papers, and without even knowing what was tucked away in the grooves, it grabbed me by the bollocks and promised me I wouldn't be disappointed (which reminds me of the ex-wife, but hey, you can't always get it right can you?). When I got it as a wet-behind-the-ears 12 year old, it meant absolutely fucking everything to me. I listened, learned and digested every last word, every note, every sound. The inlay sleeve on the beach with the bulldog and the lyrics lovingly printed became part of my everyday fabric. I'm getting misty eyed, let's crack on again....

For me, the true sign of a great album is one where your favourite track changes on a day-to-day basis. What do I go for today?

The rollercoaster of emotions that is 'Thick As Thieves', which lovingly recalls a bond that could never be broken, whilst at the same time declaring that same bond smashed and shattered beyond repair?

'Saturday's Kids', a tongue in cheek look at the working class boys and girls who live for the weekend?

Bruce's finest three minutes, 'Smithers-Jones', magically transformed into an orchestral masterpiece (Buckler's apparently), exaggerating the tale of his dad being given the heave-ho and his inevitable descent into unemployment, bitterness and resentment?

'Wasteland', with Weller at his most evocative, almost placing you smack bang in the middle of the song, in amongst the holy Coca-Cola tins and the punctured footballs?

'Private Hell', a hellish insight into the psychology of a woman/wife/mother/grandmother, with Weller almost joyously whispering into her ear how her life has disintegrated before her very eyes?

'Burning Sky', which still bends my head to this day that a 21 year old could have such a grasp of how time can have such a savage effect on seemingly bomb-proof friendships?

'Eton Rifles', Number 1 on David Cameron's iPod (which part didn't the PM get?). Hard, cool, aggressive, sneering and the greatest use of the word 'catalyst' in a top three pop song ever?

No pop-pickers, today's choice is going to be 'Little Boy Soldiers', and I could reel off a whole raft of reasons why: the whole musical idea of it, three separate movements in three minutes and nine seconds; the closing payoff with the heroic corpse and the futile medal; the production; the fact it just set them leagues apart from every other Revival band that sought to usurp The Jam's dominance in that three minutes... I could go on for hours, and I probably would, but I've got a deadline to keep.

We haven't even touched on the start and the finish yet — the headlong rush into paranoia of 'Girl On The Phone', or the adrenalin-fuelled Holland–Dozier–Holland tribute in 'Heatwave'. From beginning to end this album demonstrated the band's new-found confidence and authority, without sounding forced or mannered in any way, shape or form. Within a few months The Jam were riding high at the top of the singles charts and would continue to do so until Weller saw fit to pull the plug.

Setting Sons was the moment that the snowball of momentum gathered an unstoppable pace and knocked over anybody who dared to stand in its way, and 32 and a bit years down the line it'll always have a special place on my turntable.

"By 1979 the Jam had a very loyal following, backed up by the release of the singles, 'When You're Young' and 'Eton Rifles' – they were massive.

There were also the Rainbow gigs of that year. You had bands like The Chords supporting them as well as other Mod groups of the day, like Secret Affair. My fondest times of seeing The Jam were at the Rainbow. The Rainbow was a fantastic venue – an old picture house with all its gilt and ornate designs adourning the doors and walls. They seemed to have an affinity with the venue and that came through at the gigs. They played there for the venue's 50th anniversary. At one gig, Weller even commented that, 'We've played here so many times, I should have a bed upstairs'.

This was also the year that The Jam played the Marquee as John's Boys, on the 2nd November. That was when the glass doors got smashed. The place was rammed, to an extent whereby if there had been a fire then it would have surely resulted in tragedy. There is no way that any venue would get away with this in these days of health and safety. But such was the nature of the Jam's management to make sure each and every fan, or at least the majority who had turned up, got into that gig. The Nips supported that night.

The Jam played under three different names in their time together: John's Boys, The Eton Rifles (which was the night after the Marquee at the Nashville, The Nips supporting again) and The Jam Road Crew (but that was just a small do at The Cricketers in Woking, a charity gig to celebrate Valentine's Day). The Marquee gig was just blinding. By now there was a football crowd element creeping in, too. In some ways a destructive element, always looking for aggro against other 'tribes'. It was at the Rainbow's 50th Anniversary gig that front seats got ripped out – the band still played on, though!

Polydor always marketed any Jam release well in the music press. For some reason 'The Eton Rifles' advert sticks in my mind: a full page spread, with an image of a straw boater and hand pistol. Like everyone and his brother, it now transpires that I wasn't the only one to start collecting these trade adverts.

Setting Sons was also released this year, but it was nothing like AMC. Foxton's thundering bass and Weller's jangling three chord riffs, along with Buckler's timpani drums on 'Little Boy Soldiers' – absolute class.

I'm quite a shy person, but I remember coming home from the local record shop with a massive cut-out display of the front cover of the album – the looks I got carting it through Chatham High Street, then onto the 166 bus back home! That ended up on my bedroom wall, along with all the other posters. By this time I had also spray painted the Jam logo onto said wall. When I left home I had to redecorate my bedroom to cover it up.

Jon Abnett"

The Jam were my Beatles and the best band I have ever seen. When John Weller came on stage, the butterflies in my stomach just erupted. I was jumping up and down trying to see what Paul Weller was wearing. I first saw The Jam in 1979 in Hammersmith. I was still at school and was buzzing the next day whilst telling all my schoolmates about it. The last time I saw them was at Wembley on the last night [of their final tour], and I just couldn't believe that I would never see them again. It was a very sad night – and an even sadder night when I came out and made my way back to my scooter, only to find that someone had nicked the wheel-trims off my Vespa.

Steve V. Page

I first heard The Jam as a newly-arrived teenager. I was into The Who and then later the Two Tone era – Mod was the only way to be back in the late '70s. You were either a crusty hippie, a strange skinhead, an out-of-date Punk or a cool Mod. Music and fashion back then went hand in hand. It's not like today, where everything is mixed.

The first record I bought by The Jam was 'David Watts', the storming Kinks cover. My brother Noel was into Punk and Liam into comics or whatever kids liked back then.

Unfortunately I never saw The Jam live – it's one of my biggest regrets.

The Jam were the best, Weller was the don: he was cool, he was credible, he was smart and he could write a song.

There was a guy who lived near me called Steve Mallarkey. He was a Jam nut: he had the shoes, the suit, the hair, the lot; he didn't have a scooter though. Mind you, he was only 14.

My favourite album is *Sound Affects*, absolutely loved 'Man in the Corner Shop'.

Apart from The Jam, it was The Specials – they were the only two bands worth bothering about. I never bothered with Madness after 1979, they went too pop for me.

Someone's gonna crack on your dreams tonight…

Paul Gallagher

'Setting Sons' shoot.

I always wanted to live abroad. I was thinking of either England or the US, but I never got into American music. Then I had a chance to come and visit the UK in 1979. It was a tour that was planned by a music magazine in Japan, called 'Rock Tour in London'.

It was only for 10 days. I just felt I want to live here as soon as I arrived. Then I went back to Japan, and I talked to my parents to discuss if I could come to London again to study English, and they agreed. So I went back to study English, and at this point I planned to go back to Japan after three months, but I extended my visa and stayed longer, which allowed me to see The Jam at the Rainbow Theatre for the first time. I simply loved the UK and it's people, but I must say The Jam was the main reason. I just couldn't stand the thought of being in Japan and waiting for them to come over on tour. I just wanted to see them as much as I could!

I first met Paul in Tokyo in 1980. Gill asked me and my friend to have a cup of tea with her and Paul. They weren't surprised to see me in Brighton: I was already going everywhere to see them.

There was lots of jealousy from other fans: most were nice but just a few of them used to call me "fuckin' Jap", "slit eyes" and all sorts. But Paul used to say, "Fuck them! They're just fucking idiots!"

I mainly knew Paul and Bruce, and Paul was the one always being so kind to me; and his father was always concerned about me travelling around on my own. Paul and his family were great, down-to-earth – they never made me feel like I was with someone famous at all.

I saw The Jam 70 times from December 1979 'til the end.

Keiko

Bizarre as it sounds, the *Something Else* [TV programme] recording was actually a bit dull. 'The Eton Rifles' had not been released so we did not know the song, though we did our best to pretend we did! I worked in Manchester at the time and I think I had been tipped off by the guy in Penny Farthing Records about the recording, so I just went down and asked for tickets.

I remember the audience were the biggest load of dickheads you could put in one room: there were probably 10 Jam fans in the audience with the rest made up of 1970s student types and girls with swept back hair. There was quite a lot of standing around with nothing happening. I actually spoke to Tony Wilson most, as we lived in the same village. The band he was promoting, some fucking shoe-gazers called Joy Division, looked about as joyful as your football team conceding a last minute losing goal. We just stood there, staring at them, waiting for the main event – we really did treat them like the support group.

We spoke to Buckler most that day and I remember he had the most fuck-awful clothes on, then changed into uniform for the recording. Weller was milling about, but I was a bit too 'cool for school' by this point, having met him a couple of times before. I was a right knob!

When The Jam played Newcastle Civic Hall on the *Sound Affects* tour, the mics went during the encore, so they played *In the City* and all the crowd sang the lyrics. I swear that is the happiest I have seen Weller on stage.

Garry O'Connor

Bruce with Mark Ellis.

Above and opposite: On the coach after the Bath Pavillion gig, 22nd December 1979.

It all started way back in 1977. As a 13-year-old schoolboy I thought of becoming a Punk, but there was always a '60s thing going on due to my dad being a Mod and me hearing the music he was into.

My first experience of The Jam was hearing 'All Around The World' on the radio and thinking, who the fuck is this? I needed to know more, went and bought the '45' and was immediately hooked. I got my mates round and said, listen to this. They too were hooked – and we comprised a Mod, a Skin and a Punk – but the tune appealed to one and all.

The next stage was I had to see the band live and while reading the *Birmingham Mail* newspaper, I noticed an advert for a Jam gig at what was the Top Rank Club in town. So I set off to Virgin Records to obtain a ticket. I got to the counter, but as the girl was about to sell me a ticket, another assistant butted in and said you needed to be 18 years old. I left the store gutted but I wasn't beaten, so I asked a passerby to get me a ticket, which she did, and I was bouncing!

The night came and I managed to get in. The venue had loads of scooters parked out front and inside was filled with Mods and Punks. The Jam finally took to the stage, so loud, but awesome. I can't really remember the set but remember Weller's 'angry young man' attitude and the crowd going berserk.

I tried in vain to meet the band after every gig I went to. Finally, I bumped into a Mod lad I knew from a clothes shop in town who had backstage passes and asked me if I wanted one? Silly question! After another blinding gig tinged with sadness (as we all knew off the dreaded break up), I ventured backstage and remember being stunned at where I was. I was totally stuck for words so I got my ticket and white Lonsdale sweatshirt signed and homed in on a gap on the seat between Weller and Buckler. Some girl tried to beat me to it, but no chance!

I sat there for at least an hour just talking shit to Weller, but I must have done something right because he still remembers me all these years later!

Due to age and lack of funds I couldn't see The Jam as many times as I would have wished, but cherish the times I did see them. Brilliant. Still untouchable.

Mark Hough

My first memory of seeing The Jam live was at the Brighton Centre on Saturday 15th December 1979. That was a weekend I won't forget. I went to Coventry during the day to watch Manchester United play, got thrown out of the ground by police for swearing, got the train to Brighton, saw the gig and a few hours later (the next day) crashed my motorbike badly, ruined my parka with all my Jam badges, and spent three months in hospital recovering with my head full of The Jam. I next saw them at the Hammersmith Odeon on the 18th or 19th November 1980, when I was lucky enough to have been given a drum skin backstage after the gig by RB [Rick Buckler]. It is hanging on the wall right by me as I write this.

Of course I had no idea then that just over two years later I would be lucky enough to be on the bill, supporting The Jam at the Brighton Centre. I was, after all, first and foremost a fan.

My main recollections are of being very interested in the guitar sound and style of PW's [Paul Weller] playing, so I was always trying to watch from the crowd, about five to ten rows from the front, what he did and how he did it. He was able to make his one guitar sound like two as far as I was concerned.

In 1980, while at Worthing Art College, I joined a band in Littlehampton that had just formed, called Jump In Your Datsun, and promptly bought a Rickenbacker 330 with some of the proceeds of my motorcycle crash insurance claim.

I always tried to get backstage after the gigs I went to with the intention of promoting the band. I managed to hand PW a bunch of poems at St Austell, Cornwall, on 8th December 1980. I saw him again at the Michael Sobell Sports Centre, when Bananarama supported them, on 13th December 1981.

PW told me he remembered the poems – in particular he mentioned the name of one of them (a year after I gave him the poems) called 'The Fisherman' – which was very encouraging, but still nothing to tell the band, though.

I always kept a cassette of the band's demo songs wherever I went and at some point I was walking along Oxford St. and saw JW in traffic right by me. As far as I can remember I threw a cassette into the open front window of his car, which might have been a Mercedes, but that may well be rose tinted glasses talking... and still nothing to tell the band....

I travelled to Paris to see The Jam at the Pavillon De Balthard in February 1981. That was a great experience. The travelling fans were allowed in very early on and I watched the whole set-up and soundcheck (see black and white photos). I got PW and BF to sign something to the band that night (subliminal marketing). During the gig there was quite a big scuffle and PW got very annoyed. I think I've seen a video of this gig somewhere on YouTube. One of the photos I took shows him as he stopped a song and waited for the fight to end.

Paris, February 1981.

Dear Barrie

I received your note with interest, interest enough to Say, I cannot help you immediately with a 'Single' but I can help maybe by offering you a support gig with The Jam, on their concert at Brighton Conference Centre 13 March, if you have a band that is ready and able to play a 25-30 minute Set, then feel free to write back and let me know.

Only then after seeing the band work, maybe we can see any potential, your letter sounded Sincere, I also am a sincere person

Let me know Soon,

Regards John Weller.

P.S. Please write to this address,

The Jam,
45/53 SINCLAIR RD,
LONDON - W.14

The JAM

Manager: John Weller

45-53 Sinclair Road,
London, W.14.

Phone: 01 602 5094
01 602 6351

Telex: 919534 NOMHIR

3rd February 1982

Barry Goodwin,
'Bancroft',
Radford Road,
Tinsley Green,
Crawley,
Sussex, RM10 3NN.

Dear Barry,

Thanks for your letter. This is to confirm that Jump In Your Datsun will be supporting The Jam at the Brighton Centre on 13th March. You will be the first group on stage. Please arrive no later than 4.00.p.m. on 13th with your backline equipment.

Yours sincerely,

Gill
P.P.
JOHN WELLER

35-1708-78

MCP
GUEST
PASS

NAME: JAM
ARTISTE: 11.12.82
DATE:
AUTHORIZED BY: TGP

MCP
CREW
PASS

NAME:
ARTISTE: JAM
DATE: 18.3.82
AUTHORIZED BY: TGP

THE BRIGHTON CENTRE

SATURDAY, 15th DECEMBER, 1979 at 8 p.m.

THE JAM

STANDING TICKET
MAIN HALL ONLY £3.00

BRIGHTON CENTRE RESTAURANT
(Magnificent Sea View)
Open two hours prior to most performances
Reservations: Telephone 203130

Neither the Council or their officers accept any responsibility for any loss or damage (howsoever caused or sustained) to any property whatsoever brought on to these premises.

Tickets cannot be exchanged or refunded.

The taking of unauthorised photographs during an artiste's live performance is a breach of the Copyright Act 1956. Cameras being used in defiance of this regulation will be removed to the cloakroom for the duration of the performance. The Management may also exercise the right to expose film if so requested by the artiste.

to Jumpin your Datsun
Paul Weller
Bruce Fox

Stepping up my marketing plan, in early 1982 I drove to PW's house in Woking. I think the address was something like 45 Balmoral, or Imperial, Drive. I can remember walking up the small suburban drive and shoving a cassette and a JIYD poster through the letter box before disappearing quickly. A few days later I received a letter from JW inviting the band to support The Jam at the Brighton Centre on Sunday March 13th. I was told that the gig might lead to more gigs and an involvement with the Respond label, and although PW popped into the dressing room to say hello we weren't there at the time and I only bumped into him in the loo, so not a good time to talk, really. When I did speak to him he didn't seem particularly talkative and I guess he was preoccupied with what maybe only he knew then: that was, breaking up the band later that year.

JW's [John Weller] letter showed what a genuine man he was. He said my letter sounded sincere and that he was a sincere person. That was after six years of answering people like me, so he really must have been exactly as he appeared. JW was very friendly at the gig, too. During our set he sat and talked to our singer's mum and told her how PW had been playing our main song, 'Dead In Your Garden', all the time in the tour bus. After the gig John came up to me on stage when we were clearing up and he handed me a £50 note, and that was that.

Someone called Tim came up to me after the gig. He was an engineer at Martin Rushent's studio in Goring-on-Thames. We spent a night recording in the studio (I don't think Martin Rushent knew we were there) and we also recorded at Alaska Studios under the arches at Waterloo, courtesy of our manager, Jazz Summers, who was managing Wham at the time. We played support to Rudi, Secret Affair, The Lurkers and The Alarm. Two tracks, 'Dead In Your Garden' and '17/5', were released on a south coast compilation record called *Seaside Rock*, organised by Airship Records, and John Peel played our tracks several times after I kept loitering outside his office in Regent St. at midnight and badgering him. I have a letter from Chris Parry (ex Polydor Jam person, I think) saying our demo was one of the best he had heard, but nothing came of our meeting and that's about it.

All these years later, The Jam are still a part of my life. I rekindled my interest in playing while buying a camera from Kingsley Photographic (sadly now gone) in Tottenham Court Rd. The manager and salesman, Tim Stavrinou, was a big fan. After a year of messing about with alcohol, crisps and guitars, last summer we (www.martellandmoray.com) released an album on iTunes, called *21st Century Neanderthal Man*, which includes a couple of PW tracks, one being 'Liza Radley'.

Barry Goodwin

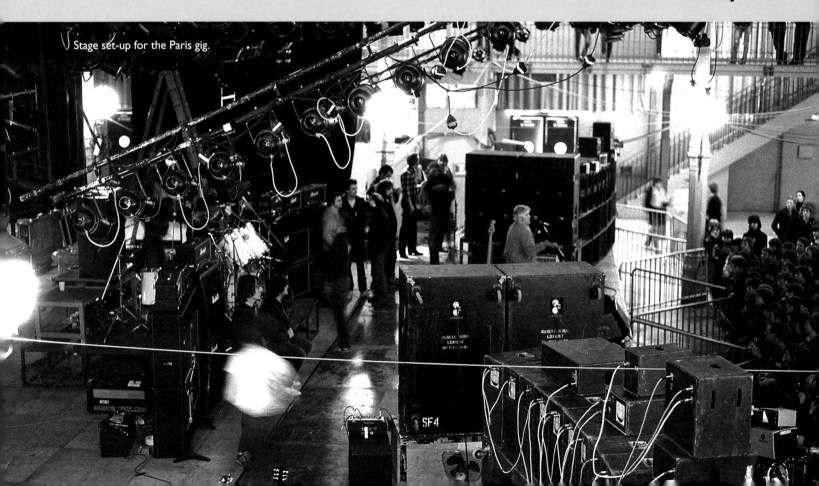

Stage set-up for the Paris gig.

Pavillon de Baltard, Paris, February 1981.

It's 1979, I'm 15 and on a coach from West London, heading for the Rainbow in Finsbury Park to see The Jam on their *Setting Sons* tour – we've somehow persuaded our music teacher to organise this as a school trip and I'm excited to bursting point. I'm a 'Saturday's Kid' living for gigs and my fortnightly trip to Stamford Bridge to sing, shout and gesticulate with the Mods, skinheads and other football herberts who make up the Chelsea support. Many of the faces would become very familiar as I saw them at numerous future Jam gigs around the UK over the next few years.

I'm dressed in a pair of drainpipe Levi's, Ben Sherman shirt, skinny black tie and mohair jumper, and I think I look the business as me and my mates make our way into the packed venue. I scan the crowd and am mesmerised by what I see: an army of people like me. We push our way to the front and watch the The Vapors perform a decent enough set, but I'm more interested in those around me, especially the Ace Faces – so cool, suited and booted, they look the dog's bollocks and they know it. Then the lights begin to dim; the atmosphere changes and you can feel the buzz going around the Rainbow – it's electric. John Weller, Paul's dad, stomps on stage and the sense of anticipation goes up another notch. Finally, The Jam hits the stage and the place erupts. It's like being in the Shed at Stamford Bridge and I love it – pure unadulterated joy. The gig seems to fly by, with every song sung word for word at the top of their lungs by the crowd. I stagger out at the end high on adrenalin and soaked to the skin. It was everything I had hoped – and more – and I was hooked.

The Jam became a religion for me – this was before the internet, so I would scour *NME* and *Sounds* for gig announcements and articles. I even used to hang out near Polydor Records, mooching through dustbins, looking for anything relating to The Jam. I'd go to all the various Mod clubs, checking out the latest fashions, and then head for the West End to track down that elusive shirt, must-have jacket or perfect boots.

As soon as ticket sales were announced I would plan an early start to queue at the venue, be it the Rainbow, Hammersmith Odeon or anywhere. The queues would snake from the ticket office and around the building from the early hours – if you wanted to go to a gig you had to work for it, but nothing felt as good as having those tickets in your hand.

Memories of those gigs are still very clear over 30 year later, and snippets come back to me all the time – standing in the foyer at the Hammersmith Odeon, looking up and seeing the older, smartly dressed fellas just standing looking down at us, myself self-consciously wondering if I was dressed correctly. I remember our little gang leaving at the end of the gig only to be confronted in the subway by some Hammersmith skins: punches were exchanged before we legged it down to the tube platform, laughing our heads off, but secretly shitting ourselves. Violence was very much part of growing up back in those days, be it at football, going to gigs or just hanging around the streets – a wrong look or stare and it could all kick off.

The Jam were a phenomenon and they inspired a movement – Weller's lyrics tapped into an army of young, streetwise youths across the country. Every record release was an event; every new Weller haircut had everyone running to the barbers; when he wore bowling shoes, within a day bowling alleys were complaining of dozens of pairs going missing. Friday night pre-going out, *The Tube* was compulsive viewing, and every Jam appearance must have had clothes manufacturers rubbing their hands as Weller belted out his anthems in paisley, stripes, polka dots, suits, blazers – you name it, he wore it – and a week later everyone was wearing the same.

Gigs were coming thick and fast and I found myself heading off to Portsmouth, Birmingham, Nottingham, Oxford, Reading – each gig mind-blowing and leaving me always gagging for more. Back to London to the Michael Sobell Sports Centre, where just down the road on the same evening The Exploited were playing the Rainbow. The inevitable happened, and a lot of Punks found out that these fashion-conscious Jam fans were handy in a ruck and not afraid to get stuck in, with countless running battles taking place in revenge for the 'Fuck the Mods' song Wattie [Buchan] was so proud of.

In 1982 the unthinkable happened when The Jam decided to call it a day. I was devastated. The last gigs were announced and the five nights at Wembley Arena started a mass scramble for tickets – I managed to get one for each night and whilst they were great gigs, they felt like a wake. But there was still the Brighton gig and five of us headed for the coast with no tickets in an old MK1 Cortina, desperate to get in somehow. We hung around the venue hoping for tickets but we had no luck. We were beginning to think that we wouldn't get in when, 10 minutes before The Jam were due on, a side door for guest list punters was kicked open and we all flooded into an already over-full venue. The rest of the gig was a blur – I just knew this was the last time I'd see them, that something that had been such an important part of my life was ending, and I was consumed by the occasion. And it did end – finally, with Weller saying, thank you and good night. It was a quiet drive back to London in the middle of the night, devoid of the euphoria you usually feel after a great gig.

The Jam was history and in hindsight, it was probably the right time. Fashions were changing and many Mods made the change. Wedge haircuts, Tacchini, Pringle, Lois and trainers were in; button down shirts, flight jackets and bowling shoes were out. The "youth" were now getting their kicks on the terraces, but those of us who were part of that movement still have The Jam as the soundtrack to our lives. Our clothes have the odd Mod touch here and there, and although many of us would identify more with Smithers-Jones these days, we often hark back to the time when we just wanted to be like David Watts.

Paul Baker

The Jam were EVERYTHING to me back then. I first saw them on TOTPs playing 'Strange Town'... the sound, the clothes the attitude, the incredible melody – they had it all, not one thing out of place – perfect. It took me a while, but I managed to get all of their records before *Setting Sons* was released. By then no other band mattered to me, only one thing was amiss. I needed to be in that band, in my head really, but that was the connection, The Jam was me. I copied the clothes, the hair, the stance; every school book was covered with a *Smash Hits* poster, the school bag was covered in *All Mod Cons*-type writing – feckin' hell, the school walls were covered in the same *All Mod Cons* writing!

Every single was bought on the day of release, the sleeve and its smell were taken in on the bus trip home, the door was hardly closed behind me as the record was put on the turntable for its first of many, many spins.... I was prepared to be critical if need be, but that never came with a Jam single, though. Just the feeling of sadness for any of the other bands around at the time, they were miles behind – years even. the flipside was always a treat, Weller didn't believe in putting out a cheap track – some of the B-sides were better than the A-sides, but that was to be expected from The Jam, they never failed on that front.

The albums, that was the most important moment of the year: a full 10–12 tracks of wonderment, months of playing, dissecting, and thinking about the grooves on each long player. They spoke to me.

Paul May

The first time I saw The Jam was on a TV programme called *Something Else*. They sung ' The Eton Rifles'. In 1979 I got right into the Mod scene and I genuinely believe The Jam started the Mod revival. I bought every single and album from then on in, including picture discs, imports, bootlegs and anything I could lay my hands on. I got most of my bits from Carnaby Street from a Chinese geezer called Henry.

I remember first hearing that The Jam were due to split when a friend told me. I was gutted and didn't want it to be true. It wasn't until I watched The Jam's appearance on *The Tube* the following week and saw the interview with Paul Weller that I knew it was true. This was to be their last TV performance and nothing was going to stop me seeing it. Channel 4 was relatively new back then and I had to borrow a neighbour's aerial to be able to watch it. I didn't blink throughout the whole performance, and as we didn't have a video recorder I soaked in every minute of it, thinking I would never see them on TV again.

Jim Tiddiman

"Mum… Can I have a pair of Jam shoes?"

I blame West Ham, and being a Chelsea fan in the '80s I wasn't the only one to be thinking that, but this was different! These lads changed the way I looked at life: my clobber (well, you've got to wear the right clothes), my opinions and most importantly, the music I listened to, still remain a part of my world today….

It started in 1979 when I was a spotty, flare-wearing 13-year-old that liked nothing more than a jumpers-for-goalposts kick-about and fantasising over *Charlie's Angels*. We would meet at the bottom of the road where I lived and play against the wood yard fence, ten of us, all the same age and just starting to grow bits and getting gobby. Then these three older, bigger lads started to join in. All three were wearing a claret T-shirt with white and light-blue trim, with what looked like a laurel leaf as a badge, Levis and desert boots, except for one who wore these black suede shoes with a white stripe running up the middle and a couple on the side… I didn't ask… I never did then and still don't now. I found out by overhearing the other lads talking about them! It became my aim in life to own a pair!

Friendships were formed and stories swapped when one day I was handed a long player, called *Setting Sons*, and I was instantly hooked: the tunes, the lyrics and the attitude. I no longer wanted to play for Chelsea, I wanted to be Paul Weller and be in The Jam!

By now the West Ham lads had scooters, wore parkas, button-down collared shirts and, most of all to a lad who had a new hero, tickets to see The Jam. But I was deemed too young to go by my mum. I have forgiven her long since but at the time I was ready to pack up my stuff and move into my Nans…. Of course, in hindsight the old dear was right, especially when I eventually did go and see them (knives and fights) but that's for later!

We move on to March 1980 and a play area in Wellingborough, where I see the older chaps jumping around like loonies because the inevitable had happened: 'Going Underground' had shot straight into the charts at top spot. It seemed the whole of the UK thought the same as us. I still hadn't left school or had the money to buy the clothes or the records and it became an itch I couldn't scratch: the frustration lasted the best part of two more years.

After weeks of saving for the annual holiday to Great Yarmouth I had an interview to become an apprentice metal polisher! The very same day I got the job was the day I left school. One of the clauses of the job was that I couldn't go on holiday, which not only left me with £43.50 burning a hole in my pocket, but I was also one week away from my first pay packet of £36.10p!

There was never any question as to what that money was going on. I withdrew the money as fast as I could and went to Revolver Records in town and promptly purchased every 7" and album The Jam had released to date. Then it was onto George Allan's for my first pair of Sta-Prest and Fred Perrys. The funds wouldn't stretch to the shoes so another week had to be endured until I got that little brown envelope, and the next day went to the market in Wellingborough, where a stall sold all The Jam shoes that had been made. Instead of plumping for the badgers, I wanted the ones Weller was wearing at the time, and so became a proud owner of some black-and-white bowlers…. I didn't care how I looked to others, I felt like I was the business, so sod all the rest!

The next aim for this young Mod/Jam boy was to go and see them live, and within a month dates for the 'Solid Bond in Your Heart' tour were announced. The West Ham boys were all going and I rushed down to Yorks Travel and nervously waited my turn, only to be told that tickets were still available but you had to be 16 to go…. "Hang on a minute I turned 16 in June and have a job", but the bastards wouldn't have it (ok, I looked 14, but that's besides the point). In the end I had to get my birth certificate to prove my point; £10 quid was handed over and my coach seat and gig ticket to see The Jam at The Granby Halls, Leicester, on 23rd of September, was finally secured…!

The gig itself turned into a bit of a blur at times: I don't know whether I was star struck or passed out from the crush, but I remember the testosterone-filled hall, flick knife and fights and not being able to see until one of the chaps said, "Pretend to faint!" I duly obliged and was carried, crowd surf style, to the front, where I was about to be dragged out when one of the West Ham boys told security I was ok now, and he would look after me. All of a sudden I felt fine and was standing right at the front, in front of Mr Weller's microphone – so close his sweat hit me, so close I got a nod, so close I remember his red-silk, button-down, black Sta-Prest, white socks and he had my shoes on….

Well you know what I mean… they came and went, it was all I expected and more. The icing on the cake was before coming back for the encore a roadie flicked something from the stage that hit the Happy Hammer on his cheek… "Not another one, Steve, you want this?" And so I was handed a plectrum that the Weller fella had been using to play, and it is still with me now (how one little piece of plastic can mean so much!).

The next day I had a row with the old dear as she insisted I went to work, but I was pleading with her that I couldn't as I was deaf…. But Mum won that one again, and once the ringing in my ears subsided it was all about when I could go again. But as we now know, after that there wasn't to be many more gigs to go to, as Weller announced the split – which, fittingly, West Ham told me about one night in October.

It hit me hard: what was I meant to listen to now? Who was I going to go see? Well, for many of us, The Style Council, casual clothing and even dancing at discos was on the horizon, but I can safely say The Jam were OUR band: no other has had the same effect as those Woking Wonders.

Steve 'Meds' Medlin

The Jam were important for many reasons: they led and others followed, or at least tried to. They may well have hitched a ride on the Punk rollercoaster, but they were sussed enough to see that it would quickly derail.

The Jam were working class, just like their fans: there had been no poncy education or middle-class upbringing for them. They did what we did: went to the same schools, lived in the same type of housing, drank in the same pubs, scratched around to make ends meet, suffered the same shit we suffered and in Paul Weller they had a writer who could document life in a way that we could all relate to. It meant something to him, you could tell: he was raw and angry and there was much to be angry about.

Weller had insight beyond his years. The middle-aged woman in 'Private Hell', cracking under the strain of isolation; that bloke who ran the corner shop or the factory worker returning home from work so knackered he just wants to sit and watch the telly. Weller had remarkable empathy and he was only just entering his twenties.

Foxton and Buckler played their part, too! This was no one-man show: they were fundamental to the over all sound of The Jam. Thumping bass lines and powerful drumming created the perfect rhythm section for Weller to bounce off.

In my mind, above all else The Jam stood for YOUTH; I can think of no other band that epitomised youth in the way they did. Ok, so Townsend may have done it with *Quadrophenia* but that was a moment in time, a concept. The Jam lived it and we loved it.

The Jam set the foundations on which I grew. These were my formative years and they took a young lad that lacked confidence and gave him direction. They set me on a journey that I am still travelling and I thank them from the bottom of my heart.

Each single, album release or gig meant so much to us. Sadly, the days of rushing to the record shop to get the latest release have long gone, replaced by the sterile world of downloads from the comfort of your own armchair.

Looking back, I have so many memories associated with The Jam, such as: being smuggled into Barbarellas when I was about 13 to see a band I'd never heard off and being totally blown away; the arguments at school with 'the rockers'; the parties, the clothes, the scooters; the power of The Jam live; the excitement and anticipation just before John Weller came on to introduce the band; the deafness that lasted for two weeks after the bomb went off at the end of "A' Bomb in Wardour Street'; the crush of the crowd at Bingley Hall and my girlfriend losing her shoe in the mayhem; *Top of the Pops*, *Revolver*, *The Old Grey Whistle Test* and *The Tube*.

Entering the charts at Number One at a time when that actually meant something; being chased around the Bull Ring by a gang of dirty rockers; being chased around the Bull Ring by a gang of skinheads; Butlins 1980; listening to The Jam on the radio at work and nearly coming to blows with a rocker who was taking the piss out of them; trying to explain to my old man why they were so good and him just not getting it; playing *The Gift* to death whilst trying to keep warm with my girlfriend in my bloody freezing bedroom; waiting for my photos from a New Street Odeon gig to come back and not one bloody picture coming out! The Barrel Organ in Brum; someone getting stabbed after the Bingley Hall gig in '82; a gang of school mates cycling like crazy to catch the train into town to see The Jam at the New Street Odeon in 1978, and the near riot on the train back home. Oh yeah, trying to break my feckin' bowling shoes in!

They say that all good things come to an end, but when the news broke that The Jam were going to split, it was as if someone had ripped out my spleen. I just didn't get it: they were doing so well – surely had much more to offer? However, as soon as I saw Weller explaining his reasons on the telly, I understood, and still do.

Paul 'Mez' Merrick

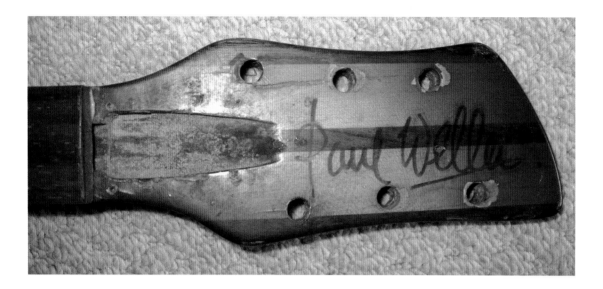

The story behind this guitar neck is that it came from one of Paul Weller's Rickenbacker 330s in Fireglo Red. I can only differentiate him having two 330s in this colour*.

I acquired the neck off eBay from a guy who worked at Wings Music in Bromley, Kent. Wings was a company where the Jam used to hire PA equipment and Paul Weller used to call in there to buy odds and ends when visiting Gill Price, who lived in the same town.

Weller broke the head of the guitar on stage at a Rainbow gig in 1979, during some over-active feedback for 'The Eton Rifles'. The broken parts were taken by Dave Liddel to Wings to see whether it could be repaired, but when it was deemed beyond repair the head and neck section were removed and kept as a souvenir. The body section went on to make the Roy Lichtenstein inspired Wham! guitar (now on display at the British Music Experience at the O2 Arena, London).

It was taken to the studio during the recording session for 'Funeral Pyre' in 1981 to be signed. I had it counter-signed and authenticated in 2011 by Bruce Foxton. In an e-mail to Dennis Munday I mentioned I had the neck and asked him if he had any recollections of the incident… he replied that he did in fact remember and how upset Paul was to have broken a favourite guitar!

Guy Helliker

*The other one being the 'I Am Nobody', that sold at Christies in July 2008 for £10,000 — see opposite.

POPULAR CULTURE: ROCK & POP MEMORABILIA
London, South Kensington
Jul 10, 2008
Sale 5397

Lot 37

The Jam Paul Weller

A 1974 Rickenbacker 330 guitar, Serial No. NG 4292, in fireglow finish, double cutaway body, single cats-eye soundhole, rounded front body, 21 fret fingerboard with dot inlays, two pickups, five rotary controls, selector switch, standard jack input, chrome 'R' tailpiece and white split level pickguard, scratched on the body I AM NOBODY; accompanied by a copy of The Jam, Extra Special depicting Paul Weller playing the guitar during a 1979 promotional film for German television; a colour photograph of Weller holding the guitar with the vendor; the original invoice on THE JAM headed stationary 'One Rickenbacker guitar 330 serial no. NG4929, £150.00'; and a letter concerning the provenance (5).

Estimate: 5,000–7,000 British pounds
Price realized: 10,000 British pounds

Back in late 1979, I think it was, I was still editor of the Liverpool Mod fanzine, *Time For Action*, and because of my connections both in the music scene in Liverpool and with lads from the Liverpool match, It was suggested I should hire a coach to take our band of merry men to go and see our favourite band, The Jam, at Deeside Leisure Centre.

The Jam, who had released *Setting Sons* that year, were arguably at the peak of their career. Certainly, singles-wise, Number One followed Number One. We *had* to go and we all wanted to go together, so I agreed.

Our ties with The Jam went back to 1978 when we had seen them at the Liverpool Empire and were hooked to the point that I was inspired to write a fanzine. We saw them again around May '79 at Liverpool University, Mountford Hall, where I actually met Weller and he invited a few of us to be on the guest list at the Manchester Apollo a few days later (another legendary Jam gig that will be remembered for all the wrong reasons).

At the time there was a coach service in Liverpool called Ribble and I went and hired a 50–60 seat coach for around £30, if I remember right. I put the word out at the match and on the housing estate I lived on, Cantril Farm (a notorious 1960s overspill estate known in Liverpool at the time as either Canny Farm or Cannibal Farm) and the coach was filled within five days. Although not planned this way, probably about 90 percent of the punters were young and had various levels of hooligan tendencies, but I can honestly say that this was not the remit when we had the idea of hiring this coach.

This was the first of two coach outings to see The Jam at Deeside Leisure Centre, both of which are kind of legendary in Liverpool, although unfortunately not for anything to do with the performances of The Jam.

The night before, a group of us had gone to see The Chords at 'Bradys' (better known as 'Eric's' before its name change that year). The Chords played a great set, but what I remember most about that evening was sitting in the dressing room after the gig had finished with members of the band and some of their London following and then a lad I knew from the match came in. He exchanged a few words with a London lad who was being typically arrogant, going on about his boxing prowess, etc, and then I just remember watching, open-jawed, as the Liverpool lad ferociously thrust a drum stick into the London lad's mouth a couple of times, smashing teeth all over the place, then walking out as calm as you like. I should have known then what might have been in store for the following evening.

We set off nice and early and in good spirits, so that we could enjoy a few beers pre gig (or "concert" as we used to say in those days). Amongst the travelling urchins were future *End* fanzine staff, members of a local gang from Canny Farm, known as the 'SRS', while the rest were a mixture of red and blues from the match. Average age was probably 18 or 19.

We decided to look for a decent alehouse to settle into. Driving past the actual leisure centre, we noticed a crew of about 200 locals on the lookout for Scousers, so we decided that we'd travel on about a mile past so we could have a few drinks without being spotted too early. We found a nice, big old boozer with pool tables and tellies – ideal.

Despite the welcome committee we had seen earlier, at this point all we were interested in was having a few scoops and going to see The Jam. Everyone was in good spirits, with no hint of trouble to be seen anywhere. So there we were, playing pool, lots of banter and singing in one room and then around 7.30 *Top Of The Pops* came on the telly in the other room. Someone shouted that Secret Affair were on, plus Madness I think, so we walked through to watch the show.

After a brief sing-along watching TOTP, we returned to the pool room. Only we now found our pool game had been taken over by a gang of local fellers. They were quite a bit older than us, and were clearly not fazed when we piled in, and they certainly were not willing to back down when we pointed out we'd left an active game on the table while we watched a couple of tunes on the telly.

So there you had it... a gang of about 20 fellers telling a gang of about 60 lads to "do one".... In seconds, all hell broke out. It was honestly, the closest I've ever been to a situation like one of those fights in those old black-and-white cowboy films! Stools, bottles and glasses flying back and forth, fist fights every direction you looked in, people being lifted in the air and thrown across the pool table... it was almost comical. Through sheer numbers and tenacity we forced them back and out of the pub, one-by-one.

Then at the closing stages of the ruckus one of their gang remained, standing his ground, still throwing punches, face and shirt drenched in his own blood; he snarled, "Yer fuckin' Deeside wools"!

For a second or two the room fell silent. Then someone piped up, "What???"

He groggily repeated, "Yer fuckin wools!"

(For those who don't know, "wools", or "woolybacks" in full, is a derogatory term that Scousers use to describe pretty much everyone who isn't from Liverpool).

One of our lot piped up, "We're from Liverpool, yer knob!"

contd.

The battered and beaten one replied, "So are WE, yer fuckin' tits"! Oops.

There wasn't much we could do about it now other than to offer mumbled apologies and patronising offerings of, "Ee'yar mate, get yerself a bevvie". We decided it was best to set off to the gig.

We jumped on the coach to the leisure centre and arrived without further incident. When we got inside it was heaving! We'd just missed the support act, The Vapors (thankfully), and the crowd were singing various songs of their own, including pro- and anti-Scouse songs.

We piled our way through the crowd to be as near to the front as we could get. The atmosphere was electric. As soon as The Jam appeared on stage it was like someone had shouted "action!" because a mass brawl broke out! After five minutes or so of absolute bedlam, it became apparent which side was which now, and it was pretty even, with Scousers on one side and the Welsh and lads from the other side of the Mersey on the other. Weller had to appeal for calm right away: "Pack it in! Stop fuckin' fighting!" etc, and there was a no man's land created down the middle of the arena.

God knows which song The Jam opened with, because as soon as they started, the crowd started bouncing, the no man's land disappeared and the two sides of the crowd clashed. Chaos ensued for three more minutes. Then the no man's land would re-open at the end of each song (each time containing more and more stray shoes/trainees and ripped clothing).

Weller would scream and shout for calm… but nine out of ten times, every time The Jam starting singing the crowd would start fighting. The only songs I can remember from that night are 'Strange Town', 'When You're Young', 'Girl on the Phone', 'Heatwave', 'Eton Rifles' and 'Tube Station' – all played at breakneck speed, all received uproariously by the crowd. The rest of the night was a blur of shoves, kicks and punches, interspersed with a 5–10 minute break in the wings, dancing with me mate's sister. What I do remember thinking was that the performance was every bit as edgy and exciting as any gig I'd ever been to and befitted the events that were unfolding on this mad night.

After the gig finished, the Deeside wools were waiting outside and we had to fight our way back to the coach. I watched in youthful awe as one of our lot just steamed into the waiting mob and they scattered, leaving the way for the rest of us to give chase and find our coach without attaining too many injuries.

Once at the coach, it was like we had just watched our team win a European Cup – everyone was buzzing. Hugs, handshakes, smiling and singing everywhere you looked. It felt like a coming of age moment. The Jam at Deeside would be cemented in my heart forever.

Not surprisingly, that was not the end of the drama. We had only been driving about five minutes when the shout of "CHIPPY" went up. The driver was a good sort and agreed to stop while we piled off to buy some fodder from a Deeside fish-and-chip shop. Most of the coach piled into this chippy, but a couple of mates, Danny and Billy, had spotted another chippy further down the road and grabbed me to join them, so we wouldn't have to queue up behind 50 hyper Scousers in the other one. We walked down, went in and calmly and quietly placed our orders. There was a group of about five or six fellers outside, eating their meals. We paid them no attention and thought they were doing the same. Wrong! When we came out they launched straight into us. Chips, fists and shouts went flying through the air, and within moments someone at the other chippy saw what was happening and gave the call… and so it was that about 20 mates came running to our rescue. Most of the other, smaller, crew had legged it before our lot arrived, but as per normal, one stayed to stand his ground, lost in the moment, not aware of the impending danger he was in.

What happened next was crazy. Without anyone saying a word he was grabbed from behind to stop him throwing punches. I assumed he would then have to take a few digs to the kipper while he was defenceless, but no: someone grabbed has feet and within a second he was being swung to and fro, until he was finally flung through the chippy window!

The poor coach driver was having a nervous breakdown now and quickly ushered us all back onto the coach and drove us back to Liverpool as fast as he could.

The next morning, the local radio station, Radio City, did a news report on the violence inside the gig, and also mentioned a lad being thrown through a chippy window (he was ok). And so the first part of the legend was born.

The Jam returned to Deeside three years later in 1982. This time, the locals were out for revenge and the coach party I took to that concert were prepared for the reception awaiting us. Deeside in 1982 was even crazier than in 1979 and resulted in me being banned from hiring coaches from city centre coach firms, but that's a story for another day.

[Excerpt from the forthcoming untitled book by Phil Jones, editor of *The End* magazine].

Phil Jones

On the band coach travelling back from the
Bath Pavillion gig, 22nd December 1979.

On my birthday of 1979 I went to see The Jam at Mountford Hall in Liverpool. The crowd was a mixture of Punks, scallies, Mods and students. It was one of the best concerts I have ever attended. Around this time the *Setting Sons* album was released and I remember being really disappointed. It just wasn't as Punky as the band's previous stuff. But in time I grew to love it.

In 1982, me and four mates set out to see The Jam again at the Deeside Leisure Centre. We travelled on our scooters and on our arrival were instantly hassled by the local badly-dressed yobs. There was a smattering of Mods and only a few scooters. Some of the scooters got attacked with bricks and a couple of the younger Mods got punched.

More and more locals started to turn up and I thought we were going to get a major hiding. Then we started hearing chants of "We are the Mods" and some Liverpool football songs. It seemed like a thousand voices but really it was only about 120 lads who confronted the local yobs and then ran them ragged over Deeside. It turned out that a load of the Liverpool FC hooligan crew were big Jam fans. The same year we went to see The Jam at the Royal Court in Liverpool. Little did we know at the time that later that year The Jam would split up.

Jon Ginny

I started secondary school in September '79, and straight away made new friends with a few other new Jam fans. Some were a year older, but all were as mad as me about the Mod revival, especially The Jam. I'll always remember The Jam performing 'Eton Rifles' on *Top of the Pops*.

Quadrophenia was on at the same time at the pictures, so the whole Mod thing was in full swing, with up-and-coming bands like The Chords, Purple Hearts, and Secret Affair, to name a few. Anyway, Weller looked the dog's nuts on the telly that night: black shades, smart French crew cut hair, sky-blue jumper, Prince of Wales check trousers, and to finish, the new Jam stage shoe. In fact, all three looked proper smart. It was around this time that the new album, *Setting Sons*, was going to be released. And another UK tour in November and December included three nights at the Rainbow Theatre. I got all excited about the tickets going on sale. In those days you either brought tickets by queuing at the venue or sending away postal orders to a certain address and hoping the postal order never came back (which meant you hadn't got one); but the hardest thing was trying to get my parents to let me go... again it was NO!

I didn't take this lying down. I wanted to be part of that "Jam Army" and be right in the middle of it all, but I never did – the best I managed was to bunk off school and go to the soundcheck.

I went with a mate from school. We got the train up and found the theatre. When we approached the venue there was a small crowd forming by the doors, with a notice reading THE JAM – SOLD OUT. We got in at 3pm, after two or three hours waiting, with around 30–40 other fans. At first, all I saw was some guy with Weller's guitar playing it, then stopping, then tuning it again. This went on for ages…. Finally, Rick Buckler appeared and signed fans items.

Then Paul and Bruce made their way out towards the front of the stage and again signed items. They then said they would be running through a few numbers. Wow: I was actually going to see The Jam play live, albeit at a sound-check… but it meant the world to me. I can't remember which songs or how many they ran through, but it seemed to be over in seconds.

Phil Potter

421 BGP3
22 ORCH.
CENTR
ORC ADULT
CAS FACT1
K 7.50
A
104 01APR

OAKLAND AUDITORIUM
THEATRE - 10 TENTH ST
BILL GRAHAM/KSAN ANN
MIDNIGHT WAVE - THE J
FRI APR 20 1979 12MI
ORCHESTRA ADULT
ORC K 104 $7.50

In 1977 I was 15 years old and living in Camberwell. I remember The Jam were on my radar but I wasn't really chasing them then – I think I was a bit too young in some ways. I never quite 'got' them until about '79. Then around that time *Quadrophenia* came out, and The Jam and *Quadrophenia* go hand in hand. By 1980 I was buying into the whole ethos of it: the clothing and the music; and then there was Weller, who I felt was a fantastic educator.

The first single I can remember buying was 'When You're Young'. The song spoke a million words to me. I was on holiday at the time, down Hastings or somewhere. Around this time, although I was living in Camberwell, I was socialising in the West End. Back then, the Old Kent Road area was a bit too 'Soul Boy' for me. Instead, I went to the West End and found myself seeking out the history of places like the Marquee, the Scene Club and all that stuff.

I was like a little train-spotter walking around, taking photographs of places like Ham Yard. And by doing this, as a young Mod I would meet other young Mods, and we would go to gigs or parties together. So, as young as 10 years old, I was going around Covent Garden and Soho with my mates; I mean a lot of them were hoisters (thieves). They would pick me up with a "We will look after him Mrs Baxter" and I would be thinking, I was going to have a day of ice creams, but they were all on the dip (nicking).

So, I found myself getting drawn into the Mod scene. I was also getting my clothes handmade: I have always been a lover of tailor-made clothing. When I was young I use to save up to buy something just so that I could have that individual look. By 1980 I was working and had a bit of dough in my bin, and a whole new world had opened up that included The Jam and *Quadrophenia*.

So I was watching Weller and wondering, where is he getting his clothing ideas and inspiration from? Then there was all the CND stuff and because of Weller I got into that a bit and went on a couple of marches, but then I found myself questioning why I was doing it and all that.... Funny, really, but Weller was having an influence over loads of us. I think Weller made a lot of people aware of politics.

In many ways I think Weller was saying things that we couldn't say. I mean the song, 'English Rose'. In that song Weller was saying what us spotty fuckers couldn't say. We would of loved to say to a bird those sort of things, but we just couldn't.

The Jam are also the greatest singles' band of all time. I love the singles, we grew up with the singles. My favourite album, I suppose, is *All Mod Cons*. Every song is a fantastic song. It's not like there are one or two decent tunes on it: every song is great, one after the other after the other. There is 'Mr Clean', which has really powerful lyrics about "fucking up your life". And then again *Setting Sons* was another album packed with great tunes, although it was also an album that had a different sound to it.

Then there is *The Gift*. To me that is a great album. The use of brass and so on gave it that Southern Soul thing. At the time that album it all: bit of brass, bit of Hammond, a bit of Northern Soul.

The soul connection really did it for me. I mean, I never really got the Mod revival thing. A couple of songs from bands like the Purple Hearts and Secret Affair were ok, but I didn't really have much interest in them at the time. I don't think any of them had the craftsmanship of The Jam.

But going back to Weller being educational: I have said to him a couple of times how important he was. I mean, only yesterday I was with him and we went to Bar Italia and then to a tailors, and there were 10 people outside trying to watch and photograph him trying on some strides. But the thing is, Weller is always moving forward, every six months he is into something else, but a lot of people are still stuck in a relationship with Weller or The Jam that they developed 30 years ago. He does understand that. But then I also remember the first time I met Weller. I have met him several times since, and for a start, he is always early. Anyway: Weller just kept asking me questions. You see, he respects graft and what are you doing with your life. I remember it crystal clear: he was throwing questions at me like, what are you reading, what was the last film that you saw, what TV are you watching. It was all very much about are you putting good stuff in there, or are you putting shit in there. So I was name-checking some Blue Note album and he would be like, "Yeah, sweet, have you heard that one". That's what he's like. I mean, when I met with him yesterday he was asking me about some Art Nuevo book that I'm doing some work with, and he starts telling me about a similar book that he has on the same thing.

The *Beat Concerto* was also an important book at the time (I've got to say that because you know I have written a few books with Paolo). But yeah, lovely book. *Beat Concerto* was a great insight into the band and the family. Especially the insight into Weller's family: Nicky, Ann, John and so on. The upbringing, the first hand reports. I learnt to admire John, as well. I mean, John and the family backed Paul to the hilt. There's not many dads who would of sold this, and sold that, just so a guitar could be bought. Then there was the working all day and then driving the band to a gig, getting home and only having three hours kip before doing it all again. I mean, fuck me, that's dedication to your son!

Mark (Bax) Baxter

Here in America, I first became acquainted with The Jam at the time of *All Mod Cons*. But even at that moment, being a fan was a lonely proposition in central New England. My first exposure, and the track that hooked me, was 'Mr Clean', which I had originally heard on an underground station broadcasting out of Boston. From that moment on, I never looked back. I became totally devoted.

Like I hadn't done since the mid to late 1960s, I learned all the words to their songs and anxiously awaited every release, whether it was a single or LP. Driving 75 miles to Boston (one way) to purchase their latest was how it had to be, as their records weren't immediately available in the United States. Each time The Jam visited the US I felt unbelievably fortunate. They were not as popular here as in the UK, and as a result were very accessible, playing small clubs and making themselves available to me before shows. I remember Paul explaining the bit of poetry on the back of the sleeve to the masterpiece, 'Strange Town', while we sat in the bar at the Paradise Club. And then there was the time I got in to see the soundcheck at the Channel, during the 'Funeral Pyre' period. We had another conversation then, this time about the merits of Orwell's *Homage to Catalonia*.

When visiting London in the early '80s, I stopped by Sinclair Road to pick up a copy of *Mixed Up/Shook Up*, a book of poetry released by Weller's Riot Stories imprint. The receptionist informed me that, "the office is closed". When I explained that I was leaving town the next day, she called up and I got the green light. Someone was upstairs that could help me. To my surprise, Paul greeted me warmly with a shout to "C'mon up!" We chatted for a while about music and all sorts of other things in between.

The Jam, like the very best of their predecessors, kept the bar moving forward with every release. As a writer, Weller kept developing and growing. Each LP had new sounds and the band were using the studio so creatively. So much has changed since then, but when I take the time to think back to this period in my life I'm reminded of total joy and limitless possibilities.

Chris Makris

The Channel Nightclub, Boston, 29th May 1981.

Top, Middle: The Channel Nightclub, Boston, USA 1982;
Bottom: 45–53 Sinclair Road, London W14, April 1982.

Setting Sons Tour 1979

Rainbow London, Sunday 02/12/79
Rainbow London, Monday 03/12/79
Rainbow London, Tuesday 04/12/79
Newcastle City Hall, Thursday 06/12/79
Newcastle City Hall, Friday 07/12/79
Glasgow Apollo, Saturday 08/12/79

RAINBOW THEATRE
FINSBURY PARK   316

M.C.P. presents
THE JAM
at 8 p.m.

Monday DEC 3
STALLS

Incl. VAT   £3.50

WW 37

TO BE RETAINED   For conditions of sale see over

Me and my mate Dave decided to do the full week's tour, travelling by train to see the only band that mattered: The Jam. We wanted to do a British tour and the gig dates, when they were released for the *Setting Sons* tour in the winter of 1979, worked perfectly. We spent ages planning it, albeit not very well, but we were both working in Newcastle and saved up a bob or two for trains, some B&B, some floors and a lot of alcohol. It started at the Rainbow on a Sunday, but we decided we needed a Saturday night out in London.

The 9am train was booked from Newcastle. We were on the platform at 8.30. Excited wasn't the word, but we were ready. Twenty-four cans of McEwan's Export, a couple of kilometres of corned beef and pickle sarnies (cheers Mam), and enough batteries for the Duette tape recorder to power a nuclear sub. We got on the train, a table, a seat: a can cracked. The train wasn't too busy, but we were already attracting attention, and by the time we got to Durham, we pretty much had the cabin/carriage to ourselves.

I can remember Dave saying, "Kev, that's four times in a row you've played 'I Got By In Time'", but I think it might have been my poor Weller impersonation that scared our fellow passengers. It wasn't long before the first complaint, and we were approached by the ticket collector to turn the music down, stop singing and sit still, or we would be put off the train at Darlington. A game of cat-and-mouse began: complaint, collector back, turned down music, goes away, music back up again! This became more difficult to do as we sank more McEwan's Export, but it was great fun.

By the time we got to King's Cross at 3pm, we were very merry and excited, but a bit worse for wear. We sorted out a B&B for Saturday and Sunday nights up the Holloway Road, but we needed a pint because – well, just because!

We made our way to Holloway Road tube station, and then followed the map sent to us from Jean, the owner. Found it, no probs. She and her husband Tom were sound. Tom was into his music and loved the Small Faces: result. So it was into our room, quick change of tops then down to have a look through Tom's record collection, which was impressive. We offered him one of our cans, so we sat having a drink – really nice people, but they could only put us up for Saturday and Sunday because they were going away. Never mind: Monday was ages away. Tom asked us where we were heading. We wanted to go to the Hope & Anchor because there was going to be a DJ playing loads of Jam. He directed us to walk down from Holloway to Upper Street, via several pubs, and eventually to the famous boozer.

There were as many people outside as in, and the atmosphere was brilliant. We met some lads (Jam fans) outside. They were top lads: Geoff, Tony and Ronnie. They would save our bacon Monday and Tuesday with regards somewhere to stay (and we became good mates over the coming years).

The Sunday was here! We couldn't wait: we were up early. We had arranged to meet our new mates in Soho in the afternoon for a trawl round the record shops and, of course, a few beers. What a cracking laugh and day we had. We headed up to Finsbury Park about 7pm, went to a pub (can't remember its name) but it was rammed – loads of people in there that had been at the soundcheck.

The gig was brilliant. I can vividly remember 'Thick As Thieves' and the whole place just moving as one – fantastic!

contd.

The Monday we got into the soundcheck, which was great, and managed to have a chat with John Weller afterwards. We told him about our tour around and he was really brilliant with us (as he was with all the fans he met) and told us to come to the stage door that night and ask for him. We couldn't believe it! The Monday night was also lush, but I couldn't wait for it to end and claim our reward.

Last encore and we were off and at the stage door. In we went. It was busy – no sign of The Jam – and then John Weller spotted us.

"Hello lads, enjoy that?"

"Yeah, brilliant mate."

"Get yourselves a beer off the table."

Ha, ha, was this really happening?!

It wasn't long before the lads were in, and loads of people wanting autographs. We were just soaking in the atmosphere and the free beer.

John came over to us with Bruce and Rick, introduced us and said, "Have a crack with these Geordie lads, they're following The Jam all over."

We stood with Bruce and Rick for what seemed like ages, chatting about our tour and train journeys. It seemed to last for ages – what a night!

The Tuesday night was great as well. We had been sleeping on our new-found friends' bedroom floors and we will be eternally grateful to them, but as we boarded the train north on the Wednesday, I was looking forward to my home town gigs and my own bed.

Newcastle on the Thursday night was strange, watching all the fans getting excited in the pubs before; we were too, but I felt like telling everyone, hey, this is my fourth time this week. Another cracking gig.

We went out after the gig and got hammered. I remember waking up on the Friday thinking, Jesus my head! Breakfast sorted me out and then Dave was on my doorstep, buzzing for tonight's gig. We decided to go up to the City Hall Friday afternoon, to see what was going on. When we got there we went around to the stage door: there was a mini-bus and the stage door was open, so we went in and more or less bumped into John Weller.

"Fuck me, you two are early."

We said, "Yeah, just seeing what's going on."

"Come in, we're just having a cuppa."

There were people all over the shop, so we just sat having a crack with him. What a really top bloke he was. He asked us how our week was going and asked, "It must be costing you a few quid?"

"Yeah, but it's worth it: we love The Jam."

With that, he said, "You're going to Glasgow tomorrow aren't you?"

"Yes, we were going to sort the train today."

He said, "Never mind the train, you can come with us. Bring your stuff here tomorrow and you can jump a lift with us."

Honestly, I thought I was hearing things; and that's how we went to Glasgow on the tour bus, sitting, chatting, with John, Rick, Bruce and, occasionally, Paul. It was something I will never forget.

Unfortunately the same cannot be said about the Glasgow gig. It was a blur and to this day I can't really remember it or the train journey back to Newcastle.

Best week of my life.

Kev Stevens

I seriously think I knew it ALL. Lived it from 11 years old and have loved it ever since. Never been shy to say The Jam changed my life. Have known there were thousands like me. BUT, I have always felt irritated that it has never been acknowledged. I love The Clash but I am chippy about the fact that they have a ton of books about them, when The Jam were – in every way, although not in every song – more important than them. It was playground, working class, fucking youth explosion – not situationist wank. (And I love The Clash!)

When I first saw The Jam at Dundee Caird Hall on 9th December 1979 I was delighted when, after another tedious outburst of "We are the Mods", Weller dedicated 'When You're Young' to "…the real fans in the audience – all the morons can fuck off". Wowee, he didn't say much, but when he spoke…. I thought (and got) that he really respected us, and that felt fucking great.

Ed Mylles

Backstage after the Bath Pavillion gig, 22nd December 1979.

1980 – I SAW THE LIGHTS AND THE PRETTY GIRLS

When 'Going Underground' crashed into the Number One spot in February 1980 Margaret Thatcher was firmly in the hot seat, with no signs of going underground or running away. The Welsh wished she and her cronies had though, especially after the announcement that 11,000 steel workers' jobs were at risk. A figure that was nothing more than a drop in the pond compared to the August estimate of 2 million unemployed.

A month after the release of 'Going Underground', the life of Radio Caroline came to an abrupt end after the boat from which the station operated sank. The '60s pirate radio station that had thrilled so many bored teenagers and introduced them to the sounds of Stax and Motown and the British Beat bands, ceased to transmit.

The summer months witnessed the Alexandra Palace being destroyed by a fire and the withdrawal of the six-pence piece. Roger Daltrey impressed a generation with his acting skills in *McVicar* and the SAS made their presence known on national television as they stormed the Iranian Embassy and rescued all but one of the hostages.

September saw the first CND rally at Greenham Common and the same month Ford unleashed the Escort Mark III and British Leyland, the Metro. One would keep many a boy racer happy for years whilst the other would be driven by first time lady drivers and your mate's Nan. A month later IRA prisoners in the Maze prison began a hunger strike. Within months this act would produce several fatalities. In November the British public were also notified of the Yorkshire Ripper's twelfth victim, a 16-year-old female.

The Jam reached the Number One spot twice in 1980, alongside 'Geno' by Dexy's Midnight Runners (from the incredible *Searching for the Young Soul Rebels* album), 'Another Brick in the Wall' from Pink Floyd, Fern Kinney's 'Together we are Beautiful', 'The Special AKA Live' EP by The Specials and Blondie's 'Atomic'.

The album charts were dominated by acts with a Two Tone, Reggae or Ska influence. *I Just Can't Stop It* by The Beat, *The Specials* by The Specials, *Absolutely* by Madness and *Signing Off* from UB40. November eagerly announced The Jams fifth album, *Sound Affects*. Nearly every other kid seemed to be either in tonic trousers or a Fred Perry T-shirt.

Television featured Trevor Eve in *Shoestring*, who's peg trousers and skinny tie influenced many a father to try and pretend to be 20 years younger. Also Children in Need began its annual charity campaign and the fantastic *Hi-Di-Hi!* got under way and made stars out of unlikely actors, such as Su Pollard and Paul Shane. Shame they're still living off it….

'Going Underground' was the fifteenth biggest-selling single of the year, shifting 585,000 copies. The single beat John Lennon's '(Just Like) Starting Over', which was a surprise, especially because the world had been so shocked by his murder that same December. The year 1980 also mourned the deaths of Ian Curtis, Peter Sellers, Billy Butlin and Alfred Hitchcock.

'Going Underground'/'Dreams of Children'

The front cover was shot in early 1980, around the same time as the video, and the live pictures on the back were taken from a gig at the Rainbow.

'Start!'

This was the first single sleeve that was purely typographical and didn't include the band image. We used hand-drawn type for 'START!'.

Bill Smith

The family holiday every year was spent in a chalet down near Bournemouth, which usually rained, and lost time that could have been spent on a sunny beach in Adidas shorts trying to look like a teenage babe magnet was spent on Boscombe pier, throwing the old man's loose change into horse-racing games and slot machines.

In early August 1980 on a particularly wet drive down to the holiday park, it coincided with hearing 'Start!' for the first time. I knew it was due out by the end of the summer holidays and after 'Going Underground' had taken the band into the stratosphere, I was double sure that even the boring bastard daytime DJs at Radio 1 would play it upfront. Unheard of before 'Going Underground'....

So it was on some rain-lashed A road near Ringwood that Peter Powell played the future Number One to my ears for the first time.

"Turn it up Dad!"

"Oh look, it's your boyfriend, son."

"Shuuuut up, will ya?!"

Me and my younger sister did imaginary dances and nodded our head to the spiky funk. Instantly, I knew they had done it again and produced pure gold. At the end of the record Powell mentioned it sounded like a Beatles tune, and instantly I thought I needed to hear that, too. The following weeks, as it got played more and more, the more it got slagged off by silly old wankers too thick to see past the 'Taxman' reference. Of course the bass line is nicked off 'Taxman', but it's more of a homage than a straight rip. The Beatles 1966 album *Revolver* had been the listening pleasure of Bruce and Paul that year, so was bound to rub off.

The lyrics were inspired by ideas expressed in George Orwell's *Homage To Catalonia*, in hinting at an egalitarian society where everyone was equal even for just two minutes, which would be a start.

The psychadelia of the earlier 'Dreams Of Children', the double A side of 'Going Underground', had been emphasised and pushed further as the dreamy "If I never ever see you... agaaaain..." was pulled up by the immediacy of Bruce's precision over the background guitar of Paul.

Stuart Deabill

Sound Affects

The album was very much Paul's idea and all he wanted me to do was put it together for him. All the images have a relevance to the actual songs, and the general colouring was my input, but he wanted it to look like a BBC 'Sound Effects' album. I took all but three of the photos and the football ground, I'm pretty sure, is Charlton Athletic's The Valley. The dog is Max, who belonged to my mother-in-law. The power station is Sheerness. The girl was a friend of mine. The phone box is in Gravesend.

   The inner sleeve shows a group picture from Townhouse Studios by Pennie Smith, who took some really great shots. The colour one was taken at 5am down in Kent. That was by Andrew Douglas, who I worked with a lot afterwards.

   'Start!' and 'That's Entertainment' are my stand-out tracks. What a great way to finish Side One.

Bill Smith

HMV store display.

SOUND AFFECTS [Review by Stuart Deabill]

The Jam's fifth album is the greatest album ever made. You can argue the merits of any classic album to me and you could tell me why it's better than SA, but it wouldn't make a blind bit of difference. I've played *Sound Affects* more than any other record or CD since I bought it. I know every word from Shelley's poem on the back sleeve [*The Mask of Anarchy*], to every lyric, which hit home like an Exocet missile.

The front sleeve encapsulates how Paul Weller saw life at that time and his take on Britain at the turn of the so-called decadent '80s. (Whoever thought the 1980s was decadent didn't come from a mining village or steel town.)

The album was The Jam's most expensive to make and missed several deadlines for completion, as the band were still writing in the studio time. Recorded between the 15th June and 22nd October, it was eventually released on the 28th November 1980. It reached Number Two in the UK and in the US, a heady Number 77. Magnificently crafted at the Townhouse Studios, Goldhawk Road, London W12, it went on to sell nearly 300,000 copies on vinyl.

First, though, my story with *Sound Affects* started a bit later than its introduction to the public. Even though I had a few albums, usually given to me at Christmas, I was predominantly a singles' man. Well, when you're 14 or 15 years old, and the pocket money and paper round dough is spent on going to football matches, you don't have a lot left. So £4.50 for a record was out of the question. I didn't have an older brother and my pals were mainly into jazz/funk, so apart from Madness's debut *One Step Beyond*, the Specials' first album, The Clash's *London Calling* and the Police's *Regatta De Blanc*, I was barren on the long player front.

I found myself in the summer of '81 looking through the racks of Sellanby's in South Harrow. There was a secondhand copy of *Sound Affects* at a reasonable price. It was in decent nick, but half of me was thinking, £2.49 is two singles and some dinner from the excellent, award-winning chippy next door....

The run-out grooves, the lyrics, trying to work out which ground was used for the picture of the football fans... the inner sleeve photo taken at 5am to get the dawn light. The record slowly becomes part of you. You might not understand the full meaning of 'Set the House Ablaze' but you know it's about the nastier side of life.

The flip of 'Ablaze' is 'Monday', though. When Weller sings, "I will never be embarrassed about love again", you know that one day you will feel like that.

'Start!', with its now obvious reference to the Beatles' 'Taxman', meant absolute jack-shit to me, as I'd never heard *Revolver*. That's why I could never understand all those wanky DJs and journalists moaning about a rip off! It had already been a chart topper and an overplayed record in my house, so was already part of my inner being.

Side Two's opener, 'Dreamtime', had an other-worldly feel that I now recognize as a certain detachedness that I felt at that age — the feeling of being an awkward teenager and not fitting in. It starts with a backward tape loop followed by crashing chords. I used to put that on especially loud and get right into tennis racket shapes, whilst shouting, "STREETS I RAN, THIS WHOLE TOWN, BACKSTREETS AND ALL, I WANTED TO LEAVE THERE, JUST NO MATTER HOW FAST I RAN...". I used to feel empowered just by the opening verse, but by the end of it shrink back into small-town paranoia!

The manic pop thrill of 'Boy About Town' and 'But I'm Different Now' had me pogoing round the bedroom. The use of the word "superb", which is rarely used in any sort of lyric, doesn't bother Weller, who's every step was watched by fans and critics alike. He throws caution to the wind and pronounces "*Superb that you're my... GIRL!*"

'That's Entertainment' is the hymn that seems to be missing from the church on Sundays. The song, written in 10 minutes after a session down the local, later turned out to be massively influenced by a poem sent to him by a fan for his newly set up publishing company, Riot Stories.

'Man in the Corner Shop' is so simple but unbelievably poignant. I used to wonder if my local shopkeeper was jealous of any of his punters. Mind you, factory owners were in short supply on my manor....

'Music for the Last Couple' which, I have to say, I used to skip because my sister used to turn the sound of the fly right up and drive me fucking mad, still had the lyric about poison trains and referencing the shift of nuclear waste through our green and pleasant land, which the government tried to hush up.

'Scrape Away', though, was the one that really made me feel deeper and heavier than any song I'd ever heard until that point. As an end to an album it really left me in a state of confusion. It's not a happy ending, it's not a nice send off. It's no 'Chipmunks Are Go' off the Madness debut LP, or 'Garageland' off The Clash's first album. It doesn't send you on your way with joy in your heart and a nice cuddle. The supposed attack on John Lydon is a real sonic assault, with its dub overtones, and has the feel of shards of glass on flesh. With Bruce's bass line, which wouldn't have sounded out of place in a warehouse rave later on, and Rick's fantastic drumming, the whole band sounded like they'd spent the last three months in a cold and rainy Berlin rather than a sunny Shepherd's Bush. I used to play the album over again just to take away the disturbed feeling that 'Scrape Away' left me with. A bit like *The Shining* with Rickenbackers....

You could see where Weller was at in 1980, desperate to move on from the classic sound that peaked with 'Going Underground'. The Jam swapped the Who for Wire and James Brown for Joy Division. Lyrically, you can almost sense his disenfranchised feeling for England and the world. Thatcher started to make big waves in the political arena and there was a real threat of nuclear war as the Soviet Union and the United States went head-to-head, trying to see whose dad was bigger. Me, I was never a happy-go-lucky kid with just Chelsea and girls on my mind. Life might have been easier back then if I had been, but then I wouldn't have had the feeling I get whenever I put *Sound Affects* on.

"March 1980 was when 'Going Underground' crashed in at Number One and The Jam cut short their US tour and returned to England (returning via Concorde, such was the status of the band now!). In February there was a small series of warm-up gigs for the US tour. The first night was cancelled and the second was a gig at the University of Kent – I remember the place was half empty but that was probably as it wasn't advertised that well and tickets should only have been sold through the Students Union. Although I was at Maidstone College of Art, I picked mine up at the Longplayer in Maidstone. At the gig, we were treated to the first ever live performance of 'Going Underground'.

At last, I finally got to meet the band. It was at the Bromley Tech gig, again a low-key 'secret' charity gig. We had got there early. There were about 30 of us just hanging about and John let us in for the soundcheck. Kenny was never that happy about so many kids getting in but John always won!

That particular gig was quite small, may be around 400–500 people. It was a real word-of-mouth gig. The venue was chosen because the band used to hire all the PA and tour gear from Wing's Music; also Paul's then girlfriend, Gill Price, came from the town. My first meeting with the band was over-shadowed by nerves; I had so many things I wanted to ask but just said 'hello' and asked if they could sign my copy of *All Mod Cons*!

So in 1980, they released *Sound Affects* (like every Jam LP, the album was a work of art to me), plus 'Going Underground' and 'Start!' hitting the Number One spot – they were the only band since Slade to get two chart-topping hits back-to-back. The Jam 'army' just grew and grew and I think this was probably the time when most people really did get into them. Mick Talbot appeared on stage at the Rainbow and he played organ on 'Heatwave' at the 50th anniversary gig.

The band also went on their first tour of Japan in 1980 – the Japanese folk took the band to their hearts. By this time, Bruce and John had taken an interest in The Vapors. The band had supported the Jam on several occasions already and although they were, on paper, the band's management, in reality they did not have the time to put in the necessary work to push the band on as much as they would have liked. However, their experience and fame in the music business did help, bringing moderate success and a high-charting single with 'Turning Japanese'. And they weren't the 'one-hit' wonders most people think they were – they had other excellent songs, like the first single, 'Prisoners' and 'Jimmy Jones', 'News At Ten' and 'Spiders'. They also released two very good albums, *New Clear Days* and *Magnets*.

That year saw The Jam walk away with every music press accolade – *NME*, *Sounds*, *Smash Hits*, *Melody Maker*, you name it – LOVE WAS IN OUR HEARTS!

Jon Abnett

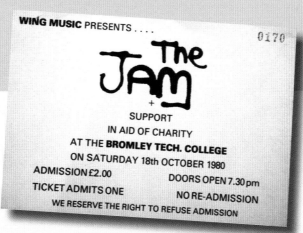

WING MUSIC PRESENTS . . . .

0170

The JAM
+
SUPPORT
IN AID OF CHARITY
AT THE BROMLEY TECH. COLLEGE
ON SATURDAY 18th OCTOBER 1980
ADMISSION £2.00   DOORS OPEN 7.30 pm
TICKET ADMITS ONE   NO RE-ADMISSION
WE RESERVE THE RIGHT TO REFUSE ADMISSION

The news that the *Sound Affects* tour would be gracing Bracknell Sports Centre for not one night, but two, in early November 1980, was something of a big deal to lads and lasses of a certain age, who'd been waiting for further action to grace this unlovely silo since The Specials and Madness had visited the previous year. The former was our first encounter with massed skinheads, the latter culminating in a stage invasion and 'riot' which had got our loved/hated new town on the front page of some tabloid or other.

The venue was handily located at the bottom of our school sports field and ideally placed for some mates to bunk off and lurk around the crisp machines during the soundcheck, until they got to meet their heroes. The conversation reportedly ran thus:

Paul: "Alright?"
Mates: "Alright?"
Paul: "You all live in Bracknell, then?"
Mates: "Yeah."
Paul: "Shithole, innit?"
Mates: "Yeah."

On hearing about this I tried to look nonchalant and not insanely jealous, while vowing to forge some kind of contact with the holy trinity on one, if not both, of the following nights.

Both shows were reliably stunning, but I suppose it's logical I remember more about the first, what with it being the first time I'd seen them live. It was a spicy old gig with plenty of sweat, tension and sporadic rucks. I remember a snapped string during 'Tube Station', and bouncers hauling one punchy dickhead out of the pit and onto the stage, where Paul and Bruce both took a swing at him before he was dragged off out the back somewhere.

Even more spectacularly, I managed to catch one of the battered drumsticks Rick flung out into the crowd at the encore as it glanced off a couple of extended claws and glided into my startled mitt in apparent slow motion.

Later on, clustering around the three at the ritual post gig meet-and-greet autograph gauntlet with the rest of my pint-sized crew (all tonic strides, unnecessary parkas and mail-order blazers), I found myself without a bit of paper for them to sign. In desperation to secure a more binding memento than Buckler's rim-shot mullered stick, I asked if they could sign that. Reasonably enough, they pointed out the idiocy of trying to write their names on a drumstick and so, instead, they all left their teeth-marks on it.

The following night I got their autographs and a 'Start!' T-shirt, which turned out about two sizes too big. I also managed about 15 seconds on the tour bus, trying to blag a lift home with two teeny Mods, who'd had a pasting from some skins (plenty of that around then, too); but John and the boys weren't wearing it.

The autograph went in the plastic sleeve on my copy of *Setting Sons* and was swapped for a bunch of Trojan 7 inches about a year later, I think. The drumstick was enshrined on a chest of drawers in my quarters and then secreted somewhere for safekeeping, where it was most likely slung out by my old dear once I'd fled the coop for a student's existence around '87. I turned the gaff inside out searching before they moved away, but no joy. A shame: the veracity of this sacred artefact is probably about as provable as the many professed fragments of the True Cross, but I reckon it'd still do alright on e-Bay.

James Papadamitres

Garry Bushell: I think it was around 1980 when The Jam recorded a song with The Cockney Rejects, who I was managing at the time. The song was called 'My England Dreaming'. I knew Weller at the time and, of course, the Rejects, but I think the main link for the project came via Grant Fleming. Grant was the number one Jam fan and one of the first Mods, one of the first 'glory boys'. He was also in a band at the time called the Terrible Twins. The song came about before Weller's political views took a radical change.

Eddie Piller: I think The Jam felt the song may be misinterpreted and that's why it wasn't put onto record.

Garry Bushell: I remember that I had not long done a piece about a Mod riot in Southend. It wasn't really a riot but the papers called it a riot. In the piece I included quotes from various Jam songs, but I heard that Weller was livid about that. But I think this was the only time I ever upset him. I first saw The Jam in 1977 when they played the Rainbow. I think it was with Sham 69 and I think it was supporting the Buzzcocks. It made the front page of the *Evening Standard* because the fans pulled up the seats at the Rainbow. One of the first pieces I wrote for *Sounds* was on The Jam, and this was about the *All Mod Cons* album. But by then I was already loving The Jam and *All Mod Cons* was a great album.

Eddie Piller: I didn't go on the first trip to Paris to see The Jam but I went on the second one. It was the first one that Grant Fleming organised where we really suddenly realised that there were like a hundred Mods in London. The Mods mainly came from South and East London, and they were getting the ideas from Weller, but at the start of '78 they hadn't really formed a scene as such. It took The Jam to crystalise the scene. The *All Mod Cons* album was really important and that had some really important imagery. I would say that the Mods claimed The Jam, but that The Jam didn't claim the Mods.

Garry Bushell: The Jam definitely upset the Punk establishment at the time.

Eddie Piller: Yeah, I mean when I was 13 I liked Sham 69, the Buzzcocks and The Jam. Those were my three bands. And when you look at them now they all had a bit of Mod about them. Bands like The Jam and The Saints had that Feelgood R'n'B sound and bands like the Buzzcocks had that angrier, modernist Punk sound, but at the time we didn't think they were different from the other Punk bands; they were just the ones that you liked. Even in '78 Generation X were considered a bit of a Mod band. They did that song 'Ready, Steady, Go', which is of course very Mod, and their guitarist used to wear a target T-shirt on stage. It was only after I got so sick of going to gigs and you had people chanting anarchy and all that I fell out of love with it. But I still loved those three bands. The Buzzcocks dressed as Mods but it was The Jam or Weller really that took it forward and became *the* Mod band.

Now, another thing that took The Jam forward was the fact that they had Paul's dad as the band's manager. John wasn't the sophisticated manager that was typical of the music industry, but he certainly looked after his boys' project, and so The Jam didn't get as fucked as lot of those other bands at the time.

Garry Bushell: I was at one of the 'John's Boys' gigs at the Marquee. I remember seeing [x] and [x] with these scaffolding poles, trying to smash their way in. I think [x] and [x] had been in the venue earlier, but had been thrown out, so that's why they came back with the scaffolding poles. I remember I was working for *Sounds* at the time and somehow got linked to it, and also got some of the blame.

Eddie Piller: I saw The Jam at least 60 times all over Europe from the age of 14, and that included one of the last ever gigs at Guildford Town Hall, and they did a lot of great songs. Weller once said to me that I am the only one of his mates who thinks that *This is the Modern World* is his best album. 'Life From a Window' is just a fucking genius song. And Paul always thinks that's odd, because people are always talking to him about *All Mod Cons* or *Setting Sons*. By '81 I had fallen out of love a bit with the band's direction and I was glad when he set up The Style Council.

Live, The Jam were just brilliant. In terms of atmosphere you just couldn't beat walking into the Rainbow twice a year, from late '78 onwards, and seeing the same hundred faces at the bar and then seeing The Jam. And that was it really, seeing The Jam was about the experience of the event as well as the genius of the music.

Garry Bushell and Eddie Piller

103

Garry Bushell and Eddie Piller

What can you remember about the Cockney Rejects/Jam single? Who wrote it and where was it recorded?

Back then, a lot of Punk bands would run a mile rather than mix with the Rejects, who scared the hell out of them. But there were a few were exceptions, like UFO, Joe Strummer and Paul Weller. Paul, Joe and the Rejects used to bump into each other at Nomis rehearsal studios in West London from time to time and would always have a friendly chat around the coffee machine. Paul and Mick in particular had links via fans, and good mutual friends, like Grant Fleming. The Rejects admired The Jam and found Paul to be an alright geezer, but they never had any plans to work together. It all came about by accident. Here's how: Mick was at a loose end in EMI's demo studios in Manchester Square. He had an instrumental that he wanted to lay down called 'England'. He called up Pete Way, UFO's bassist, and the Rejects drummer Sticks, and asked them if they wanted to come over and record it. They got together that evening, and did so. Mick liked it but decided it needed some piano. He called up Pete Wilson at Polydor a few days later, and Pete told him to bring the tapes over so he could play on it. When Mick got there Paul was in the studio laying down his own demos – this was around the time of 'Going Underground'. Mick played the track, Pete played some piano and they all had a few beers. Weller really liked the track, but thought that it could do with a vocal. So Mick said, "You got any ideas?" Paul responded: "As it happens, I do. Do you mind if I write some lyrics and give it a go?" Later that afternoon Paul called Mick and said he'd written the words. Mick went back to the Polydor studio and Paul recorded the vocals there and then. That's the story: it was never intended for release, it was nothing to do with The Jam or the Cockney Rejects, it was just Mick and a few pals doing it for the fun of it. And it sounds cool to this day, I reckon!

What can you recall regards the 'John's Boys' Marquee gig?

I was walking up Wardour Street on the way to the gig and the first thing I saw was HT and some of the Glory Boys attacking the front of the Marquee with scaffolding poles. There had been an altercation in the club earlier, and a couple of the lads, including Barney (of Barney & The Rubbles) had been thrown out. The word got out, and a few mates got outraged on their behalf. Chaos ensued. I think there was a bit of history, with security men throwing their weight around in there. Or that's what the punters thought, at any rate. The gig was superb, once the trouble had died away; the atmosphere was genuinely electric. But as I said: when I called the club from the Sounds news desk to get their response to the mini-riot, I was told that the trouble had been "led by Garry Bushell". Not for the first or the last time, I got the blame for something I'd had nothing to do with.

Can you remember your reaction when the band split up?

I was surprised for sure, because they had enjoyed such a golden period, and disappointed too – but probably not as surprised and disappointed as Bruce and Rick! But looking back, it made sense artistically and probably (for Paul) commercially.

Do you have a fave single or album?

Tough – so many great singles, all in a row. The Jam really were the most important band in England for a long time. For me, probably 'Down in the Tube Station at Midnight' because not only was it a great song, it also perfectly mirrored the paranoia of the time. But the next four singles were absolute belters too: 'Strange Town', the glorious 'When You're Young', 'The Eton Rifles', 'Going Underground' – everyone a gem: great tunes, clever lyrics, anger, and hooks that could land Moby Dick, just superb.

In July 1980 myself and two other Mods travelled over to Shepherd's Bush market on our Vespas to try and find an old 1960s clothes shop that still had stock from that era! I can't remember if we bought anything but I do remember riding down Goldhawk Road and seeing Rick Buckler with some 4x2" on his shoulder. We rode past, did a double take and turned around. It was Rick and he was buying some wood to take home. We asked him what he was doing and he told us they were recording an album at Townhouse Studios.

We asked if we could come along and he said, not today but come on Wednesday, so we returned to the Townhouse Studios two days later. We were met by Kenny Wheeler and a sound engineer, who took us down to the studios. We sat behind the huge mixing desk and the producers on a leather couch and saw that Weller, Buckler and Foxton all had separate areas to record in behind the glass and also had pieces of corrugated iron in each section where they played.

The sound engineer kept answering the phone and saying "Führer's bunker" every time someone called, which was pretty funny. When we got to the studio The Jam were playing an instrumental track, which had no name at the time but ended up being 'Music for the Last Couple'. We sat behind Coppersmith-Heaven and Parry until lunch, then we all went upstairs and played pool with Buckler and The Chords, who were recording there at the time.

We then went out to check our scooters. Paul Weller came out and asked me about my Vespa 50, which to be honest was quite beat up and had a huge toilet-shaped green fly-screen with 'London Mod 1980' on the front. Weller posed for pictures in his 'Smash Hits' T-shirt, and we went back in for the afternoon. At no point did anyone want to kick us out.

In the afternoon they started on 'Boy About Town', which we all thought would be a number one, as it sounded brilliant. During a break a crate of Carlsberg beer was produced, and we all sat on the huge sofa at the back of the studio, drinking and listening to *Sound Affects* take shape.

At 4-ish The Jam all came to our side of the studio with the producers and engineers to watch a TV screen that was above the mixing desk. I'm not sure what show it was, but it was a repeat of The Jam singing 'All Around the World' on the Marc Bolan show years earlier. Weller and the band all took the piss out of themselves and their suits and how they'd changed. There was lots of laughter and beer drinking.

We sat and chatted with Weller for 20 minutes and he ate a sandwich while we asked him about his writing. We left at 5pm having been there for 7 hours. We were made to feel welcome, had beers, chatted to the band, had pictures taken and thoroughly enjoyed our day.

I'm not sure if any other band would have let us sit in on a recording session; at the time The Jam were huge after 'Going Underground' went straight in at Number One, which made it even more of a privilege to be there.

Steve Butler

Dear Greg,
I'll wait until you do the
other demo ok and enclosed are
4 tickets for the Rainbow.
good luck
Paul Weller.

The following are letters from around 1980, from Paul to Greg Swatton, concerning the band Greg was in at the time. Paul always took time to write to fans and was keen to support and encourage up-and-coming bands.

Dear Greg,
I recieved a letter about your band (spice) from one of your friends, which I replied too, dont know if she got it. Anyway I would very much like to hear your band, but at the moment there is no plans for our own record company. Time being the enemy mainly.
We're going to U.S.A. on Friday for about 5 weeks, but if you want send your tape to me after that ok
send it too
45/53 SINCLAIR RD
LONDON. W. 14.

all the best with your band
Paul Weller

Diary entry of a 13-year-old: Tuesday 8th April 1980

Went to the Rainbow: me, Bev, Dad in the car. Met Allan and that lot up there. Our seats were second last row, but we took seats in the first row. The support group, The Records, weren't bad but The Jam beats them all. Paul Weller lovely. Part way through string broke, mike stand fell over. Got back about 12.30. Beverly slept over.

Songs included 'Smithers-Jones', 'Modern World', 'Little Boy Soldiers', 'David Watts', 'Billy Hunt', 'All Mod Cons', 'Strange Town', 'Butterfly Collector', 'Reach Out (I'll be There)', 'Going Underground', 'Down in the Tube Station at Midnight', 'It's too Bad', 'Dreams of Children', 'Away from the Numbers', 'In the City'.

My brother Allan was a big part of why I got into The Jam. He had gotten into them very early on. But because he was four years older there was this natural rivalry, so I was determined not to like what he would like. So, he use to go around scribbling on things "In the City" and I use to go around rubbing it out. But then the next moment I use to sneak into his bedroom and look at his records.

I recall my dad taking Allan to see The Jam in, maybe, 1977 in Canterbury. My dad use to take us to see bands separately. I mean the same year I went to see The Jam for the first time was the same year I also went to see David Soul. I guess my life could have gone one of two ways. I think I took the right route.

My dad took me to my first Jam gig at the Rainbow with a cousin. She was two years older than me. So, my dad took us up there and I remember what I wore. Not very cool (but I was only 13), but I had these red sparkly jeans with some piping down the sides and a white T-shirt, and my cousin wore these super tight trousers that made me really envious. We got some seats in the front row of the balcony and everything about it was just fantastic. The song I really remember was 'Reach Out', by the Four Tops.

In time I was into The Jam in my own right. Up until then I didn't want people to think I was just following The Jam because of my brother. By this time Allan was getting attention because The Prisoners were playing out. In those days The Prisoners were practising in our house so I use to take loads of photographs. So yeah, I was well aware of music and bands by this time.

Looking back I was really fortunate. I mean I was getting taken to gigs at a really early age. My friends at school and I mostly lived different lives. A lot of people at school were into the New Romantic thing instead of The Jam. I think my dad now looks back and thinks that I saw things at an early age that I shouldn't have seen. I mean especially along with The Prisoners, because I use to go with them to all their gigs.

Another Jam gig I went to (I went to six in all) was at the Michael Sobell Sports Centre. I think this was in '81. They played with a group, which turned out to be Bananarama, but we couldn't even say it. But I remember the girls came on with their dungarees and their check shirts and sang to a taped background. Let's just say their music wasn't appreciated. The audience thought it was a joke and the boys just letched.

I use to catch all the support bands because I was too young to go the pub before a gig. The best support band was The Vapors. They were my dad's favourite band. I think Bruce Foxton managed them along with Paul Weller's dad. 'Jimmy Jones' and 'Here Comes the Judge' were my favourite two songs. The Vapors were really good live, they were just powerful. Another support act was The Piranhas, but I only remember because I wrote it in my diary.

One of the funniest things about The Jam gigs was when Weller would come on stage with a new haircut and all the boys in the crowd would still have his old haircut. You would just know they would all be heading down the hairdressers in the morning to get an up-to-date haircut. Very amusing really.

By the time of my last gig I was buying my own records and clothes. I remember that I made a special dress for the last gig, at Brighton. I found some '60s pattern and made a dress. It was a black wool dress with this V-neck cut down the back. It had three-quarter length sleeves with darts on them and it was very fitted. I was 15 now and into my four button suede jackets, which I use to wear all the time, so I was either boiling hot or freezing cold. I use to go up to Kensington market and the shop, Sweet Charity, which sold all the hipsters, and look for shift dresses and so on. I remember coming home one time with some ski pants that were obscenely tight and my mother banned me from wearing them. A lot of us around the Medway towns were into that look at that time. I mean, we had The Prisoners, who dressed all '60s.

Elinor Crockford

It's a golden and magical period, that moment when you first feel the thrust of the teenage kick, when your imagination is captured, ignited and catapulted into an intoxicating world of thrills and excitement, experiencing the adrenalin rushes of life for the very first time. Absolute beginners.

I consider myself very fortunate to be of a certain age, be it fate or destiny, that my initial sensation of the teenage rush of adventure could not have been timed any better. As 1979 turned into 1980 there was never a more perfect moment to become a teenager. Of course I'm sure every generation would beg to differ but I wouldn't swap my explosion of youthful escapades for anything. Why? Because we had The Jam. The Jam was our band. The Jam gave us inspiration, identity, information, intelligence. The Jam helped me make sense of being a teenager, providing a musical and political education. By the time I was 14 I'd read Robert Tressell, Colin MacInnes and George Orwell, I'd seen Curtis Mayfield and I was wearing Tonic and mohair. Paul Weller probably showed me more than most of my secondary school teachers could have ever dreamed of. The Jam sound-tracked our young lives.

They first arrived in my world when a list of records circulated on the school playground. It was 1979, I was in my last year of middle school, and I suppose I had always been into collecting stuff. Panini football sticker books were all the rage with kids of a certain age, embroiled in scenes of frenzied card swapping to try and complete their books; but then records started to turn up, 7" inch singles, LPs, coloured vinyl, picture discs. They looked so alluringly attractive and they seemed cool.

Keith Ricketts was a local Punk and a 'face' on that scene. He was several years older than us. It was his list of records for sale I was clutching – I made a note of Keith's phone number and hastily arranged to meet him after school. I bought as many pieces of that seductive round plastic wax as my limited budget would stretch to.

I was elated at my purchases and rushed home to play them. I can no longer recall what they were, certainly they included Devo, 999 and quite possibly The Dickies, but almost immediately I was taken by one particular record. I became transfixed by its cover: a photograph of a band pictured beneath what looked like a flyover, two blocks of high rise flats standing in the distance. The band are all neatly dressed in sharp button-down shirts; the singer, who's the only one staring directly at the camera, is sporting a jumper with two arrows tacked on to it, pointing in vertically opposite directions. It was called *This is the Modern World* by The Jam. The album was everything I wanted it to be. It still had the energy, drive and anger of Punk but it contained more style and substance; in fact my favourite two songs from the LP, 'I Need You (For Someone)' and 'Tonight at Noon', could almost be described as love songs. I wore the grooves out on it: little did I know at the time that this would turn out to be their weakest album.

I had some catching up to do.

1980 was a momentous year for me. The most important records in my life were both released that year – Dexy's Midnight Runners debut, *Searching for the Young Soul Rebels,* and *Sound Affects* by The Jam. If my house was burning down these are the possessions I would have tried to rescue. *Sound Affects* was, and still is, my favourite Jam album. I love its dense, stark atmosphere, its psychedelic overtones. I also think it is a uniquely English sounding record and has stood up remarkably well to the test of time. It certainly contains some of Weller's finest compositions.

1980 was also the first time I got to see The Jam. The *Sound Affects* tour arrived at the cavernous Bingley Hall in Birmingham on 11th November. I had just become a teenager, I still find it hard to describe just how unimaginably exciting this was to an impressionable but already obsessed 13 year old. I recall spending weeks prior to the concert just staring at my ticket and imagining how it was going to be. Wondering what Weller would be wearing? What would I wear? Where would we stand? Would I see ok? What songs would they play?

As anyone who has ever witnessed them live would confirm, a Jam gig was not just another show, in fact it wasn't a show at all: it was the real deal, it was an event. The sound that the three of them made was so immensely powerful – which has to also stand as a testament to the often-overlooked abilities and attributes of Foxton and Buckler, too. They were an absolute powerhouse and the force and directness of those songs played live at a thunderous volume was just immense, this colossal sound created by just three people. Also,

contd.

the crowd and atmosphere it generated was just magical. I don't think I've ever felt anything like it since.

I could put on a Jam record today and I'm almost instantly reminded of that golden period: huddled around a portable radio at lunch time, listening to the new single, 'Funeral Pyre'; rushing to buy the *NME* to find they had cleaned up in every category in the readers' polls; taping the charts on a Sunday to find out if they had gone straight in at Number One; being cautioned at school for wearing a mohair suit ("It's not strictly school uniform is it, Sheasby lad?"); pissing my 'O' level English literature exam as it asked me to write a short piece using a number of titles, one of which was 'Down in the Tube Station at Midnight'; my heart sinking and shedding a tear in Gales newsagents as I read the statement and news of their imminent split.

More than anything, they gave me the strength, belief and confidence to feel like I was somebody at such a young age. Great groups will define their time and place in musical history: The Jam also defined ours.

Neil Sheasby, Stone Foundation

I first came across The Jam on one summer's day in 1980, when 'Start!' was Number One in the Top 40. As an 11-year-old, I was not really into music, but hearing this song for the first time on Radio 1, started a love affect with The Jam.

It would be another year before I purchased my first record by the band – 'Absolute Beginners'. I can still remember going into Woolworths in Kidderminster and buying the single for 99p with my pocket money. This was the first record I ever bought and today it still sits in my record collection, with all the band's singles, which are the pride of my vast record collection!

By now I was gripped by the Mod scene – well, the tail end of the late '70s and early '80s revival. As a 13-year-old I thought I was the business in my Harrington jacket, Fred Perry polo shirts, Sta-Prest trousers and loafers. Living in a small rural town in Worcestershire, I thought that I was ahead of my friends by being into music and the Mod scene in a big way.

'A Town Called Malice' would be the last single I would buy while the band was still together. It did not hit me how much the band meant to me, until I heard of the split while watching the old BBC programme *Nationwide* one evening in December 1982. I can remember Paul being interviewed on Brighton Pier and explaining the reasons for the split.

By 1983–84, I was old enough to travel into Birmingham on my own, and armed with my money from my Saturday job, I was able to start assembling a collection of the band's records. I started off by buying the albums, which were still readily available from the record shops. I was also getting more heavily into the mid-1980s Mod scene, and shopping at places like Melandii and the Cavern, who had shops in Birmingham at the time. I had bought a copy of *A Beat Concerto* and would copy what Paul was wearing and even the way he had his hair cut!

My favourite all time song by the band is 'Ghosts' off *The Gift* album, which always gives me goose-pimples and cold shivers when I listen to it! It's one of those incredible songs that slowly grows on you: musically, the structure of the song is simple and yet so understated, with lyrics so poignant and true, allowing the listener to relate to the words in their own way, relevant to their circumstances. The song has not aged in the 30 years since I first heard it – true brilliance!

Mark Watkins

Tokyo 1980 – First tour of Japan.

My first gig was at the Rainbow Theatre in 1980. The ticket was three quid, bloody hell. This was actually my first ever gig in London. The only gig I had ever been to before that was Secret Affair, down in Canterbury. That gig sowed the seeds. Me and my mates thought, this is good, we are having some of this. It was loud and people were crowded in. It was great.

I remember we arrived at the venue and it was vast. There were lots of people, it was hot and when you looked around people were all dressed like you: I mean we all had our aspirations of being Mods by then.

Anyway, The Jam came on and it was like, 'wow'. It was loud, the music was brilliant and when you came out your ears were ringing. I remember I was trying to see what they were wearing and I could see Weller's shirt and his shoes. I wanted to get copies of them. The whole thing was just brilliant.

By now, I was smitten with the gig thing and my next gig was a few months later, in Bingley. It was just me and Malc who made the long journey for this one. The venue was like this bloody great agricultural warehouse in the middle of a field. It was huge inside and teaming with people. I think the band, Apocalypse, were the support band. I remember they didn't go down too well and got things thrown at them – you know, drink and spit.

I remember The Jam were playing some new stuff, I guess new singles or something. There was one point in the show that went very quiet and Weller was like fiddling with his guitar, tuning maybe or something. Then Weller shouts out to the crowd, "What do you want", so I shouted back, "'When You're Young'". Anyway, he must of picked out my southern accent because he pointed at me and the next thing The Jam are playing the song. That moment just made it for me. That song is probably my all-time favourite song.

Following the Bingley gig was a trip to the Brighton Conference Centre. This was one of my favourites. It was also around this time that I saw them in London. They were like on this float, driving around the streets. I think it was some kind of CND rally or something. I watched them do a few numbers whilst they were along the Embankment.

A little while later the announcement was made [about the split] and I couldn't really fathom it out. I mean, I kind of get it now, looking back in retrospect, but at the time it felt like something was being pulled from underneath my feet. It felt like a big part of your life was being taken away from you. I always remember the interview with Weller (I think it may have been on Nationwide), sort of trying to explain it. I watched it and thought, I'm still not getting it.

Then it was announced that they were going to play a final gig at the Conference Centre in Brighton, so we went down although we didn't have tickets. In fact we could have had tickets – they were offered – but they were well beyond our price range. Anyway, we spent the day having a jolly around Brighton, went on the piss and so on, and then it's coming up to the gig. By now we were trying everyone, bumping into everyone with all the bravado going, "Got any tickets, got any tickets for The Jam", but nobody's got any tickets. Mind you, we did get this shady tout who tried selling us these tickets in a doorway for forty quid, but we couldn't for go it – that was like a week's wages.

So the whole thing ended in an anti-climax. All these people were on a buzz as the gig got closer and were going inside the Conference Centre, and it's thinning and its thinning; and then it's just me and my mate outside, kicking our heels and mumbling to ourselves, fuck it. And on top of that we could hear the music inside, and it got louder as people opened doors and so on. So, we eventually gave up and took a slow walk up to the train station via a Kentucky, or somewhere. So yes, that was the last Jam gig that I never got to.

Dan Derlin

APOLLO THEATRE, Manchester
M.C.P. presents—
The Jam
PLUS SPECIAL GUESTS
Friday, 31st October 1980
Evening 7-30
FRONT STALLS
£4.00
C   32   1
No Cameras or Recording Equipment.
No Ticket exchanged nor money refunded.
Official Programmes sold only in the Theatre.
A. B. Cooper (Printers) Ltd, MANCHESTER
Retain this portion.

It was the summer of 1980 when a few of us decided to visit Paul Weller. See, we were Mods and Weller was our leader, so it was a bit like a pilgrimage really; and when I say 'visit', we decided to go uninvited to his home town of Woking and call at his house. No one actually knew where we were going (we were from Acton), but we did know that it was somewhere in Surrey, and that it was also where Chessington Zoo was.

So that was it, armed with his address – 44 Balmoral Drive, Maybury Estate, Woking, Surrey – we set off in search of our holy grail. First stop was the bus to Ealing Broadway, where we picked up the number 65 to Chessington Zoo; well it had to be somewhere near there, surely?

As the bus terminated at the zoo, we asked the conductor if he could direct us to Woking, which is when we discovered we were miles away. Anyway, he told us the best thing to do was take a train from the nearest station, which we did. We arrived in Woking and set about finding Paul's home, which we knew was near Shearwater County School, so we started to ask for directions in local shops, etc. Surprisingly, we found the school pretty quickly, and we soon found ourselves on the estate looking for the 'Modfather'. From the top of the hill we could see down into rows of back gardens, and spotted an old scooter round the back of one of them. The excitement started to build and we raced down to the road, which turned out to be Balmoral Drive.

The house with the scooter turned out not to be the one, but that didn't matter, as we were now stood in front of No.44, which had a wagon wheel on top of the porch. After some discussion about what to do next (we were not sure we actually believed we would get there), I was volunteered to knock on the door. The door was opened by a large geezer with grey hair, which we recognised as Paul's dad, John, and the only words I could muster were, "Is Paul in?" John chuckled and explained that Paul now lived in London and he would get his wife, Ann, to speak to us. Ann came to the door and we explained that we had travelled from West London to see our hero and were just amazed to have actually made it. To our surprise Ann invited us in and we duly joined the fan club whilst sat in Paul's bedroom, which was home to a piano, guitar, and numerous framed discs hung on the walls.

We left Woking buzzing that afternoon, clutching various mementoes of the day courtesy of Ann, and couldn't wait to get back to Acton to boast of our adventure. I think Ann was probably a busy lady for the rest of that summer, but I was happy in the knowledge that I was among the first to cut this particular style!

Steve O'Neill

Tokyo, Japan 1980.

After the release of *Sound Affects* the group played a series of charity gigs in Woking, one of which was at the YMCA. Seeing as Paul was back in town we took the opportunity to go for a beer or two, so we took a long walk to the Anchor, a boozer on the River Wey. It was a warm day so we sat out in the sun drinking, chatting and laughing. After several pints we thought we'd better make our way back to the gig. We were feeling the effects of the booze by now, and we had miles to walk to get back home.

It became obvious we weren't gonna make it in time. I swear this is true, but my older brother drove one of those rubbish carts, and he spotted us staggering along the road, pulled over and delivered us to the gig! Paul Weller arrived at the gig in a dust cart! (As a postscript Paul played the concert slightly merry in a gig that included several broken strings and a few damaged guitars…. Paul's mum, Ann, used to egg me on to do my impression of PW struggling with 'Little Boy Soldiers' – you know, the "We ruled the world, we killed and robbed, the fuckin' lot.")

I remember getting the first LP. Paul had given me a handful and told me to make sure everyone got a copy. I took them down the Princess of Wales that night, one each for Dave Waller and Tony Pilott (both of you RIP). They didn't show up, so I left them with the barmaid for the lads if they came in; of course she recognized the faces on the cover….

By now we were getting advance copies of the singles. I recall my brother Pete, who used to drive for the band, giving me 'Start!' in the pub one Saturday lunchtime. Pubs used to close in the afternoon back then, so when we were chucked out I thought I would take the record to the music shop and ask them to play it (I hadn't heard the finished single yet!). So a few of us marched into Arcos and asked, "Have you got the new Jam single yet?" Of course, he said it wouldn't be released for another three weeks. So with a flourish I handed him the mint copy and said, "Can you play this one then?" The look on his face was priceless! We would stand around while he played it to a packed shop ("both sides mate") – childish and big-headed I know, but funny when you are drunk.

The best job I ever had

I was 24, I had deliberately taken a year off work, but the bastards had cut my dole money 'cos I wasn't actively looking for work. So I had got off my arse and got a job. A day or two later I was walking into Woking to have a beer (to celebrate, or drown my sorrows) – I wasn't looking forward to returning to factory life.

"Oi, Tufty!" (everyone in the gang called me that). It was John Weller. "Have you got a job yet?" "Err, not really John, why?" I asked. "Well, we've got a tour coming up, and I wondered if you fancy coming along and helping us sell T-shirts. What do you reckon?" I weighed up the possibilities – 7am to 5pm working in a factory, or selling T-shirts on the *Sound Affects* tour?! Now I really could celebrate (my dad couldn't believe I had turned down a perfectly good job for a month on the road). As an added bonus, John said I could travel on the coach with the band. Selling merchandise, seeing every gig (we always packed up the stall as soon as The Jam came on stage, figuring no one would want to miss the show), travelling in style, drinking with the lads AND GETTING PAID!

I remember about the third gig in, after seeing the show a few times and listening to the previous night on a Walkman, watching from the balcony, thinking, "This is the best band in the world".

And yep, that certainly was the best job I ever had.

Steve Carver

1981 – LOVE WAS IN OUR HEARTS!

The British public breathed a sigh of relief in January as the announcement came that Peter Sutcliffe, the suspected 'Yorkshire Ripper', had been arrested. In May he was convicted for the murder of 13 women and sentenced to life imprisonment. The year also saw John Lennon's killer, Mark Chapman, sentenced to life imprisonment.

The year was going to be a restless one, with riots igniting in Leeds, London, Luton, Manchester, Derby, Preston, Birmingham and other down-trodden, pissed-off towns and cities. Unemployment had reached 2.5 million and skinheads would clash with Asians in Southall in April. Groups from these inner cities provided the background music to the unrest, such as UB40, Steel Pulse and The Specials. The type of peace that Lennon had fought for was not going to get a look-in during this year. Moira Stewart also became the first black newsreader, on the BBC.

Pedal pushers and soul belts were the fashion items of the day with the high street kids, as the downtrodden celebrated Charles and Di in a fairytale romance that was anything but.

Tenko and *Brideshead Revisited* were the big shows this year, but for us they were overshadowed by the darts quiz, *Bullseye*, hosted by Jim Bowen. Nothing amused us more than thinking about John Thomas from Uttoxeter winning a speedboat and having to park it outside his tower block, where he lived on the ninth floor.

March saw the first London Marathon. Bucks Fizz won the Eurovision Song Contest thanks to a showing of knickers, and *Chariots of Fire* was a massive cinema hit. Adam and the Ants were telling us 'To Stand and Deliver'. In September, Soft Cell made it to Number One with a version of Gloria Jones' Northern Soul classic, 'Tainted Love'. Three months later the infamous club and mecca of Northern Soul, the Wigan Casino, closed down forever. Cricket legend Ian Botham lost his England captaincy due to a shocking start against the Aussies, but spearheaded the return of the Ashes to its rightful owners in one of the most thrilling Test series in decades.

The Jam released two official singles in 1981, 'Funeral Pyre' and 'Absolute Beginners'. Also out that year was 'Green Door' by Shakin' Stevens, 'Vienna' by Ultravox, 'Body Talk' by Imagination, 'Don't You Want Me' by the Human League, and 'Happy Birthday' by Altered Images.

It was also the year Wings disbanded, Billy Idol left Generation X to go solo and Kit Lambert (The Who manager after Pete Meaden) fell down the stairs and died.

'That's Entertainment'

Not an official release but a best-selling import from Germany, which reached Number 21. The cover was an abridged version of the *Sound Affects* sleeve with six squares rather than the 22 on the LP.

Summer 1980 and Paul's on his way home from the pub...

Right nice little session that, with the chaps. Five-minute walk and I'll be back indoors.... That poem I got sent by that kid Paul from up north, for Riot Stories, was blinding. Proper fired up my imagination....

That's Entert...ain...ment.... That's Enter...tain...ment.... Must get this song down when I get in, keep thinking about the everyday things that we all see and putting it into a three minute song.... Hopefully the missus won't start giving me earhole.... Pimlico, drives me mad, dunno why I moved opposite a school. Kids ringing on the bell – rather be on tour. At least I get me afternoon snooze. Should let Kenny sort 'em out, he'll probably twist one of the little fuckers ears off though.... Still, not far from the river and I can't deny, I love being a stone's throw from 22 Westmoreland Terrace, where the Small Faces lived. What a gaff that must have been, loved to have got on it with them....

Fucking hell, struggling with that key in the lock, must have been that last pint Paolo bought....

"Is that you, Paul?"

"Yes, love."

Who else is it gonna fuckin' be? I know I wrote about someone having their keys lifted in the tube station and getting a visit, but the chances of it happening are a bit rare. Grab a beer....

"Love, I've got this song, gonna work on it for 10 minutes. Most of it's written in me head, just got to get the melody right."

"No worries darling, I'm watching Reggie Perrin, so keep it down a bit, yeah?"

Keep it fuckin' down? Just had me first Number One, which is paying the rent on this gaff and I've got to play at low volume? Acoustic it is then, I suppose... quick tune up... LA LA LA LA LA LA LA LA ....

A Police car and a screaming siren, pneumatic drill and mixed up concrete...

Five verses later.... This is going well, bit unsure about these lines at the end:

Two lovers missing the scream of midnight, two lovers missing the tranquillity of solitude, getting a cab and travelling on buses, reading the graffiti about SLASHED SEAT AFFAIRS!

Yeah, that does work... number of Routemasters these days with the top deck seats in bits.... Paul loves Gill, get in, ha, ha....

Right: demolish that beer, and see if Gill likes it....

"Err love, wanna hear my new one."

"Yeah, Reggie's finished so let's have a listen."

...Days of speed and slow-time Mondays, Pissing down on a boring Wednesday...

I'll get in the studio with Pete tomorrow to get that down; don't need to bother the others....

"That's well good Paul... right – Chinese or Indian babe, I'm starving..."

Paul Weller actually wrote 'That's Entertainment' in a caravan in Selsey Bill, but never let the truth get in the way of a good story.

Stuart Deabill

THE YOUNG VIC
THE CUT, LONDON. SE1 8LP

£3.00

30 NOV 1981

TICKET OF ADMISSION ONLY–
NO RESERVED PLACES

195

FOR CONDITIONS SEE BACK
TO BE RETAINED

'Funeral Pyre'/'Disguises'

The sleeve was based on Munch's painting, *The Scream*. Paul was keen to use that and be an actual 'Funeral Pyre'. I shot this in Horsell Common near Woking. The band got their friends involved and other locals came with their torches. It was funny because at that time the whole video shoot game was very heavily unionised and as I didn't have a director's ticket I couldn't be the director as such! So we had some guy who came on set who had a director's card and sat in a trailer all day while I directed! That was my first video and I still like it, the book burning, etc – and the band looked great. We started in the middle of the afternoon and finished up about 2–3am. All shot and edited on film, before the digital era.

Bill Smith

'Funeral Pyre'

'Funeral Pyre' was released in May 1981 and reached Number Four in the charts. The intro to this song immediately sets the tone and hints at the song's direction. There is a steady 4/4 beat from Buckler using his bass drum and Weller introduces parts of his guitar lick. Foxton supports the bass drum and occasional snare drum flurries. The song builds and Buckler introduces more marching drum style patterns before exploding into the verse.

The accompany video was brilliant and shows a bunch of kids (lucky Jam fans, I always thought) carrying paper and wood, reflecting the lyrics, to the funeral pyre being built.

I remember playing this record loads but not really paying attention to the lyrics. Then one day I read the lyrics that were written on the rear of the picture cover and noticing that Weller had been singing the word "pissing" in one of the verses. After that I was conscious to choose my moments to play the record because I didn't want my mum or dad hearing the swear word. Not that they would have given a shit anyway. The song is often remembered for the way Buckler's marching snare drum carries the song through. He even gets the final word on the song with a snare strike after Weller has stopped singing about feeling so old and feeling so young.

B-Side: 'Disguises'

This song was credited to Townshend and on the whole is a fantastic version from The Jam of the Who song. The guitar sound is very Who-like and has a Who feeling. Buckler bangs around the tom-tom's in a very Moon-like fashion and the rhythm always impressed me. Weller's voice sounds youthful on this track and he sounds like he is doing his best to capture a certain feel.

The song is close to the original in arrangement and includes an interesting instrumental break that relies on the instruments being heavily affected with delays and echoes. The guitars screech and have a psychedelic effect, too, and continue through the outro before Buckler's use of the tom-tom's again have the last word.

Snowy

'Absolute Beginners'/'Tales From the River Bank'

This double A-side was released in October 1981 and reached Number Four in the charts. The photo on the front was taken by Rick from the Marriott Hotel, Leicester, when the band were on tour, I believe. The back cover photo was taken in Chiswick Park by the photographer Derek D'Souza.

That would have been the last sleeve I worked on with the band. I worked on the video with my friend Gered Mankowitz. We used the same crew that shot The Specials 'Ghost Town' video. The band agreed the storyboard, but when they arrived they proved completely uncooperative. We shot it all and I did the first edit and sent that to them. Didn't hear anything back for a few days and then they said there's a couple of bits in there that we don't like, blah blah. I started the re-edit but then didn't hear anything until Polydor rang to say, don't worry, we've shot a new video, and by the way we're not paying you. The video I did was mainly studio with some outside shots, but I think Polydor just scrapped it, never to see the light of day. It did leave me with some resentment, no question, as my work had been rejected.

With the videos I had ideas from 'Going Underground' onwards, but 'Funeral Pyre' was the first time I actually got asked to shoot one.

Looking back, The Jam were an important catalyst for me as a designer within the music industry and they started me thinking more and more about design and also in terms of putting images to music. So I think they gave me a clean slate from which to work as they had no history, and you don't get that very often. Musically, their songs still stand up today and Paul Weller is one of the great half a dozen British songwriters. No one else could have written 'English Rose'. They stand apart from everyone else and although it ended the way it did, I still had a great time and loved working with The Jam.

Bill Smith

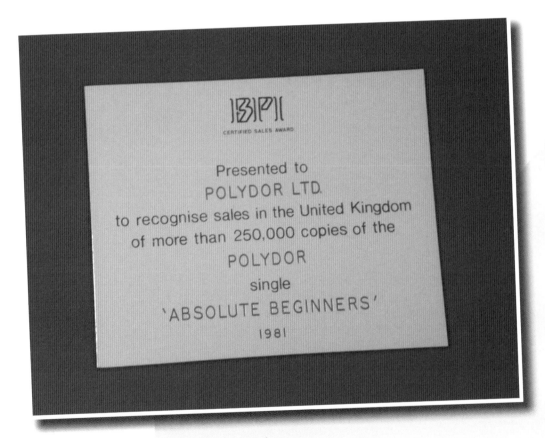

Detail of BPI Award.

It was a hot summer's day, I was walking across some sticky black tarmac (this bit is made-up, but it sounds good) on my way to the town centre where I lived. I had my pale blue Sta-Prest trousers on, a white Fred Perry polo shirt and beige desert boots. Stuffed inside one of my trouser pockets along with my door key, and trying to not fall out of the hole made by said door key abuse, was a 50p piece. It was my 12th birthday, and the 50p was some of my birthday money. It was the 6th June and it was hot and sunny. In my childhood years, every one of my birthdays was always hot and sunny.

I strolled on my own, taking little notice of my surroundings: a large grey prison wall, an assortment of Ford Cortinas and Capris, the traditional working class pub, also shared with the local squaddies. I was bouncing, I was excited, I was on my way to Woolies to spend my 50p.

Within ten minutes of leaving my house I had passed the first few shops of the town centre. On my right there was a pub. It was shut, not 11am yet. On my left was the best menswear clothes shop around for miles. Huckles' shop window was displaying its latest deliveries. I paused, but not for long: I needed to get to the big red-and-white store to spend my birthday money. But I stood long enough admiring a pair of red, white and blue bowling shoes and a grey Lonsdale sweatshirt. With a sigh I ambled away and toward my destination. A few steps more and I pass Barry the Mod's hairdresser. It's where I go to get my French-line cut back into shape.

A further 20 yards and I can see the window of the store. I get a rush of adrenalin. I glance to the right and look at the albums hanging up in the Our Price shop window. A colourful collection of '80s bands peer back at me through the window. Duran Duran, The Police and the Human League. I dismiss them with ease – almost a mental spit – but I am not that bothered really.

I quicken my pace now that my target is in sight. I reach the large glass doors and am about to enter when I hear a familiar voice, "Oi". I sigh again, halt and turn around. It is my sister and three of her schoolmates, Debbie, Lisa and Laura. They send me a mixture of smiles and sneers. I just know they are going to take the piss, but it's not me that looks like I have had a dozen tins of paint thrown over me.

"Happy birthday," says Debbie.

"Happy birthday," add Lisa and Laura.

They are being friendly, so that's a result. They ask me a few questions about what I got for my birthday. I offer them a couple of examples, like socks and book vouchers, and then tell them about my favourite present from my parents: a pair of dark black, wrap-around plastic glasses. Debbie wants to see them but I tell her that I left them at home, next to the socks and book vouchers. It was a deliberate act because I am saving them for a special occasion that is coming up after lunch. It's the day of the annual fete on the heath near to my house, and I want to make an appearance later in my new shades and Jam cycling shoes that I have recently acquired.

I am itching to get away from my sister and her mates. The smell of the pick 'n' mix draws my attention back to my destination. I say my 'see you laters' and push the glass door wide open. I step inside and brush up against an old woman with a head scarf wrapped over her pink-rinse, thinning hair. She must be hot, but she is not the sort to leave home without a head scarf, even if it is 80 degrees outside.

I snake my way in between aisles of kettles, picture frames and lampshades until I reach the record section. I clock the rows of albums and singles. It all looks so ordered and still. Then I see what I want and reach out my hand. In one swift motion I am holding between my thumb and index finger a copy of 'That's Entertainment'. I am buzzing inside. I now feel that within minutes I will own my very own copy of the 7" record. Not only does the touch of the paper cover feel great, but it looks fantastic.

My eyes dart around the front cover picture: why is it pink? What is the meaning of the pound sign? Why the jukebox? Ah, the jukebox, that reminds me of my local youth club. That jukebox gobbles my 10 pences, week in, week out, because it has 'Going Underground' and 'Start!' on it, and my mates and I can't get enough of hearing them two songs.

"Can I help you?"

I am jerked back into life and forced to accept the reality of what exists in the big store. There is a female shop assistant glaring down at me. I hold up the record and she escorts me towards one of the tills, where

contd.

she nods to the younger girl working the till. She holds out her hand and I let go of the record. It all happens so quickly but it's ok, the quicker the better, so I can get home and play my record. I know, for certain, that I will be marching home in a double-time the local Royal Engineers Regiment would be proud of.

There is a speedy exchange of record in brown, pink and white paper bag and me parting with my birthday money. Then with bag tucked under my arm I exit the shop, keep my head down to avoid any further engagement with my sister and her Human League clone friends, and I race home.

On the way home I pass one of the local tramps, Pig-Bin Billy – he is harmless, he doesn't bother anyone and people leave him alone. Next, I pass the Mustard Man, not a tramp exactly, but a regular face around town because he is always pushing his old trolley with a bag that advertises English Mustard. He is a poor soul and people respect him because we all know he suffers from shell shock as a result of some incident from World War II.

As I turn right towards the prison wall I notice the familiar figure of my dad walking off to work at the Post Office. He must have bagged some much-needed overtime. See you later, Dad.

It's the home stretch now. I can see the bottom of my road. I remind myself that it will not be long before I am gently placing the needle onto the record. I desperately hope that I don't pass any more people I know. I don't have time to chat to anyone.

Head down for the last 20 yards. I pass the hairdressers and homebrew wine-making shop and then I am home, No. 57. I bounce down the stone steps that lead to the basement and push open the door. It's not locked, so Mum must be indoors somewhere. She is: in the kitchen making a Bakewell tart. She knows it's one of my favourite afters and well, it is my birthday.

I hastily show her what's in my bag and she smiles. She knows all too well what The Jam mean to me. I charge up the three flights of stairs that lead to my bedroom that is in the attic area. The sun is beating through the skylight window that Mum has pushed wide open to let some fresh air in and some (almost) teenage boy odours out.

I fall onto my knees in front of my record player that sits on the floor next to my growing record collection of Northern Soul, Jam, Ska and Two Tone 45s and 33s. I quickly and carefully remove the 7" that I had left on the deck from the previous night. There you go, 'Fortune Teller', by Benny Spellman, I mutter and respectfully ease it into its sleeve.

Then cometh the moment. I pull 'That's Entertainment' out of the bag and in one swift movement allow the shinning oily vinyl disc to fall onto my palm. It looks brilliant, but, what is this, something is missing? Bollocks. I repeat it again but with more venom. Bollocks, shit, bollocks. I stare down at the 7" record and focus my attention on the missing bit in the middle. The middle bit is missing, and without the middle bit I can't play my prized birthday present.

Still clutching the record I shift copies of the *Melody Maker* and *Sounds* and flick through my other 45s, but I cannot find a spare middle bit. I'm looking but I know I don't have one. I use to, but I am reminding myself that the spare middles I had were pinched by one of the older Mods at the last Howard De Walden disco.

I place 'That's Entertainment' back into its pink, purple and white sleeve and leap up onto my feet. I'm sweating. I'm annoyed and pissed off. Within seconds I have left my bedroom and my house and am hurtling back down the street, retracing my steps back to Woolies. I must have a middle for the record. I need it quick....

This is just one my special moments from my personal memories of what I consider to be the best band of all time. I had an old head on my young shoulders and having an older sister who was liked and respected by her peers done me a whole world of good. Via my sister I was in contact with older kids. These kids accepted me and allowed me into their worlds, and included in their worlds were their record collections. And it just so happened that in our part of town, every other kid was either a Mod, skinhead or Rude Boy. It was these Mods and Rude Boys that ran the Howard De Walden youth club. It was these kids that took charge of the record player at the discos, and what they played was The Jam, Secret Affair, the Purple Hearts and a healthy dose of Northern Soul, Reggae and Ska. It was wonderful. It was also something that would stay with me for the rest of my life and contribute towards shaping who I was to become.

Snowy

1981 saw the band play The Cricketers pub as The Jam Road Crew, a charity gig in celebration of Valentine's Day. Sadly, a punch-up saw Ann and Nicky being escorted away by Kenny Wheeler! They also played the Sheerwater youth club and the YMCA fund raisers. One thing that could always be said about The Jam was that they always remembered their roots and were keen to support the people who had helped them on their road to success.

It was in October that Paul Weller produced and presented the *Something Else* TV programme, after writing in to the programme's producer. The band also embarked on their second Japanese tour.

A lot of fans were really into the whole CND thing by now, but it meant nothing to me. I didn't buy into any of it. For me, The Jam were always about the music, the sound. A lot of people wore a CND badge on their parka only because Weller wore one. Loads of people were sucked into it because of Weller.

I remember we went up for a CND march at Hyde Park only to be told it had moved to the Embankment. So we went there instead, legging it around London. There weren't many people, maybe a hundred. The band played on the back of a lorry. I remember Weller was wearing a beret and a red denim jacket. Vaughan Toulouse was there as well. The band played four songs and that was it. They also played that night with the Gang of Four, again in support of CND.

One of best gigs of 1981 was at Golders Green Hippodrome – Radio 1 aired the concert – it was a fan club only invite. I think this was the only gig of this nature from my recollection. From memory, a letter announcing the gig was sent out by Ann and Nicky, and then you had to 'apply' for a ticket. Managing the fan club was a family affair and a full time job for Ann and Nicky. If you wrote a letter to The Jam, you always received a reply – mostly from the band if they weren't recording or touring.

It was also the time of the Sobell dates, with the acts like Rudi and Bananarama. I remember the Bananarama gig well because the backing tape broke. People just weren't interested in Bananarama and started to get restless and boo them off stage. Time was given to bands like The Questions and Department S, but not Bananarama.

If you listen to the bootleg from the first night, you'll hear a thud and a long intro to 'The Gift'. Paul rushed on stage, picked his guitar up and promptly fell on his arse. Both nights were recorded and like half a dozen 'live recordings' still sits in the Universal vaults waiting to see the light of day.

The two single releases 'Absolute Beginners' and 'Funeral Pyre' could not have been further apart and the latter saw The Jam on the song writing credits for the first time.

It was also the night that there was a lot of trouble with some skinheads. There had been a skinhead band (The Exploited, I think) playing just around the corner. This was one of the many Mod/Skin/Punk/Teddy Boy fights that took place over the years.

I recall the Skegness Pavilion gig that year being really good as well. I stood at the back for the last few numbers and all you could see was a cloud of steam rising to the roof. 'In the City' was back on the setlist. We had bumped into Paul Weller during the day in an amusement arcade. As always, he had a lot of time for the fans.

Weller also famously remained in his seat in the front row at The British Rock and Pop Awards, slouched back with arms folded while Rick and Bruce trudged up to collect the award.

Paul was already starting to diversify; he appeared, looking rather nervous, at the Poetry Olympics in London at The Young Vic, on 30th November.

Jon Abnett

'Absolute Beginners'

Most Jam fans will have a favourite single or album. Generally, all the songs are loved in an equal kind of way but for most of us there are a few songs that just claim a slight edge. The reasons are numerous. It could be that a particular song was the first song the person heard by the band, or maybe it was the song the band were playing when they were spotted on TOTPs or *Swap Shop* even. Maybe the person was just at an age that was right for them to discover and connect to that special song. 'Absolute Beginners' is up there with my favourites and I think it was because by the time the song was released I had been actively buying the back catalogue and also buying the new releases as they appeared (for me there had only been 'Funeral Pyre' before 'Absolute Beginners'). But buying 'Absolute Beginners' on the day of its release gave me a sense of belonging. Now I felt that I was properly a part of The Jam army. Now I was connected to something that was live and direct and still strong.

I like the song for many reasons. I like the up-tempo rhythm and use of the horn section. It's a song that people could dance to (easier than 'Funeral Pyre', anyway). Buckler delivers a solid drum pattern that stabs and punctuates in all the right places. The bright snare sound keeps order and clips every phrasing, leaving the song with moments of abruptness. The song is on a level, punchy and to the point, and Weller sings of having love in eyes and hearts. The song ends with the horn section sounding like something off of a late '60s Beatles' song.

The video was also worth watching and shows the band members running through the streets of W14. Weller looks good in a pair of boxing boots and whistle swinging from around his neck, though he's blowing out of his arse after 50 yards. There are shots of the band playing their instruments in a white room. Buckler plays his white Premier kit, and unusually, Foxton is playing a white Epiphone bass.

'Tales From the River Bank'

The song is introduced with a few gentle plucks on the bass strings, backed up with rim shots on Buckler's snare drum. Then the guitar comes in and builds the song up. Weller sings about having hope in your heart. The medium tempo unfolds and with it the haunting atmosphere of the song.

When I first heard this song I was blown away. I couldn't compare it to any other Jam song at the time. It was another song that I grabbed my drum sticks and tried to play along to. It was the first song that I practised using the rim-shot technique and then swapping the rim for the snare drum skin whilst changing from tapping the Hi-Hat to the Ride cymbal, just like Buckler did in the chorus. Also, I remember really liking the sound of Buckler's snare drum. It didn't sound as full and flat as usual and seemed to have been recorded with added reverb. It added to the atmosphere of the song.

The song progresses into a middle-eight section that includes a piano part. This piano reappears on the outro along with Weller's strange guitar noises. This is one of my favourite vocal parts from Weller and also includes my favourite Jam lyric. Those words about the dream being true and being mixed with nostalgia provided the frame upon which I wrote my novel, *Long Hot Summer*, some 30 years after first hearing 'Tales from the Riverbank'.

The picture on the cover of the single was also atmospheric and evoked a presence that supported the song. When I hear the song now I think of river bank scenes: it is early winter time, it's cold and foggy and the path beside the river has a carpet of leaves. There are also golden brown leaves drifting down the river on the water's gentle current. There is a stillness and there are not many people around. My mood is reflective and my emotions are nostalgic. It is a good place to be. 'Tales from the Riverbank' is a song close to my heart, thankfully.

Snowy

I first got into The Jam through Punk really. I was 14–15 when Punk happened and buying loads of singles, and then I bought a Rickenbacker copy bass because of Foxton. A mate of mine used to see them all the time, from the Red Cow days onwards. He once said to me, even though your into Punk, one day you'll be into Bowie and Disco and Soul, which The Jam used to do on the B-sides, so he was right! Because of that I used to go out and check out all the bands they covered, so through buying a Supremes LP I'd check out other Motown stuff, and through them covering Wilson Pickett I'd check out the Stax label, which to me was a cooler version of Motown.

The first Jam gig I saw was at the Hammersmith Palais in December '81. I got Foxton's autograph before the gig. The Soul music they did was our Soul music, but with socially aware lyrics.

I was at a party and vividly remember a *Quadraphenia* moment, where someone stopped the record that was playing and stuck on 'Going Underground': everyone went ape-shit, and that seemed like a seminal moment for myself and the band. After that I went out and bought everything I hadn't already got, and they're the only band I've got every picture sleeve and non- picture sleeve single.

After the '81 gig, me and a group of mates went to as many gigs as we could. We weren't Mods or Punks, but we used to wear the flight jackets, jeans and trainers, such as Sambas. As I was playing the bass I was quite in awe of Foxton and used to love watching him. Although I missed out on seeing them earlier around the time of 'Going Underground', they were still shit-hot live.

'Burning Sky' off *Setting Sons*, where he writes it as a letter, is pure genius. And as I turned my hand to different things, I always remember the closing lyrics from 'In the City': "If it don't work at least we still tried…" It's always been my ethos, and if it doesn't work out at least I've given it a go.

And another Jam link that I've put on the flyer for our hotel was, *THE HOTEL PELIROCCO HAS MADE YOUR BED, YOU BETTER LIE IN IT.*

For the last gig in Brighton a car-full of us went down, but we couldn't get in. We didn't have the dough that the touts wanted for tickets. I was desperate to get in and was totally heartbroken when it became impossible. Normally, there's a way in somehow to most events, but this one was an absolute lock-out. There were a lot of long faces that night outside the venue in the cold wind.

Mick Habeshaw Robinson

Diary entry – 12 December 1981

The Jam. Well, I went up on the train before Neil and Mark to take the sleeping-bags up to Audrey's. It was very cold. I went all the way up to Queensbury for about an hour, then went back to Victoria to meet Neil and Mark. I had 20 minutes to spare so I went over for a couple of nice pork sandwiches at a tiny café.

I met Neil and Mark and we went to Finsbury Park. Got out and walked past the Rainbow. Who's playing? The Exploited. Oh! (Potential Mod/Punk clash.)

On to the Sobell. Unnerving to see the ambulance outside, but we went in. Pepsi only, no alcohol on sale, and right into The Questions. Pretty nondescript. Then Bananarama, who brightened things up first with the single, 'Aie a Mwana', and then the sixties-type thing 'Really Saying Something'. Then Department S, who got quite a rousing reception for a support band, especially after 'Is Vic There'. Actual cheers. Of course there were a few "fuck offs" consistently from four or five Mods, between songs. Personally I found them a bit monotonous. Apart from 'Vic', they played 'I Want', 'Going Left Right', 'Ode to Cologne: The Stench of War', 'Age Concern' and a funky type thing at the end. The drummer excelled.

Gary Crowley was the compere. He got things thrown at him and he told a joke or two and did impressions (thrills!). Also, between bands there were records, mostly old Soul and R'n'B, none of which I recognised.

Then after a long wait and much crowd enthusiasm, The Jam stormed out onto the stage and the surge forward occurred. No messing about as The Jam got into a powerful new thing ('The Gift'). Then old songs: 'David Watts', 'Tube Station' (rather early), 'In the Crowd' (far too truncated – no psychedelia), 'When You're Young' (last number of the encore), 'Little Boy Soldiers', 'Going Underground' (great, but to be honest, it was quite a shitty un-together version, especially because of the brass, which didn't fit at all).

Then there were new songs: 'The Butterfly Collector', 'Ghosts', 'A Town Called Malice', 'Happy Together', an instrumental ('Circus'), 'Give Me Just a Little More Time', and 'Precious'. There was also a slideshow on the back of the stage. The new album's going to be great.

Bob Collins, The Dentists

'Belief is All'

These were the last words Paul Weller penned on The Jam's final album *Dig the New Breed*, and I fondly recall where I read them for the first time. It was 8th December 1982, late afternoon, and I was sitting in a Wimpy bar in the centre of Birmingham with my brother and his girlfriend, killing time whilst waiting for the doors to open to see The Jam at Bingley Hall. We were not alone, as the burger bar was packed with like-minded fans, mainly smartly dressed Mods, and I can say with pride I was one of them. As it was the early 1980s, pubs would shut between 14.30 and 15.00pm, to open again at 17.30pm, so it wasn't just the school kids munching on quarter pounders with cheese, washed down by milkshakes or cola.

It goes without saying, that the main topic of conversation was The Jam. Fans were swapping jokes and anecdotes about the band, and a few had purchased their final album, as copies were being passed from table to table until, somehow, a copy landed on my lap. As I studied the track listing and sleeve notes, which had all three members, Weller, Foxton and Buckler penning their final thoughts on the band, it was Weller's closing sentence that made the most impact on me, and still does to this day.

As I passed the album onto someone else, I gazed upon all the fans, and thought everyone of us, including the band, had been on an amazing journey to reach this point of excitement, reflection and hope. The band gave so much to these people – education, ambition, guidance and principle – as well as music and fashion.

Prior to discovering The Jam in May 1979, I was already an avid reader of novels and poetry, and The Jam enhanced these passions no end. For a start, the band's lyrics were pure poetry. The Jam also introduced me to two poetic movements: Adrian Henri ('Tonight at Noon' from *This is the Modern World* album) and Percy Bysshe Shelley (back sleeve note on *Sound Effects*, with an extract from *The Mask of Anarchy*), and from these small discoveries I started to study the works of the Merseyside poets and Romantic poetry (Shelley), which in turn would take me to other poetry movements, like the Beat poets (Ginsberg et al) and New Wave poets like John Cooper Clarke. This in turn gave me the confidence to start writing poems, short stories, articles and lyrics, interests that I still hold dear today.

As I was a schoolboy throughout The Jam's career, and school failed to provide me with any real worthwhile knowledge, it was Weller's interviews, be it in the *NME*, *Melody Maker* or whatever, which became like personal lectures to me. As well as studying his attire, I would read his words for guidance and other cultural reference points. Even though the iconic shoot of Paul Weller reading George Orwell's *Nineteen Eighty-Four* was taken whilst he was in The Style Council, it was from his Jam days that he first cited Orwell, and resulted in me reading every word that Orwell wrote, leading me on to discover the works of Aldous Huxley and Jack London.

I was fortunate enough to have two close friends who shared the same creative spirit inspired by The Jam. You have to remember we were still schoolboys, and we certainly looked our age, so it was sometimes hard for us to attend some gigs and clubs, even with our mums' permission. For sure, we did the Saturday kids things, by hanging around the town centre, and we tried to form a band: it was certainly Weller that inspired me to strum my first chord.

We even invented a role-playing game called 'Mods and Rockers', on a rainy school holiday, which was loosely based on the Dungeons and Dragon's format, where Mods, skinheads, Rockers and Soul Boys replaced Wizards, Elves and Goblins, and instead of a dungeon, it was Brighton or the streets of London. In hindsight, we should have patented the concept, as I am sure we would have been millionaires by now. Yet it was The Jam that helped to enhance our imagination, due to their passion and the intelligent deliverance of their music.

I soon discovered the joys of Motown and Stax, thanks to The Jam's coverage of Wilson Picketts' 'Midnight Hour', Martha Reeves and the Vandellas' 'Heat Wave' and Arthur Conley's 'Sweet Soul Music', and was inspired by, of course, The Action. In 1980, when Edsel released a compilation of all The Action's original UK singles, called *The Ultimate Action*, with Weller penning the sleeve notes, that album didn't leave

contd.

my turntable for months. And then the search began again for more like-minded bands of the 1960s: The Creation, the Small Face, The Eyes and such like.

Due to my family, I had already formed left-wing views, and when I heard songs like 'Man in the Corner Shop' and 'Eton Rifles', my socialist views developed further, as did my support for the CND. It was a cause that Weller openly supported, and how proud I was to turn up at my school disco in a beret, paisley scarf, wearing eye liner with a CND badge on my Levi denim jacket, while the boots-and-braces boys and Soul Boys stood back in admiration at my confidence to stand out as different.

Also in times of emotional rescue, The Jam acted as a support to me. I remember having to face the headmaster over a spot of trouble at school. I won't bore you with the details, but the night before my hearing, I played The Jam, record after record, and their words and music gave me the strength to face and accept my punishment.

On the surface, The Jam seemed an aggressive alpha male band, yet there was a strong element of sensitivity, intelligence and humanity. Moreover, as a Mod, I certainly adopted the different personalities of The Jam, depending on the situation and my mood. But I had better stop here, because I am starting to sound like Jimmy from the sleeve notes of *Quadrophenia*...

So from being a fan, The Jam certainly helped to create a social, political and psychological foundation for which I have no regrets. Moreover, from the fans I have met over the years, I was not alone in this, as The Jam were much more than a band: they were a guide to a generation, as The Beatles were to their generation. That is how powerful The Jam seemed to us.

Thirty years later, Weller has forged a successful solo career, Foxton is still performing Jam songs with From The Jam, which saw Buckler on the drums until he left in September 2009, showing that The Jam have never truly gone away. In addition, fans were delighted to see Bruce and Paul record and play again in 2010, which seemed impossible even in 2009.

As for me, I am now the editor of an online magazine called *ZANI*, and through other fanzines I have had the pleasure of interviewing Paul Weller and Rick Buckler, and even pen the sleeve notes for The Jam's greatest hits. I still have the ambition of a young man with *ZANI*: the journey so far has been successful, opened many doors of opportunity and made me some amazing friends, and the reason why is simple: "Belief is all".

Matteo Sedazzari

More detail of BPI award.

On my way to a mate's one day, this fellow comes up to me and calmly tells me: "That group you like, you know the Mod band, The Jam?"

"What about them?" I said.

"Well, they're over at Red Bus Recording Studios."

"WHAT!" I said. "Are you winding me up?"

"Yeah, they're over there, have a look if you don't believe me."

I rushed off towards the recording studio. My heroes were just behind these big wooden doors. The questions were flying round outside, like how long have they been there? Will we get to meet them? Which questions was I gonna ask if I could meet them, I had thousands to ask… SHIT! What about getting one of my albums signed?

Remember that this was in the days before mobiles, of course, so ringing home meant finding a phone box that worked, then getting a member of my family to bring an album to me. I'm sure if I went myself I'd have missed The Jam by the time I'd got back, so in the end my sister brought the *All Mod Cons* album over.

It was now heading towards 9pm and getting colder; a few more fans had decided to call it a day, but not me: no way was I going to let this chance to meet the band slip away. I'd again phoned home to tell my mum I was still waiting, and I can still remember her reply: "Make sure you have something to eat and don't be too late getting home." Righto, Mum… food was the last thing on my mind.

But another hour went by and I was starting to think about going home – perhaps The Jam had left by a back door. But Rick Buckler's car was still parked across the road…. Then just after 10pm the doors opened again. This time it was John Weller and in his deep gravel voice he said, "Hello everyone, thank you all for waiting, the boys are very busy tonight." My heart sank: I knew he would say the band are unable to come out. But no… "Paul and Bruce will see you for a few minutes if we keep it nice and easy." With that he opened the doors wider for the eight or 10 of us that had stayed.

Weller was dressed in a navy shirt with white polka dots on black trousers and black bowling shoes; Bruce, a bit like Rick, was more causal from what I can remember, in his Lonsdale sweatshirt and jeans. I can't remember what shoes he had on but Weller looked so cool, every bit the Steve Marriott. Someone asked where Rick was, and to our amusement Weller replied, "having a shit" – a broad smile went across his face.

I finally managed a question through a dry mouth. I asked what they were recording. Bruce said, a few numbers for a record due out next year (1982). I passed my album to Bruce, who signed it for me. I said, thanks so much for letting us in. "Pleasure" was the response. Then I had to make my way toward Paul because of the amount of fans and also the voice of Kenny Wheeler saying, "Come on lads, the boys are busy, move along, please." John Weller just stood by the desk, looking very proud. He always had time for the fans, what a great guy.

I finally got to Paul, shook his hand and asked if he'd sign my album. I watched him sign across the sleeve of *All Mod Cons* and within seconds he'd handed it back – thanks so much, Paul. I looked down upon my new prized possession. Paul and Bruce made their way back to the recording studio, and that was it. We were shown the main door and thanked again. I ran home and couldn't wait to show my sister my signed album.

Phil Potter

The JAM

Michael Sobell
Sports Centre

December 12th 6.30pm

To be given up

Nº 1058

The Badge

I got the badge out again yesterday. From time to time I disturb it from its dusty reverie, fetching out the small, dark, dovetailed wooden box smelling of beeswax and the past. I rummage amongst the badges and baubles, ticket stubs and trinkets, until I find the right one. I hold it, letting my fingers rub across the contrasting surfaces, the front smooth and easy, the back pinched and sealed, with pin and hasp. Sometimes I play flip-and-catch on my thumbnail and palm, or squeeze it tightly in a balled fist, imagining that when I slowly release my grip and stretch out my hand, the badge will be gone. Occasionally, I press hard on the convex front to bend it in and listen for that curious metallic popping sound made as it flexes back out to right itself. But I do that less so now, as I fret that after one pop too many, the badge will refuse to bounce back, forever thus facing inwards, concave, ruined.

Mostly though, I just like to look at it, three quarters of an inch or so across, two thirds white divides sharply into one third black. Two words, one above the other from right to left, colourings reversed, and in a bold, spidery scrawl, push their way out from the stark background.

For a while, 35 years or so ago, they were a big deal, badges, or 'button badges' as they were called back then. Mushrooming out from the corkboards of post-gig street corner hustlers to market stalls and music paper small ads, through to fan club freebies and record shop window displays. About 25p a throw or up to eight for a quid (not to mention any number of complicated equations involving cash, cigarettes and other badges, if swapping), the relevance of these otherwise insignificant little roundels of paper, plastic and tin was implicit in the message. Sub-cultural loyalties, slogans, signs, or band names, the wearer displaying a deliberate statement of intent; what does your badge say? Are you friend or foe?

Those two words, the two on my badge, when glimpsed as graffiti through a grimy train window, scratched into the toilet wall of a pub, club or concert hall, or mirror-imaged on another's own badge, acted as a simple, straightforward code. And with all the zeal of an evangelist at the altar, I learnt, we learned, that code.

The high priest of the code, raw suburban seer, sage, poet, and prophet, wove his absorbing, observational lyrics in and around the declining spirit of the age. Aloof but not alone, his pulsing, melancholic laments to the lives, loves, losses and loneliness of the everyday ordinary were fused into a supercharged, melodic crescendo by the percussive fire at his back, and rumbling bass thunder to his side.

For those of us who read the runes, and were alive to the traps and snares laid by their contemporaries (who promised plenty but delivered little), we were more than willing disciples, glad to be held firmly in thrall to this rock & roll holy trinity. Zigzagging our way through the human zoo of a late twentieth century English adolescence, this band became our band, and through them, through their style, music and message, we were nurtured, guided and formed. In tandem we grew, us bathed in the sodium glare and sonic blast of recordings and live performances, they through quality, hard work, and experience, plus no little recognition and reward. With a sometimes almost eerie prescience, they found the means to tell the tales of our past, present and future.

But then, after half a decade of virtually relentless forward movement and almost completely unexpectedly, the crown slipped. Seemingly at their very zenith as a creative musical force, the self-inflicted denouement was, apparently to all bar one, an unwarranted bolt from the blue.

Once again in a curious parallel, and as the band and what they had stood for slowly unravelled before us, we, in our bit-part role as fans and followers, would also unwittingly experience our own loosening of the ties that bound. The true currency of youth, the gift of time and the attendant freedom to act spontaneously with no fear of consequence, had begun to slip through our fingers.

The spell breaks on my idle daydreams and I move to put the badge back in its box. As I do so the wistful, whispering ghost of a little teenaged monster tempts me to wear it again, pinned to a lapel, the breast pocket of a Levi jacket, or the front of the still blood-stained Korean War US Army parka moulding away in the attic, like I used to, like we used to. But I catch sight of my reflection, the reflection of a face nearly thirty years older than the badge itself, and, putting both the badge and the little ghost monster back where they belong, I allow myself a rueful little smile. And the two words on the badge? As if you didn't know....

Mark Smith

Unlike a lot of people, I don't really know where it all started; I can't remember an epiphany or a special moment. There was no special accidental viewing on TOTP whilst waiting for someone else, there was no stark realization of their brilliance, or a single moment in time that I can relate to... but I do know that I bought 'Absolute Beginners' from the ex-chart singles section at Littlewoods in deep winter, for some insane price like 49 pence. I played that song (and the B-side 'Tales from the Riverbank') over and over and over (ad infinitum) 'til every lyric, drumbeat, guitar lick and bass line was ingrained into my 12 year-old brain. The very soul of both these special tunes was a turning point in my musical (and political) education.

Skip forwards a month or two (light years to a 12-year-old) and there was a new single. I'd caught the bug, I was hooked – The Jam were now 'my band'. I bought 'Town Called Malice' on the day of release. I had to! Scooting off to my local record shop N.E. Reads after school and holding the prized possession in my mitts, that grim photograph on the cover and those arrows, that imagery, on the rear. Just like 'Absolute Beginners', both songs were played over and over – misheard lyrics were sung a plenty ("Hanging out your old Lambretta's" instead of "love letters") until I had a chance to fully learn the lyrics from the latest pull-out poster in *Smash Hits* – the one with the Lonsdale top, whistle and the Marriott cut. Paul, Bruce and Rick stared down at me from my bedroom wall, approving of my due diligence in learning the words correctly.

The fact that it had gone straight in at Number One was massively significant: this didn't happen unless you were a super group (unlike EVERY Number One these days); a direct entry at Number One was highly unusual, but such was the mass fan base that 'my' band had, it meant that they were a super group.

The 12" of 'Town Called Malice' was my next purchase, just for that cool sleeve in the black and pink candy stripe. I wasn't that much of a fan of 'Precious', it didn't have that same sense of urgency I needed at the time, that need to consume a song that was brash, dark and had meaning – just like the decade we were living in. If truth be told I didn't really understand it, perhaps it was that next musical level that I wasn't quite getting.

The next, and final album as it happened, sorted this out and introduced me to Soul good and proper. *The Gift* for me was, and still is, a musical revelation. It was the first vinyl Jam album that I owned, again bought on the day of release after going hungry for a few days – and that candy-striped, paper-bag covered album lived on my record player.

By this time I really was hooked, all my school books were covered in Jam logos – the Punk one, the modern one, the small faces one, the *Sound Affects* one – all lovingly copied from the albums, which I'd bought in just a few weeks with begged, borrowed or stolen money. Nothing could stop me owning these items and playing them over and over.

In that heady summer of 1982 I became a Mod proper (or at least in the eyes of a 12-year-old) and I pestered my Mum for new clothes. A Jam tour jumper was one of the first things; followed by dogtooth trousers, Jam Gibson shoes and a parka. My outfit complete, I could walk down the street safe in the knowledge that I followed the greatest band in the world and people could see that I did (oh how foolish we are in youth).

And then at the end of October, our world fell apart. Weller decided he had taken the band as far as he possibly could. I can still remember where I was when I heard: Lower Brook St, in Oswestry. I was bewildered and ran home to try and find something on the news – nothing, but then the radio that night confirmed my worst fears. That was it.... They would split by the end of 1982, no more studio albums. I'd never get to see them live. Devastated is an understatement: I was beside myself. How could he have done this? Why? What on earth was he thinking? This was The Jam for christ's sake, the fucking Jam, the voice of a generation. What were we expected to do now, Paul?

'Beat Surrender' came and went, another Number One, which was of course to be expected. Then came the slew of re-released singles – the charts had never seen such a thing, all the singles in picture sleeves back on sale. Again I snapped them all up, being careful not to buy the ones in Woolworths, where they punched a hole in one corner to hang it on a hook – heresy! I now had all the singles, all the albums and the video.

As time has passed, the loss has eased, and Weller has, of course, gone on to make some truly special music. But The Jam are, and always will be, that one special band in mine and a generation's psyche. I feel privileged to have experienced just one year in their history and nothing but jealousy for those who lived through every album and single – what a huge feeling of pride I would have if that were me.

Col Baker

Ady Croasdale

I went to a lot of their early gigs at the Hope & Anchor, Islington, in particular. I was well into Punk but as a black music fan loved their more moody/Soul approach. Eventually, after seeing them a lot, I approached Paul and told him that if he was after any Soul records he should give me some lists and I'd try and get them for him.

Yes, I followed them from the early days and bought all their records. I remember being particularly taken by 'Strange Town', which had a lot of relevance to me, as my family had moved about and I could associate with being a newcomer to an established town gang.

I DJ'd for them on the 'Trans Global European Express' tour and the odd one-off event. Rather sweetly, Paul had me spin a few at one of his shows at the old Town & Country venue, the Forum, about six years ago. He was great with my kids, who were having a hard time of it then.

I'd have played Northern Soul, like Maxine Brown, Chuck Jackson, Kim Weston, etc. Some Modish things, like The Quiks, Bert's Apple Crumble, John Mayall & the Bluesbreakers ('I'm Your Witchdoctor') and probably some Faces, Kinks or Who. Classic R&B by Bo Diddley, Bobby Bland, John Lee Hooker and mainstream Soul by the Isleys, Temps, Billy Stewart, Lou Johnson, Sam & Dave, etc.

Not on the tour: it was a bit of a quiet one, the band were in bed by 11pm. I hung out with Paul's girlfriend, Gill, who was great fun, and Brian Byron the T-shirt magnate; we whooped it up a bit more.

Paul was the only one into the sounds really, and his requests were mainly from his wanted list. The big record of the tour should have been World Column's 'So is the Sun', as the title song of the LP and tour name borrowed a lot of inspiration from that track.

I always loved the Hope & Anchor pub gigs in Islington. Rammed to the rafters and the full energy of Punk and New Wave sweeping all before it.

No, I'd moved on by then — my mate Tony Rounce took over as DJ from me for a while but I'm not sure they had a DJ for that gig.

I'm a South London boy and lived round Peckham way. I came from a jazz background as my Dad had his own band when he first came over from Guyana. He had perfect pitch and used to score for other people. Early on, I didn't get much involved with it – like most kids, I just used to have a blow on the recorder. I took it a bit further after that because I learnt a bit about reading music and did some classical numbers with the music teacher. Learnt a bit of guitar, a bit of piano. I was in the Salvation Army band for a good year-and-a-half, playing cornet and then moving onto sax.

In 1979–80, I was into the jazz/funk scene and knew the boys in Light Of The World and Central Line, and even Paul Hardcastle. My band, Brothers Of Funk, split up and went into Pressure Point. From there I went into a brand of music I really liked with Marcellus Frank, who still produces now. We were really tight and did a lot of recording together. We did six or seven tracks and then thought, how do we get these released?

We met up with Ray Carlos, and he said that Radio DJ Robbie Vincent was looking for some players and a saxophonist. So I phoned him, more to try and get some input into getting these tracks released, but he said, look I'm managing a band called Second Image (who came to prominence on some New Faces-type show), why don't you come and try out? So I went to this studio near Stamford Hill and did a bit of rehearsal – got on really well and did lots of gigs with Frank as the trumpet player. It was a good band to express yourself in. They were signed to Polydor, so there's the initial connection.

Robbie phoned me one day and said there's a guy at the record company called Dennis Munday who wants to have a word, do you mind me giving him your number? "No, not at all." He rang and said there's this band, The Jam, that wants to meet you and who are interested in adding brass to their recordings. "Yeah, not a problem." I was always open to doing other stuff and around that time I played on a right strange track, called 'A Million Hamburgers', which was a bit goth!

So Dennis hooked up a meeting with John and Paul Weller. I got Kenny involved, who was up for it, so we went to Polydor's offices, met up, and it went really well. John was a great geezer and Paul was a bit quieter, but chipped in when needed. John was saying, you'll be a member of the band, you can write songs, etc. I was right yeah, sounds good. I didn't know anything about them, bear in mind!

This was the spring of '81. We went up to Nomis to rehearse, great studio, and me really loving it. I still didn't know who they were, but was introduced to Rick, Bruce, Dave Liddle and Kenny Wheeler. It was a strange situation as the boys had roadies and a proper team!

They played a tune and Weller asked if we had any ideas to go with it? So yeah, we had a couple of things to go with songs they already had, like 'That's Entertainment' and some stuff off *Setting Sons*. Also 'Move On Up', to get the swing and it was great, really enjoyable. We did a couple of weeks of rehearsals and then we did a gig in either a college or a university in London to rapturous applause and with me still not knowing! I thought, this is a good band, I'm quite liking this!

I then heard something on the radio mentioning The Jam and I thought, hold on, is that the band I'm involved with?! I then asked my older brother about them. He said, "Do you know who they are?"

"Not really."

He then started filling me in, ha ha.

I only knew about Punk because I went to a club in Charing Cross called Global Village (Heaven) and there were a few pogoing downstairs. It was a very good time for mixing rock or Punk with Soul.

I was still with Pressure Point at this time, who were a fusion-type band, and I'd be enthusing about stuff I was into and Paul would do the same. I'd think: fucking hell, where did you get all this stuff?! He used to hide away in the room to play all the records. On tour we'd do the gig and then have a chat with the fans and then disappear inside. I loved the fact he brought this portable record player with him that played both LPs and 7"s. That was his thing to be inspired by.

contd.

I remember doing a lot of shows in Europe. The Swedish TV show we did in late '81 was memorable: coming back from the gig, all we could talk about was "Chicken in a Basket"!

The four London dates started at Michael Sobell Sports Centre in Finsbury Park, which was new to me. I liked the fact I could get home from there! I liked that gig and the Ally Pally [Alexandra Palace] – to play an iconic venue like that wasn't going to come along often in life, so it was a big thing. Doing the soundcheck is when you see the real size of a venue. To get the levels and build up, Paul was very specific in his guitar sound and I loved the sound of Rick's drums. He was a seriously tough drummer: taught me some strokes and it took me a while to get them.

It was good backstage when the fans were about, and I remember in Tokyo John jokingly saying to me, "What's up with you then?"

"Do you know what John, I really don't feel up for it."

"What, you'll take my money and you won't go and say hello to the fans?"

I just pissed myself laughing as he had a fantastic turn of phrase, and immediately replied, "You're right." I went and said hello to the fans and did my bit.

I remember the Dolly Mixtures, Department S and Bananarama. They got some stick but they could handle it – in a way I think it pushed them on to achieve what they did.

Recording *The Gift* at Air Studios was brilliant. I love recording and there would be complete songs that I'd have to add some parts to. Or there were times when we'd jam on ideas. 'Shopping' came around like that, so I did that flute solo. There was always a lot of talk about what would be an A or B side. With 'The Great Depression' they wondered whether they should release it as an A side.

'Precious' was another one where we moved it forward through jamming. In some of the tracks you don't even realise I'm doing backing vocals, like 'Trans-Global Express' and 'Stoned Out of My Mind'. What was endearing to me was that behind the scenes, I was really involved.

I met Steve Nichol through various connections, including Frank, which was six months before I met The Jam. When Frank had to bow out – "I can't really do this anymore, I've got to concentrate on what we're doing" – I went and saw Steve and said, do you fancy doing this gig I've got? He was like yeah, let's do it. We went to Nomis and he fitted in with the others, no problem.

We were on the road from late January, if I remember rightly. We did some CND stuff down on the Embankment. Doing TOTP was obviously a historical moment as The Jam was the first band to do a double-A side since The Beatles. I didn't know that until after. It's especially good because of the way Bruce is in that performance. He was making everyone laugh with his movements and facial expressions.

The New York Palladium was a real big gig for me. I loved New York and I was a big Marvel Comics buff, which used to amuse the band no end, so playing there meant a hell of a lot. Weller with his cup of tea on stage….

We did a gig in Stockholm and then we went to this bar on the piazza. We had a really good night, dancing on tables and having a right old crack. Paul, though, was proper ratted and he threw up. He said the next day, that's it, I'm off the booze. Fairplay to the geezer, he stuck with it.

There was tension, but there's gonna be, especially the amount of time these guys hung out together. Sometimes Christmas is enough!

I was devastated when John died, he was as close to family as you could get. I think the last time I saw him was at Joe Awome's funeral, who was a lovely fella.

The Jam were hardcore. Jam mania…. There was a time in Brighton when there were lots of kids running towards the coach and I was like, what the fuck! I just stood there and all these kids are asking, what colour pants does he wear? What toothpaste does he use? In the end I was telling them Gibbs SR or Colgate or little fluorescent ones…. Cheers mister! Japan as well. Proper fanatics, fucking incredible. We met the Go Go's on the bullet train as they were coming back from somewhere.

Paul Weller was the sort of bloke who you might not always agree with but I always respected him on every level. I had to put up with some horrific racism on the North Peckham estate. One day I was telling him about it and he told me something about Malcolm X. At that time I'd didn't know who Malcolm X was but I went and read up about him, which was something I'll always be grateful for.

Sometimes I'd do a gig and have no idea what I was about to play, as my mind went blank as I put the sax to my lips; and then a split second before the start I'd hit it and be ok. I was most vulnerable during 'That's Entertainment' as it was just me and Paul and me thinking, fucking hell everyone's looking at me, but once I got over the initial thing I'd be ok. There were nights when everyone fucked up, but it would bother the individual more than anyone else. Most of the time, though, we were really tight. Sometimes, we'd do something a certain way and think, bollocks, I wish we'd recorded that.

'Trans Global Express' live was great: it had that Pigbag thing, a proper lift to it. Intense.

I know Paul listened to a lot of Jazz because I was always banging on about it. For me it's the highest form of music you can achieve. He liked people like Julian Joseph, who came out of the English Jazz scene – he was really into it.

The Jam was amazing for me as a young musician. Everything was new and I'd never done anything like this before and a lot didn't sink in 'til way after. It was a really positive time. To get to see the world that way was brilliant. I was just sad that we didn't get to India or Australia, but I ain't complaining!

Keith Thomas

A Teenage Diary – Magnum Leisure Centre, Irvine, 30 June 1981

My first Jam gig was at age 15 and I was lucky enough to see them another three times before they split the following year, in 1982. Each time I saw them, the experience was unique, and I always had a special story to tell. Here is my diary entry for the first gig....

The day of the gig dawned and a school friend and myself arrived at the Magnum Leisure Centre in the early afternoon, having been driven some 60 miles by an aunt and my mum. The gig in Irvine was part of The Jam's 'Bucket and Spade' tour. While hanging around I bought a number of Jam souvenirs: T-shirts, badges and two scarves, which the band later signed.

I tracked down the merchandise stall and thought I recognised the female behind the counter as Gill Price [Paul Weller's girlfriend]. I asked Gill for a copy of 'December Child' (I got this signed by the band later on) along with a few Jam badges.

The first support band was pretty good, but I didn't think much of the second group so I went back to speak to Gill. I asked, "Gill, is there any chance of you getting The Jam's autographs for me?" Gill replied that she would see but they might not be there. She collected pen and paper and passed through a restricted area. Shortly afterwards Gill came back with two slips of paper. She explained that Rick was not there and handed me Paul and Bruce's autographs! I tried hard to contain my excitement! Not wanting to appear to be a pain, I then got my friend to ask Gill if there was any chance of meeting The Jam after the gig. Gill said that after the show, the band changed and if after 20 minutes there aren't too many people left then they are let back into the hall. She told us to come to the stage door.

The Jam were dynamite on stage. Bruce had us clapping during 'David Watts'. At one point Paul's Rickenbacker was playing up and he angrily kicked at the cable. 'Heatwave' live was so much better than on *Setting Sons*. 'Funeral Pyre' was introduced with Paul saying, "This is what happens when our money runs out". This got the best cheer of the night.

All too quickly the gig was over, but to my delight they came back for two encores, which included 'Going Underground'. I took my time leaving the hall after the gig and then headed outside to search for the stage door and we were let into a corridor to wait.

Eventually a door was opened by John Weller and we were let in to where The Jam was. Straight away I saw Gill and she was sitting next to Paul on an exercise bench. Gill spotted me, smiled and got up to let me sit next to Paul!!!! I couldn't believe what was happening, but I had to remain calm as I sat right next to PAUL WELLER. I can't recall exactly what we spoke about, but I do remember how shy Paul was while we chatted and he signed my bits and pieces. I then moved on to speak to Rick and Bruce. Rick signed the pieces of paper that Gill got Bruce and Paul to sign previously. I found Rick to be very funny, chatty and cracking jokes, but found Bruce to be a bit grumpy!

I came away from Irvine that night in total disbelief that not only had I been to my first ever Jam gig, but I had actually met Paul, Bruce and Rick. A totally amazing and wonderful experience!

Ann Kerr

An Absolute Beginner ... Derek D'Souza

I was hooked since first hearing 'In the City' on the radio in 1977, and have been a fan ever since. I first saw the band live in 1978, and went to see them as many times as possible, mainly in and around London, but also travelling wherever possible, home and abroad. In the end I saw them over 80 times.

The Gigs

Stafford, Bingley Hall 1981. Me and two friends, Pete and Keith, travelled up from London for the gig. The night before we bumped into Rick outside the station – he was picking up his girlfriend, did we need tickets? Thanks, but we were fine, and Rick was on his way. We went for a beer in a pub and a friendly game of pool. This ended up with us reluctantly playing pool for money with some locals, which developed into growling and threatening. We didn't think we'd get out of the pub alive, especially when my friend Keith (a Sunderland fan) diplomatically enquired: "So have Stafford got a football team, anyway!" Shortly after we made a swift exit and headed off to our B&B.

The next day, when we got to the venue, there were so many people having turned up for the soundcheck, that none of us got in. The gig itself was heaving, so hot and so frantic – it was less about singing along and more about staying on your feet and not flaking out. Bruce made a comment about it being like a football match in here, and started singing the theme tune from *Match of the Day* – the whole crowd joined in, with Bruce shouting, "Stop!!" The gig was loud and hectic, but that's what made the band so good. We were all one on nights like this.

I saw the John's Boys 'secret' gig at the Marquee – it was mental. Whatever the capacity was there, add another 200 and it will give you some idea of the chaos. People coming in through the back, rushing the doors, windows being put through…. The sweat dripping off the ceiling, running down the sides of the walls – proper intense!

I am not a fan of clichés, and people use words like 'awesome' far too easily in my opinion, but The Jam gigs were truly EVENTS. I have seen some of the live videos, but they never captured what it was really like: the anticipation, John Weller coming on stage to introduce the band, the sound, the energy, unbelievable! Everyone has good and bad days at work but these boys never seemed to.

I had taken an interest in photography when I was 18, with my dad buying me my first 'proper' camera, a Petri MF-1, on a family holiday. It just seemed natural for me to start trying to take photos at gigs, and it was very much a learning curve, taking shots under stage lighting conditions, etc. (Not to mention the frenzied crowds at Jam gigs – sometimes it was hard enough to stay on your feet, let alone hold a camera steady.) It was simply trial and error to start with and then a matter of waiting for your prints to come back from Tru-Print and seeing how bad and how blurred they were! With no Google available, I had to figure this out myself and with time and experience results improved.

I sent some photos from gigs, plus a few I took of The Jam off the TV (from the 'Start!' video) to the fan club and got a letter back from Paul, saying how much he liked them as they had some weird colours, and looked different.

I had come up with many ways to sneak my camera into gigs, having friends carry in films and lenses separately. I remember one time at the Rainbow I had put the lens down my sock and wore baggy trousers. To the great amusement of security the lens started to fall out, so I was kneeling there in full view, trying to hide a 10-inch lens so that it wouldn't get confiscated. I was easily rumbled by security and they pointed me towards the office where I was to deposit my lens during the gig. As soon as they turned away I took a diversion into the main hall and was back in business!

In June 1981 (I would have been 22, but looked about 16) I gave Paul some photos that I'd taken previously. The band was very accessible and I'd spoken to Paul at the Rainbow gig in June and at the gigs at Guildford Civic Hall on the 7th and 8th July. At Guildford, Paul was giving out passes to fans after the soundcheck. As I wasn't a pushy type I wasn't going to fight to get one, and he singled me out to hand me one (well in my mind maybe), which was really nice.

I sent some more photos in the post to the fan club, and then a few days later I was on my way home from work and popped in to the snooker club to have a beer with my dad. Just before I was about to leave he said, "Oh, I forgot to tell you, some Weller woman was on the phone for you about doing a photo session." ...Whaaat?! "Don't worry – she said she'll be calling you back."

I ran home as quickly as I could and waited for the phone call – this was a Tuesday or a Wednesday.

Stayed in, no phone call, Next night the same. I stayed in five nights – which was a record – and had pretty much given up, then Ann Weller rung and said, "Sorry I lost your number, you haven't been waiting in have you?"

"No, no," I lied.

"The band really liked your pictures and would like to meet up with you, and talk about doing a photo session."

For me, they were my favourite band and I just couldn't believe it. Especially as I wasn't an experienced photographer, but it was The Jam!

I went to the Weller's house in Woking and as I didn't drive Ann came and picked me up from the station in a Fiat X19 she'd just bought. When it came to dropping me back Ann couldn't work out how to turn the lights on! So she kindly dropped me back to the station in John's car!

At that time I had broken my fingers in an accident, so I had my hand taped up to my elbow and John Weller shook my hand so tight I thought he'd broken them again!

I went back a couple of more times, and dealing with Ann was fantastic, a truly lovely lady – always helpful and always took the time to explain things and give advice. Ann was also kind enough to pick me up and drop me back at Woking station!

Eventually, I got to meet up with the band at Air Studios, overlooking Oxford Circus, where they were recording 'Tales from the Riverbank' and 'Absolute Beginners'.

It was a daunting prospect. I'd spoken to them a few times after gigs but this was obviously a different scenario. Anyway, I got up there and was introduced to everyone – they were working on 'Riverbank'. At one point I was actually allowed to sit in the studio and was sitting opposite Paul when he was doing the feedback at the end of the song! I did actually get a couple of shots, but I didn't want to disturb them as they were working.

They said they were having a break and did I fancy a game of pool? Paul said, "Come on, me and you against Kenny and Joe". So I find myself playing pool in the studio and I'm on the same side as Paul Weller! And we won 2-1 – as satisfying as any football result! And then I started playing Kenny for money and I don't think I got a look in....

We discussed the photo session and Paul had the idea of wearing dark suits in Chiswick Park as it had great natural backgrounds and would contrast with the suits. What I didn't know at that time was that The Beatles had been photographed there many years before.

I didn't really have a clue what I was going to do. I had a Pentax ME Super, which was an expensive camera for the time, but an amateur camera nonetheless, and I had a couple of lenses. The good thing was I was familiar with my kit, so that was one less thing to worry about!

I told a couple of male friends and two female friends about the session (not very professional, but I was a fan first and foremost, and so were they). We all went along. The boys hardly said a word the whole time; I think they were pretty overawed with the whole experience and after a while they left. The girls, Suzanne and Melissa, were really chatty and the band, Dave Liddle, Kenny Wheeler and Joe Awome were great with them.

I was so nervous that it was hard to really know what to do, especially as it was my first photo session ever. We did the session and I chipped in with a couple of ideas, like the reflection of the window shot on the inlay pic, which looks like it's been taken through the glass. We did a few round the statues, but because they were so tall, when you actually take a pic of a six-foot bloke next to a 15-foot statue it's not ideal. I did get some nice ones of the band and some good individual shots – but would love to be able to do it again!

Silly things that stick in my mind after was Bruce ringing me several times to make sure they'd got my name spelt correctly, which was really nice as it was going to appear on the inlay sleeve of the next single, 'Absolute Beginners'. There is nothing worse than having you name misspelled, even more so on something important.

When the single was released there was a cock-up with the pressing and the inlay sleeve wasn't done, which was rectified. It was a fantastic job to do, despite my nerves and everything. Financially, I didn't do as well out of it as I had hoped, which was as much down to my own naivety as anything. But looking back I'd have done it for free, as they were my favourite band.

The nice thing after was being on first name terms with the band and crew and getting photo passes for gigs, etc. Again, had I been pushier, perhaps I could have asked for better access and who knows what photos I may have got.

I took a stack of photos to one of the gigs at Hammersmith and left them with the band to look through, and they signed every one! I was a bit disappointed at the time as I couldn't afford to get another set printed straight away, and I had only left them for the band to have a look – but they were so good like that – they always had time for the fans. In hindsight, they actually did me a favour doing that, and over the years, while I do confess to selling a few of these pics, I actually gave away far more to other fans! Whilst I have been lucky enough to gather some great memorabilia, I didn't see the point in having 50 plectrums if someone else who was also a huge fan didn't have one – so I did give a lot of items away.

In the winter of 1981, John had asked me to take some more photos, and while I did have a photo pass, it didn't offer me great access for the gigs at Hammersmith Palais and the Michael Sobell Sports Centre. At the Sobell gig, the band had just signed a sponsorship with Lonsdale, and just by coincidence I happened to be wearing a Lonsdale sweater, as did the chaps. I was well chuffed! The crowd the next night seemed to be wearing wall-to-wall Lonsdale and Weller was wearing a Fred Perry T-shirt (I think!).

We did what we could to get fellow fans into the gigs and we didn't charge them for the privilege. Sometimes we used to get people in on the guest passes by writing "plus one", or get a mate to hand over his and do the old jibbing trick of going outside and pulling someone in. We used to come in different entrances so we wouldn't get clocked by the same security guards.

I remember going to see the band play at the Amsterdam Paradiso in 1982. There seemed to be more English than Dutch at the gig. Walking up to the venue around the time of the soundcheck, there were hundreds milling about and one of the security guys recognised me and said, you'd better come in, the other photographer's already in there (Twink). Even though I wasn't there in any official capacity I gladly accepted and me and my mate Pete walked in. There was just the crew and band going through some numbers, which made me feel very privileged. I got some good pictures but didn't want to overdo it, as I wasn't actually supposed to be there! At the gig I got a couple of plectrums and a whack in the face! Luckily, some helpful Dutch guy helped me back on my feet…. And despite seeing stars it was on with the gig!

On the last tour, by buying tickets through the fan club, I went to four out of five at Wembley (one was a front row thanks to Ann) and also, Poole, Manchester and Guildford! I got some great photos from two of the nights at Wembley. Despite the obvious feeling of disappointment amongst the fans that this was the last tour, the band was, as ever, in great form, and the shows were a massive success.

Brighton, THE LAST NIGHT, 11.12.82 – The additional final gig after Guildford. There were no tickets, no way of getting one, but we were determined not to be beaten. I was with two good friends, Peter Deering and Tony Porter (both huge fans!). We went round the back of the centre, where there were about 20 others in the same boat. We managed to climb into the back of the venue, almost like an SAS mission! All very hush-hush, and we got into the backstage area undetected. Once the lights went down in between songs, five at a time we quietly ran through into the arena. It was a like a scene from *The Great Escape*!

All of a sudden the lights came up and suddenly it was like being caught in the headlights: Kenny Wheeler is coming towards us and I've just run for it and done a 'Superman' dive over the barrier and into the crowd. There was no way I was going to get chucked out of the last gig! I'd already missed a few songs, but to be honest the gig was such an anti-climax. People chucking bottles, anger, frustration, knowing it would be the last time, etc. People walking round dazed and stunned and in some cases devastated after it had ended.

Later on, I had some more of my photos used for compilation LPs and various books about the band. Dennis Munday was a great help in getting me some money from Polydor for some of the shots, and an all round top fella. Dennis also gave me some of his own Jam memorabilia, which is now amongst my own treasured collection!

These remain some of the best times of my life. The Jam were my favourite band, and I was both proud and privileged, and consider myself incredibly lucky, to have had the chance to work with them – especially as at the time, they could probably have had their pick of named photographers. But so typical of them, they chose a complete amateur who was a fan! Would this happen with a band at the height of their fame nowadays? Unlikely, in my opinion.

First and foremost, I was a fan and it was great to be associated with a band that meant so much to me. The gigs were always amazing events, and I never saw a bad one.

I am still a huge fan – having seen Paul, Bruce and Rick with later bands – and two years ago, my wife Krissie and I went to see Paul play two shows in New York. Fantastic! Even to this day, The Jam songs get a special response when Paul plays them – it shows how much they still mean to so many.

Thanks to Derek D'Souza for allowing the publisher permission to reproduce the following images.

ir Studios, 24th August 1981 – recording 'Tales from the Riverbank'.

Wembley Arena,
2nd December 1982
– and *opposite*.

The following photographs were taken at Chiswick Park, 31st August 1981 – as part of the shoot for 'Absolute Beginners'.

Guilford Civic Hall, 9th December 1982.

Hammersmith Palais, 14th December 1981 – and *opposite*.

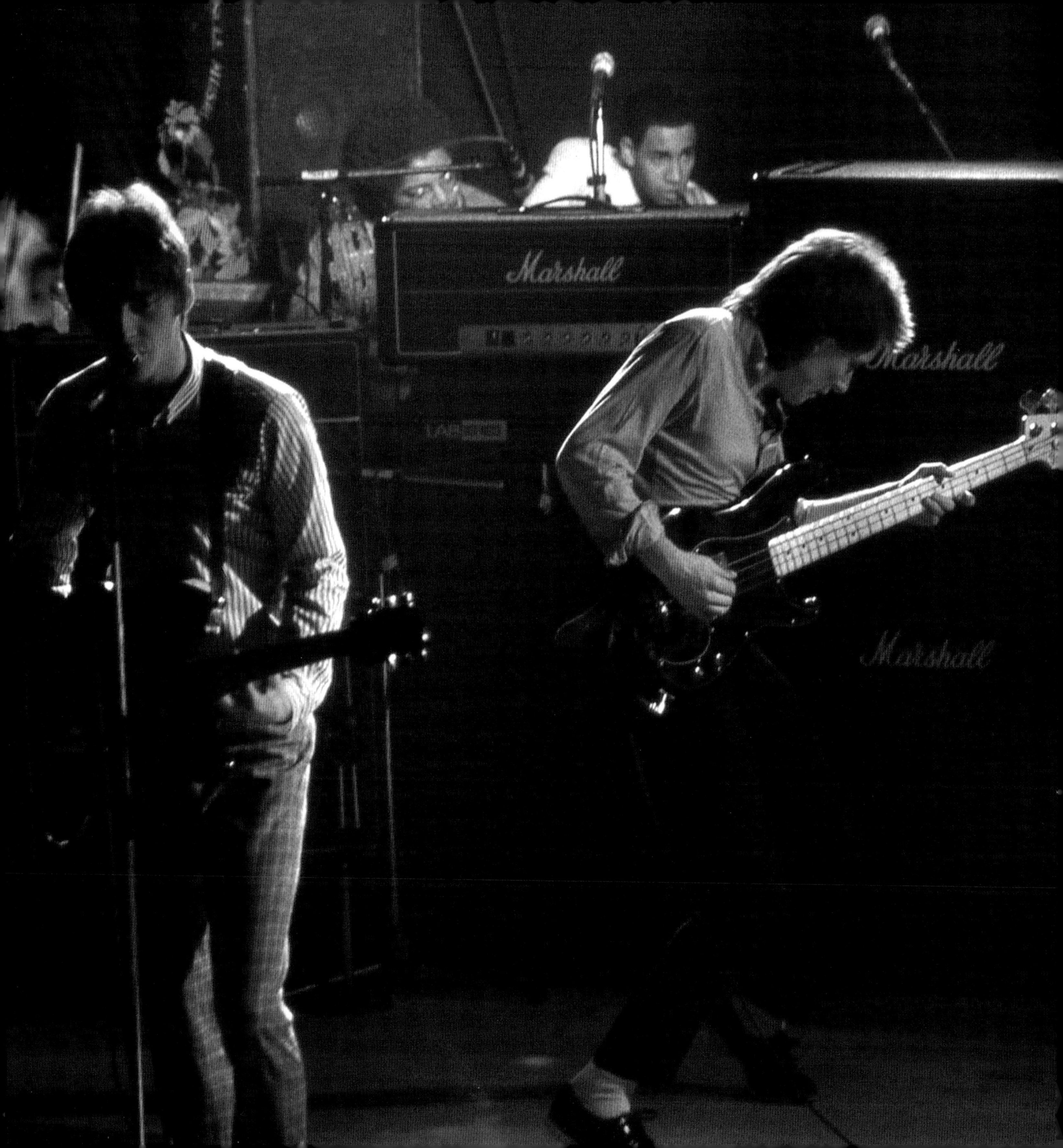
Marshall
Marshall
Marshall

Hammersmith Palais, 15th December 1981.

Guilford Civic Hall, 9th December 1982.

Guilford Civic Hall, 9th December 1982.

Clockwise: Paul and Bruce, Hammersmith Palais, 15th December 1981;
Michael Sobell Sports Centre, Soundcheck 12th December 1981.

Guilford Civic Hall, 9th December 1982.

Rick says farewell to Guilford, 9th December 1982.

In the early days of The Jam we cut our teeth playing covers we enjoyed in any venue that would have us, with an audience that were there mostly because of the low price of the beer. For us, being part of a band with a band ethic, as we saw it, along with the likes of The Beatles, The Who, The Kinks and others, and the musical influences they gave us, was important.

At that time the overblown mega groups that fostered an unapproachable divide between themselves and their audience seemed false and pretentious, so when we found our own audience at our own gigs, a bond grew that was also reflected in the strong observational subjects of Paul's songs, a 'common ground' quality that people still relate to today.

It is often forgotten that without the fans, a band is nothing. I personally feel very proud to have been one of the Saturday's Kids that is The Jam.

Rick Buckler, March 2012

1982 – A WHOLE STREET'S BELIEF

1982 was the year that unemployment in Britain reached 3 million. The Jam would also release three singles. The year included the start and end of the Falklands War, which pushed Maggie up the popularity charts no end and caused *The Sun* to sink to new depths in headline writing. It was also the year that Ozzy Osbourne shockingly bit the head off of a live bat on the stage at one of his gigs, and made him far more interesting than pretty much anything he'd ever recorded in his career.

'Come on Eileen' was a monster hit for Dexy's, as were dungarees – if you liked the unwashed look. 'The Lion Sleeps Tonight' did well for Tight Fit. The movie *Fame* hit the big screen and then flooded the charts with songs from the Kids From Fame. Children everywhere would jump off cars outside schools, pretending to be Leroy, and generally prance about with vests over T-shirts and leg warmers. The ship *The Mary Rose* was raised after a couple of centuries, a London banker was found hanging from the Blackfriars Bridge and Michael Fagan broke into the Queen's bedroom in Buckingham Palace to have tea and biscuits with Her Majesty, whilst telling her that he once wrote to *Jim'll Fix It* and ate six Topic chocolate bars in a row.

This was also the year that the music show *The Tube* kicked off on Channel 4's opening night, which saw The Jam play their last ever TV gig. The *NME* writers' single of the year was Grandmaster Flash and the Furious Five's 'The Message'. Social consciousness NY style was so raw it blew a hole through my dad's speakers as I tried body-popping for the first and last time.

The Jam's last album *The Gift* (their only Number One) shared the hit parade with *Dare* from the Human League, *The Lexicon of Love* by ABC and, of course, the *Kids From Fame*.

A cold December was the month that 30,000 women joined hands to form a link around the perimeter of Greenham Common, in an anti-nuclear weapons protest. John Peel's 'Festive 50' was won this year by New Order's 'Temptation', narrowly beating the haunting Elvis Costello song, 'Shipbuilding', covered by Robert Wyatt. Stick that up your *junta*, Maggie.

Anti-Complacency League, Baby!

I need to make a confession. I owe Polydor a fiver. Why? Because I stole my copy of *The Gift*. There, I've said it. After all these years living a lie, I've finally absolved my guilty conscience and admitted my crime.

The person I pinched it from will remain nameless in case he ever comes across this book and tracks me down via Facebook and demands it back with threats of violence; although I should add that it's technically his fault for lending it to me in the first place and for being an Adam & the Ants fan and never fully appreciating the genius of Weller, Foxton and Buckler's finest moment. I'll just let him forever think that I gave it back to him a week later and that he "…must have lost it down St Matthews Church Youth Club on Friday night, mate…".

I must also thank him for diverting my attention away from Madness, The Specials and the other Two Tone outfits that my mates and I were nuts about, and finally opening my eyes to "*The best fucking band in the world!*"

I remember thinking how sophisticated I must seem, lying on the living room carpet with my headphones on, listening to The Jam carve out the gritty, funk-laden grooves of 'Precious' and 'Trans-Global Express', instead of being out with my mates on our BMX bikes, shoplifting Panini football stickers and packets of Opal Fruits. Yep: this was year zero to me – the album that sculpted everything else musically that followed. This was a proper grown-up's album that I could impress my mates with and, more importantly, girls at school.

I look back now and think it's a real shame I was just too young to have got into The Jam right back in their early days, but I'm thankful that my nameless pal inadvertently gave me the chance to submerge myself in them before they split. Yes, there are plenty of Jam fans out there who will tell you that *Sound Affects* or *Setting Sons* is the band's defining moment, but for me *The Gift* has the edge on those albums, just because it's so personal and takes me back to a time when life was no more complicated than choosing which coloured Fred Perry to wear with your Sta-Prest. This was the sound of a band throwing off the shackles and finding its soul.

Whilst writing this I've revisited the album in its entirety for the first time in 18 months, and it still sounds as fresh and as tight as it did when it was first released. I still get that old familiar buzz when the opening chords of 'Happy Together' kick in. Then of course there's the eerie lament of 'Ghosts', followed by the tight-as-fuck 'Precious' and the everyman anthem, 'Just Who Is the 5 O'Clock Hero?' Good enough for you? No? Well there's more. How about the sinister 'Carnation' or the now perennial jukebox classic for all blokes of a certain age, 'Town Called Malice'? Even the steel band coda of 'The Planner's Dream Goes Wrong' (which many a Jam fan will tell you they shy away from) is a cracking slice of pop that retains its social message.

Halfway through comes the albums centrepiece and, in my opinion, the greatest song they ever recorded. 'Running on the Spot' sums up everything you need to know about The Jam in three minutes and six seconds of fire and skill that still brings a tear to my eye and stirs the fire in my gut. A call to arms to open our eyes and question everything we were ever told. This was Weller at his cutting and acerbic best, and we fucking loved him for it.

So there you have it: amongst all the Mod revival, Rude Boy and New Romantic nonsense my pals were into, there was a little corner of West Drayton that would be forever Weller. An album sneered at by some, tolerated by others and truly loved by a few, which opened my eyes properly not only to The Jam, but to Soul, funk, Motown and Northern Soul. And for that I'll always be grateful to Paul, Rick and Bruce.

Rob Haynes

The Gift [Review by Andy Nykolyszyn]

1982 was something of a watershed year for the decade. The simmering anger that surfaced during the riots of the summer of '81 was still fresh in the memory and a conflict was about to loom large over a small island thousands of miles away that would be used as a vehicle for Thatcher to maintain her tightening grip on 10 Downing Street. The meltdown of Punk that had resulted in a good few years of healthy musical progression and experimentation was about to take another step forward, with many of the leading figures of that time taking a step into more black music influenced waters (The Clash and Elvis Costello being prime examples).

Prior to their final studio album, The Jam had been somewhat reticent to show on record their obvious love of R'n'B that was apparent from the band's very beginnings, with R'n'B becoming a staple of their live shows. Occasional glimpses ('I Got By In Time', 'Heatwave', the album version of 'Start!') peaked through, but by and large the blueprint set down in the recording studio was of a band putting a traditional British stamp on their own work. *The Gift* changed all that, and opened up the floodgates for Weller to explore his love of black music over the forthcoming years with The Style Council. As a historical document, it's the first clear sign (alongside the preceding 'Absolute Beginners' single) that Weller was looking at a future away from the band in order to spread his musical wings.

"Now for those of you watching in black and white, this next one is in technicolour... BAAAAAAAAAAAAABYYYYYYY...."

Those barely audible words at the start of 'Happy Together' ushered in the band's final studio hurrah. Foxton's cry brought in a bubbling bass, closely followed by a descending guitar riff and then Buckler's explosive drum licks — they were off and running, with Weller tongue-in-cheek informing all present that he was an angel waiting for his wings. The song breezes speedily through with an urgency and a new sound courtesy of new producer Pete Wilson at the helm. As it ends with Weller almost menacingly claiming "We're happy together NOW", the soulful intro of 'Ghosts' sweeps in, rimshot, chiming guitars and solitary bass notes. For me (and many a Jam fan), it's the album's highlight. Weller reaching new vocal heights, alternating from mournful narration through to soulful pleading for the listener not to "Give up to your given roles, there's more inside you that you won't show". It's almost a clarion call to the army of Jam fans who were blindly devoted to the band to open their eyes and minds and create something new and beautiful. Adding in a touch of measured Stax brass, we were suddenly entering a new musical soundscape for the band. It's barely mentioned in any reviews I've ever read, but Buckler's drumming on this is sublime. Beautifully restrained, subtle hi-hat chimes dipping in and out of verses, it adds a real gravity to an already marvellous song.

Track 3 and we were now on a journey into "Brit Funk". Weller had made no secret of his love of the burgeoning British funk scene, bands such as Light of the World, Beggar and Co, Incognito and even Spandau Ballet (who alongside Beggar and Co had whipped up a funk gem in 'Chant No.1' in the summer of '81) had put a typically British spin on their US counterparts' more polished offerings. 'Precious' was his initial foray into funk on record. You won't need me to tell you that the bass line borrowed heavily from Pigbag's 'Papa's Got a Brand New Pigbag'; you won't need me to tell you that the lyrical content was a world away from anything he'd done previously; and you also won't need me to tell you that it was quite jaw-dropping to think that this was the same man who sang 'Girl on the Phone' only two-and-a-half years previously.

In interviews over the years, Weller always appears to be quite dismissive of his vocals during this period and throughout TSC, but for me, his voice was never better. Growling, impassioned and pleading, like a Woking Marvin Gaye (circa 1970s), set against a backdrop of wah-wah, punchy brass, insistent bass line and percussive madness (what is that sound?), his voice soars and swoops to places we'd never been before. It's one of those tunes I'd love to see given an occasional live airing now, but like a lot of songs from that era, it's in a range that the Weller voice of today can only dream of reaching. Initially previewed as the lesser played A-side of the 'Malice' single, it was a clear marker for where his future lay.

'Just Who Is the 5 O'Clock Hero'? I remember reading some years down the line that Buckler had the hump with Weller, claiming that the songs on *The Gift* weren't ideally written for him to drum to, which yes, on the face of it sounds a little bit like a youngest child not getting a Raleigh Grifter for Xmas. It's in this song where I can clearly hear the conflict between writer and musician. Clocking in at less than two minutes, Weller explores the idea that the daily drudgery that the vast majority of us wade through in order to get the money is something that nags away at all of us, and that we all share the notion that somehow, somewhere, there's a better and easier life for us all. It's the cry of the lottery ticket holder but a whole decade and a bit before its advent. Musically, to my ears, and set against the previous three tracks, it's clumsy. The song bursts in with drum rolls and descending bass, and never really settles down before its end, set against some discordant brass.

'Trans Global Express' is Weller's rallying call to the masses to rail against those who wish to keep us where we are. It seemed to be the lyrical blueprint for the album. As a 14-year-old, I wasn't familiar at all with World Column's 'So Is the Sun', but once I'd heard it I was astounded at how Weller had borrowed lock, stock and barrel from it and hadn't given any credit whatsoever to the writers. All that withstanding, I love this tune. Steaming in on a driving Foxton bass line, a brass hurricane and Buckler's authoritative drums, it dabbles in Dub, Funk and Soul and tidily sews up Side One.

Flip over to Side Two (kids, ask your parents) and we're just 'Running on the Spot'. A good friend of mine who's always had a love for The Jam, but in a casual, passing kind of way, caught the Roundhouse gig that Weller did in 2007. the first thing he said was that he'd forgotten just what a perfect tune ROTS truly is. It's all of that and much, much more. It opens up with that familiar guitar refrain that nags away at you all the way through the song, and hasn't got an ounce of fat on it. Lyrically, it's an album highpoint for me, Weller fully recognizing the sense that his every word, movement and statement would be parroted by kids across the country; and instead of encouraging, he implores the listener to discount what's being foisted on them and instead, follow yourself. "Intelligence should be our first weapon." Not exactly the call to arms of N-Dubz now is it? It's definitely in my Top Five of all time Jam songs. As the voices echo into the distance at the song's end, we then go to the album's loo break. 'Circus' is a filler. Simple. It fits in sonically with the rest of the album but the impetus of ROTS is halted somewhat by the band's instrumental offering.

'The Planner's Dream Goes Wrong'. This song takes a lot of stick – unnecessarily so. I put it down to the steel drums; they'd never have cropped up on *All Mod Cons* really, would they? I love the quirky, jaunty nature of the song, sweet Caribbean-style brass flourishes, nice off kilter drums, playful vocals and a great idea for a song, Weller rightly having a pop at the brains that decided that what we have in place as accommodation are fucking eye-sores. Throw into the mix *coitus interruptus* (I had to ask my brothers what that meant), and I'll always have a love for this track.

'Carnation' is a thing of wonder. A simple melody, set against a plaintive backing – dark, moody and uplifting all at the same time. It's also one of the earliest examples of Weller's ongoing lyrical theme of self-doubt and self-analysis. "With me there's no room for the future, with me there's no room with a view at all" he tells us, in what was probably a thinly veiled message to his partner of the time, Gill Price. The song reappeared at his very first set of solo gigs at a time when Weller candidly admitted his insecurities and doubts about his place in the musical landscape, and for me, this song captures those concerns perfectly.

Track 10 and it's the Billy Elliott song. The years have come and gone and 'Malice', out of the whole Jam cannon, has had more exposure than an *X-Factor* winner; familiarity breeds contempt and a Weller gig can't pass by without this being played as an encore. However, you can't deny the majesty, power and intensity of the song. This was the song that gave the band back that vice-like grip on the nation's hearts following the relatively less than successful offerings of 1981. A classic Motown pastiche, and a set of lyrics that Weller is rightly proud of (remember, he was only 23 when he wrote this). Again, it's lean and mean, at no point does the song drift off and the band go for the jugular straight from the get go. As the song builds up to its climax, with Buckler's trademark gunshot snare rolls driving it along, Weller tells us he'd go on for hours but he'd sooner put some joy back in. Mike Read ran the Radio 1 Breakfast Show back then, and I always remember hearing this for the first time one school morning and knowing instantly that they'd hit the jackpot.

And like all good things, they have to come to an end. In this case, it's with the title track, the final song ever to be played live by the band. To my ears, it's a slowed down version of the Small Faces' 'Don't Burst My Bubble', which is no bad thing in my book. A growling Hammond organ (again, another nod towards Weller's immediate future) ushers the song in, and repeats the central themes of the album: self-belief, self-confidence and the desire for unity.

And that was the final studio album. The gigs that supported that album echoed that positivity and desire to shake things up with three support bands on the bill for the London gigs, but fan devotion now was at such a fever pitch that Weller's words in 'Running on the Spot' for the fans to use their own minds and words to express themselves, were falling on deaf ears. The support acts got short shrift, and Weller must have sensed he was heading down a cul-de-sac with his vision for the band.

It's impossible to look back at *The Gift* without anything but love and admiration. Musically, it's the stepping stone between The Jam and TSC; lyrically it's a statement of intent and positivity after the mixture of wistfulness and bitterness of *Sound Affects*; and visually (check the inlay sleeve) it's a clear pointer to the future.

Andy Nykolyszyn

'Town Called Malice'/'Precious'

(Recorded in December 1981 at Air Studios, London; released 29 January 1982, reaching Number One)

"What sort of music do you like, Sir?"

"Err, Deabill, any chance you can finish this experiment?"

"Why? It's shit! Did you see The Jam on *Top Of The Pops* last night, Sir?"

"Yes, great band, really liked the 'Precious' song, love a bit of Stax and Motown, right up my alley, be buying that at the weekend…. Anyway, at least try and look interested Deabill…."

"Yeeesss Sirrr…."

You always remember the name of a good teacher and Mr Stevenson was a decent fella for a bloke who still wore flares in 1982. Why I took Physics as an option was beyond reason but at least Stevenson never put it on you, unlike the other wankers who still couldn't believe that the grammar school they so cherished was now a comprehensive. They secretly hated the fact that the likes of myself and Terry McGlynn could just walk through the gate instead of passing the 11-plus like the old days. Fuck me, did they let us know it as well.

That day made me see 'Precious' in a different light. The first band since The Beatles to do both sides of a single on TOTP was exciting enough but 'Town Called Malice' was such an amazing song that I only flipped it over once in the week that I had it. Weller had already proclaimed that he was looking for a fresh sound, a unity to force the message of the upcoming *The Gift* LP, with its brass section and soul vision.

The Jam had an unlikely influence in Spandau Ballet. With their previous summer's hit, the superb Brit-Funk 'Chant No. 1', with a horn section borrowed from fellow Londoner's Light of the World, the dye was set in Weller's mind on the direction to go next. The bass-line was similar to Pigbag's 'Papa's Got a Brand New Pigbag' (which was another massive white Funk record of the era). It's delayed wah-wah guitar confused the fuck out of me until I was old enough to know better on how that sound was achieved, and the continuous four-to-the-floor ended up being one of the few times The Jam got played in the capital's dance clubs. The newly-found temps in Steve Nichol on trumpet and Keith Thomas on sax pushed The Jam into a higher place.

Poetic licence carried through the lyric. "Your distant shoe clicks to the midnight beat…" One of the first songs recorded for *The Gift* and in a heartbeat Weller had just influenced a generation to check out home-grown Soul and Funk records. I hope Mr Stevenson has still got the candy-striped vinyl amongst his Wilson Pickett and Four Tops LPs. Bless him.

Stuart Deabill

'Just Who is the 5 O'Clock Hero?'

(Released on 3rd July 1982 and reached Number 8 in the charts.)

The thing I remember that grabbed me about this single, apart from the songs, was the way the rear cover read Face 1 and Face 2. The actual single didn't and I remember being disappointed at this. I never quite got the meaning (if any) of the image of the microphone against the vivid blue on the front cover.

I was still young when the record was released and it felt special, buying something as a Dutch import. I was also still at school and so couldn't exactly identify with the lyrics. I mean, I never really came home from school covered in shit, or with any aches or pains... well apart from the left over's from PE or the occasional scuffle with some other lad. But I did find something to relate to when I put my dad in the frame. I often saw him return home from doing his over-time down at the Royal Mail. I could certainly get the lyric in the song about the dawn to dusk thing.

I also liked the small photograph on the rear cover. There was something I liked about the image of Weller in a hat, boating blazer and Doc Martin shoes. But there was something about the photo including the horn section of Steve Nichol and Keith Thomas that bothered me. I can't recall why now. Maybe it was jealousy, maybe I just felt they had outstayed their welcome. After all, they had already been included in a picture of the band playing live on *The Gift* album cover.

The song itself bursts into life from the very first note. The entire band are in at the same time, horn section included. There are parts of the song that hint of a Beatles-like influence and some of Buckler's drum ride cymbal patterns are quite jazzy. The whole song has an unusual rhythm, punctuated with sparing guitar parts and walking bass parts. I always liked the opening lyric in the song. I loved the way the man in the story greets his wife and announces how he is feeling. I must of done the same thing thousands of times over the years since the song has been included in my record collection. On stage, Weller tags on a couplet lyric from Sam Cooke's 'The Chain Gang' at the end of the song: "Just the sound of the man, working on the chain... gang" to great effect.

'War'

Face 2. This version of the Edwin Starr classic was credited as being produced by The Jam and Tony Taverner. I remember playing it and being left feeling unsure if I liked it or not. The semi-instrumental track was funky, groovy and included some punching and stabbing horns. There is also a section where the horns get very jazzy, playing what seem to be almost random notes, John Coltrane style, but it all works and helps keep the song interesting. This song has got to be one of The Jam's most explorative studio tracks. It's packed full of strange sounds and effects.

'The Great Depression'

I found this to be an instantly likeable tune. I also liked the way the hand clap or percussive slaps backed up Buckler's drumming. Later in the song the snare drum is affected with a phaser-type sound. It works. The rest of the song is built on swirling, almost psychedelic guitar strums, a horn section and reliable bass parts. Another Jam B side that was as important as its flipside counterpart. The trumpet is almost mournful and defeatist in its playing. Fantastic track, you rarely hear outside of your own environment.

Snowy

'The Bitterest Pill (I Ever Had to Swallow)'

(Released on 10th September 1982 and reached Number Two in the charts.)

When I was young and seemed to have bundles of time on my hands I spent hours in my bedroom. I lived in the converted attic area and for several years shard the space with my younger brother. I surrounded the immediate wallpaper around my bed with countless posters, cuttings from *Sounds* and the *NME* and any other papers and magazines featuring The Jam (and other Mod-related images). I would quite happily camp out on my bed and read the music mags and play records.

Another thing I really enjoyed doing was sketching. During my years where that attic was my bedroom, I sketched dozens of pictures. My favourite thing to sketch was record picture covers, and one that I spent hours working on was a pencil sketch of the front cover to 'The Bitterest Pill'. I loved the picture on the cover of the man in a cell. It was brilliant to sketch because there was so much room to capture an atmosphere through the use of shading. I never really connected the meaning of the lone man in the white shirt in a cell with the meaning of the song. I still don't think I understand it today.

In this song Weller sings of white lace and wedding bells and of misery and love. There is a sense of sadness and melancholy that captivates the listener and draws them in. It is as if the song wants to share itself with the sympathetic listener. The song includes a string section that was arranged by Weller and Pete Wilson and there is also the inclusion of Jenny McKeown from the Belle Stars, who adds a perfect-sounding harmony. Weller said that he wrote the song with great sweeping drama and humour.

"Summer's breeze blows through Autumn's leaves…".

There is a break in the song where Weller sings about the promise of a kiss. This is a lyric I have sung along to numerous times. The song remains one of my all-time favourite Jam songs. Only years later did it take on new meanings for me, because at the time of its release I still wasn't that interested in girls and certainly had no cause to feel sad because of some failed or denied love.

'Pity Poor Alfie'/'Fever'

The song bursts into life with a horn section that gives it an immediate jazzy feel. Buckler endorses this feel with a jazzy swing beat, although played more crudely than a jazz drummer would. I can picture myself now sitting on my drum stool behind my new Premier APK drum kit that I had recently purchased on HP. I had never attempted to play anything with a jazzy feel. I tried to swing along with the song but failed miserably. I realized then that jazz was something I needed to learn about. I accepted that the only way to play jazz was to understand it. I also needed to get hold of some jazz records. Within months I had acquired *Café Bleu* and stumbled on who would turn out to be my all-time favourite drummer, Steve White of The Style Council. I also discovered that I wasn't alone in my pursuit of jazz. The Style Council were responsible for introducing a generation of young people to jazz music, but looking back, it started with The Jam's 'Pity Poor Alfie' and 'Fever'.

The tempo of 'Pity Poor Alfie' is upbeat and swings along as Weller tells the story of poor Alfie. There is a trumpet solo break and then the song cleverly slides into 'Fever'. Buckler continues with his swing beat, and the horn section and backing vocals persist. There is also a piano part that bounces off the horn section. The Jam's cover of 'Fever' easily conjures up images of a period in London when young cats ruled the clubs and found themselves in a novel like *Absolute Beginners*. There is a freshness and a vibrancy about 'Pity Poor Alfie' and 'Fever' and I have always felt that Weller sounds happy singing these songs. Perhaps he knew what was on its way.

Snowy

161

'Just Who is the 5 O'Clock Hero?'

For '5 O'Clock' the image was part of a *Sound Effects* sleeve Paul had found lying around at Air Studios, and we modified it to fit with what Paul wanted!

'The Bitterest Pill (I Ever Had to Swallow)'/'Pity Poor Alfie'/'Fever'

That is Vaughan Toulouse on the front cover. He was friends with Paul and as we needed a model he fitted the part perfectly! He saved on the time and expense of choosing and then paying for an agency model. He looks good in the picture and was very easy to work with — very direct.

Alwyn Clayden

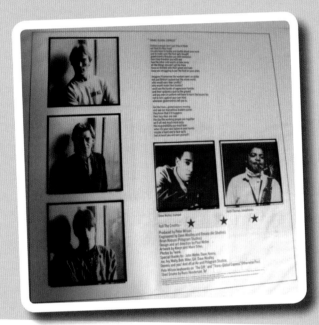

Original artwork by Alwyn Clayden
for Polydor Records.

The Jam announced another major UK tour called 'Trans-Global Unity Express'. Again I never did get a ticket when they went on sale. But my luck was finally in when I got offered a ticket for the Brixton Fair Deal. My parents finally gave in and let me go – the build-up was just as good as going. I had my white Levi jeans, red Fred Perry polo top and even polished my bowling shoes, all laid out on the bed. But I didn't have the ticket yet, though my cousin said he would bring that with him. I must have played all the albums that week, day after day, to the build-up.

My cousin came to collect me. We got the train down to Brixton. The crowded train was packed full of Jam fans, from Weller look-a-likes to the older fan, whom the music was more to them then looking like Weller. We got off the train and headed towards the venue. I was so excited: I'd waited for this moment since 1978. I remember seeing THE JAM SOLD OUT! sign and having heart palpitations!

We finally got into the venue and a cheeky pint of lager was handed to me by my cousin. The place was packed. You could see the steam rising from the fans down the front. The support band had just finished and the crowd was getting right in the moment. Then the lights went down, a roar went up and John Weller walked to the middle of the stage: GOOD EVENING, HOPE YOU ALL HAVE A GREAT NIGHT, PUT YOUR HANDS TOGETHER FOR THE BEST FUCKING BAND IN THE WORLD... THE JAM!

Phil Potter

In 1982, everyone was looking forward to another great year of all things 'Jam'. Little did we know what was in store – the most successful UK band since The Beatles disbanding! But we were to be treated to three UK tours that year.

The year started off well with the release of 'A Town Called Malice' – which was a massive hit, The Jam at the top of their game. They appeared on *Top of the Pops* and played 'Malice' and 'Precious', again another milestone for the band.

The single cover for 'Bitterest Pill' had Vaughan Toulouse from Department S and the video featured a receptionist from Polydor, along with a back of head shot of Den Munday!

The final studio album, *The Gift*, was received with universal [sic] praise from the fans. The cover featured Paul, Bruce and Rick 'running on the spot'. Twink took the photos and the other shots from the contact sheet can be seen in the book, *The Jam Unseen*. *The Gift* was, surprisingly, the band's only Number 1 album.

It was also the year of their sixth and final US tour and also spawned a live gig filmed at Bingley Hall, Stafford. This gig was part of the highly successful 'Trans-Global Unity Express' Tour. For the fans it was business as usual and we were grateful that after five years we finally had live footage of the band for ourselves, even though the complete footage did not surface until some 30 years later.

In September the 'Solid Bond' tour commenced; still, the fans did not know about the impending split. To give an idea of how big the Jam's fan base became in the final few years, 'Just Who Is the 5 O'clock Hero' was a Dutch release only, but got to Number 8 in the UK charts as an import; likewise, 'That's Entertainment' was a German import that also charted in 1981.

The July of that year was also the third and final tour of Japan. Weller had decided to call it a day but we didn't hear about it until October. (There were issues with Bruce, where he wasn't going to do the final tour.) The news was leaked then and a statement hurriedly put out. Even *Nationwide* covered the split at the Brighton gig on 11th December.

November witnessed the band's last TV appearance on *The Tube*. They appeared on the first episode and played eight songs; the dressing room interview aside, Paul seemed very relaxed.

The final tour was hastily arranged, to let as many fans as possible pay homage (or to make more money?). Wembley was chosen and all the dates rapidly sold out. I went to as many gigs as I could (work permitting); the 9th December gig at the Guildford Civic Hall and then the extra date at Brighton on the 11th, plus all the Wembley gigs. The mood was upbeat. Big Country were supporting. Rick had recorded some demos with them by this time. The Jam could have toured for weeks up and down the country but the bottle throwing marred the final gig. The band would have been right to just walk off and leave it at that, but Bruce made an announcement and the gig continued.

To honour the Polydor contract, the live album *Dig the New Breed* was released – but the album sounded rushed. It was originally going to be entitled 'A Solid Bond in Our Hearts'. (The artwork for it still exists in a private collection.)

The very last song that The Jam performed at Brighton was 'The Gift' and then that was it. Paul stood aside and let Rick and Bruce say goodbye…

Jon Abnett

The Jam had the common touch, and we're smart enough to do TOTP and Saturday morning TV shows and play the game to certain extent, but also cool enough to be apart from everything else. Weller wore his influences on his sleeve, such as The Kinks and the Small Faces.

They were like cartoon characters to a kid like myself: the images were so striking, with the black-and-white suits, Jam shoes, jumping around.

In 1982, by the time I was 11–12 years old, I knew every single song, as I borrowed all my brothers' records. *All Mod Cons*, *Setting Sons* and *Sound Affects* – what a holy trinity! They're the ones that I love.

I specifically remember talking about The Jam in my school playground in Birmingham after they did both 'Precious' and 'Town Called Malice' on TOTP. It's quite incredible to think that even at that early age the influence they had on all my friends and myself.

Weller's hair from the 'Funeral Pyre' video… though I remember the uncool kids saying, "See his fucking hair, looks fucking stupid – what a fucking poof!" But my brother went out and got my Dad, who was a hairdresser, to give him that French A-line the next day. He looked like a little Stevie Marriott!

Matthew Priest, Dodgy

In the summer of 1982 I was 12-and-a-half and lived in a crappy small town in the east of Scotland called Carnoustie. I'd also just started secondary school and musically, up until that point, the records I was buying were either by Adam & the Ants or The Police. By 1982 the Mod revival in my town was in full swing, but it was starting secondary school that exposed me to all the other music out there. I'd been listening to '60s stuff for years, thanks to my Dad having fairly good taste in music, but it was all clicking together, The Who, The Animals, The Yardbirds, Rolling Stones, all playing a medley in my head, and then I heard The Jam.

I must've been aware of them over the years, in fact I remember religiously taping the Top 40 every Sunday and 'Going Underground' being Number One. That was probably the song that "Jennifer, your tea's ready" is recorded over, with "but I'm taping the charts, Mum" making an appearance, too. So, 'Just Who is the 5 O'Clock Hero', 'The Bitterest Pill' and 'Beat Surrender' and then that was that. Bugger, whilst I was listening to The Police and *Ghost in the Machine*, I should've been listening to *The Gift* – arse!

Jennie Baillie

A
WHOLE
STREET'S
BELIEF

'Trans Global Unity Express' Tour

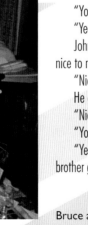

It's Sunday morning, 21st March 1982. Four of us have travelled down for this one: me and one of my best mates, Pete, plus Robbo (who's already been to five gigs on this tour alone) and Sandy, Robbo's fucking gorgeous bird, looking every bit 'the ace face' and super Modette couple. We've caught the train from Piccadilly station in Manchester down to Birmingham for the second of The Jam's two shows here. Tonight is the band's eighth gig of a 25-date sell-out tour of the UK.

Bingley Hall in Birmingham is a big warehouse-type place, an all-standing venue holding 8,000 excited, faithful followers. It's a proper shithole and fucking freezing, are my first thoughts when we arrive. We see cameramen outside and find out that its being recorded for the BBC.

We're really early and Robbo's been asking some guys from the crew that he knows what time the band will be here for the soundcheck. Walking back towards us, he says, "Gonna be here any minute lads, coz of this telly stuff," looking pretty pleased with himself.

There's a bit of a buzz going up down the street outside the venue, and sure enough the coach arrives. The coach stops rights next to us and two big guys get off: first Kenny Wheeler, the tour manager (you seriously wouldn't want a whack off him). He scowls and holds out his arm, so we all stand back and Kenny forms a one-man channel between the coach and the entrance to allow the others off. John Weller comes down the steps with his familiar silver teddy boy quiffed hair and black leather bomber jacket. John gives a couple of friendly nods as he walks by, quickly followed by the band. First Rick Buckler, wearing his green scooter jacket and red boxing boots; then Bruce Foxton wearing a long black Crombie-style coat — he looks at Sandy and winks (typically); and finally Paul Weller himself. Fuck me, he looks cool: he's wearing the long, black corduroy coat he wore on the 'Funeral Pyre' set, with a green striped university-style scarf, black peaked cap, black Melandi bowling shoes, with what I'd call 'Rupert the Bear'-style pants.

The coach door shuts and the other kids disperse towards a side door of the venue, hoping to gain access to the soundcheck. A couple of minutes went by and we could hear the sound of drums as Rick warms up inside. Once all the other kids have gone there's just the four of us standing by the coach, when other familiar faces climb down: firstly Gill Price, Paul Weller's ever-present girlfriend. Right behind her is merchandise manager Brian Hawkins, who we all know. Robbo knows Brian, and they chat for a bit.

A bit later, Brian gestures us into the venue with him with a flick of his head and we all sneak inside calmly, so as to not attract too much attention from any other fans. There's another door: "Just act cool and wait here," insists Robbo as Brian walks off to his crew. We wait for a minute and can see the back of the mixing desk now. The band starts playing bits from 'Midnight Hour' — very different from the old version, almost 'swingy'.

I can't believe it, we're just in the right place at the right time, the only kids in there and we're about to meet John and see the soundcheck. John knows Robbo's face from loads of previous gigs and acknowledges him with a nod, waving him in. We get the nod too from Brian, and follow quickly before anyone else decides we shouldn't be there. Standing before us is John Weller — not only The Jam's manager, but Paul's dad — and I have nothing but respect for him!

"Alright, John mate, how's it going?" asks Robbo very confidently.

"Well mate, very well thanks, bit brass monkeys in here though, eh?" says John in that very distinctive London accent.

"You come down from Manchester today," he asks looking at the four of us.

"Yeah, on the train, early this morning. This is Sandy, me girlfriend, and my mates Denny Woo and Pete."

John smiles and holds out a big hand, then he says in his gruff, '40 cigs a day voice': "Alright kids, nice to meet ya, we gotta a great show for you tonight, fantastic," as he firmly grips my hand.

"Nice to meet you, Mr Weller," I say, like a total wanker.

He chuckles and says, "John please, John will do, son."

"Nice to meet you, John," I say, as I feel my cheeks going a little red.

"You all seen the boys before?" he asks.

"Yeah loads: first time in '79 at the Apollo," I say enthusiastically. "I'm only 15 like, but my older brother got me into it all and now I wanna be at every gig possible," I continue without taking a breath.

Bruce admits to a fake Rickenbacker — as used on 'In the City'.

"Nice to hear it," he pauses: "Sorry, what's your name again?"

"Den… Denny Woo to me mates," I say, growing in confidence.

"Right," he smiles.

The band starts playing 'Midnight Hour' and we all turn to watch for a minute.

"Are they playing this tonight, John?" asks Sandy.

"No love, just getting some sounds for the crew," he says.

"Shame, it sounds really cool," she says.

"Where are you from love, that's no Mancunian accent, is it?" John asks, intrigued by Sandy's super sexy voice and giving her an approving quick once over (well, you can't blame him can you!).

"Melbourne John, been here since the summer – always been a fan though," she confirms.

"Fantastic love," he adds. He turns to Robbo. "You want to bring the kids back afterwards, Robbo?"

"Great John, yeah… please, we'll love that, and they'll behave themselves," says Robbo, looking at me and Pete starring pathetically at John in disbelief.

Den Davis jamming with Bruce at home.

"Well, we'll see you later then kids, and get you into meet the boys properly alright?" He smiles in a very cheery manner. What a nice bloke he is, really down to earth and makes us feel right at home. "Well, you go and enjoy the show," He says pointing to the stage, nodding approvingly for us to get to the front before everyone else. "I want to let some other kids in now so you get a good spot down there."

Me and Pete don't need asking twice and we dash towards the front. We watch the sound check: 'That's Entertainment', 'Move On Up', 'Precious'. Then we're all asked to clear the venue by Kenny and another even bigger guy, when Robbo comes to the rescue: "Those two are with me Kenny, John's taking us backstage, if that's ok?" Kenny frowns at us but accepts it and tells us to wait by the stage. John is soon there to greet us and takes us behind the stage and up some steps to a large lounge area.

"Come on in kids, the boys are all sat over there, we'll get you introduced in a minute or two," he says taking care of us and making us feel relaxed about it all.

I'm not usually nervous, I'd say I'm overly confident, but I'm actually shitting it! By the look on Pete's face, he is too! We wait politely for John's call. Backstage I can really feel the 'family love', not just between the fans and the band mates but most noticeably between John and Paul. I stand for a few minutes and witness the man hugs they give each other; it's total affection in every sense and I am truly intrigued by this.

We join the band on the sofas, my stomach is churning a bit but my head's shouting at me to be cool, and thankfully I am. Smiling and shaking hands with them all and just fitting in like part of the furniture. We all know Paul hates hero worship and hysteria, so we all act like we've done this all before and it's just another day.

After a while Kenny shouts he's getting some more fans in. "What do you want: boys, girls or both?" he asks.

Bruce jokes, "Oh, boys for me!"

Rick adds, "Yeah, as long as they're all under 12."

"I reckon the TV might cut that out later," I whisper to Pete.

After having a mesmerising time backstage we take our places at the front of the stage, soon to be joined by 8,000 eager fans all wanting to get as close to the band as possible. The house and stage lights go down, a single light illuminates Bruce's mic and John Weller appears on stage. There's a huge, rib-crushing surge from behind as, in typical fashion, John shouts: "Put your hands together for the best fucking band in the world – The Jam!!"

On stage enter Paul, Bruce and Rick, collecting their instruments. Without saying a word, there's a stick count and they're straight into 'Strange Town'. The force of the bodies surging from behind us is almost unbearable but the passion, power and energy displayed in front of us keeps us all going, even Sandy, protected by Robbo's arms. Song after song, each one an anthem, each one greeted by mass cheers of appreciation. This is what The Jam are all about, this is what a Jam gig is all about: being at the front, fighting for your life and singing every word before your lungs give out.

The gig is fucking unbelievable, 24 energetic classics each greeted by massive cheers and 8,000 kids singing along to the very end. What a night! And this one is only the first of many more to follow over the next 10 days!

We missed the last train from Birmingham and had to hitchhike through the night to get home. There's no way I was getting up for school in the morning! I lay on my bed, absolutely knackered, but with a smile on my face! I didn't get undressed, just pulled the covers over me and pretended I'd been there all night!

Den Davis

Jennie McKeown (Matthias), from The Belle Stars

How did you get the 'Bitterest Pill' job?

Paolo Hewitt, who happened to have interviewed The Belle Stars for a few music magazines, was also a very good friend of Paul's and Paul asked him for an introduction. It so happened that Paolo was working for Melody Maker, doing a celebrity coverage of bands reviewing other artists' albums. Paul was asked which female artist he would like to be on the front cover with, and he said Jennie Bellestar. We did the photo session and Paul asked me a few weeks after that.

Did you like The Jam even in your Two Tone years, or did you feel separate to what was going on with The Jam and their fans?

I didn't know much about Paul Weller at the time, or indeed The Jam — I was more of a Clash person, coz we were hanging with them at the time and touring with them and Madness, but I knew that they existed. My friends knew more about them than me. I only got to know about them after I met Paul and whilst we were sharing TV slots.

Do you recall the day you laid down vocals on the penultimate Jam single?

Yes, I did, and I will never forget it because I felt that I let down Paul badly. I was very naïve in those days and didn't even know what a harmony was — God love Paul, he was extremely patient and very sweet.

Were The Jam in the studio?

I can't remember seeing the others — from what I can remember, it was just me and Paul.

Did you have any idea then that The Jam were splitting up?

No, like I said I was real busy doing The Belle Stars, TV, gigs with The Clash and Madness, so once work was done with Paul I would have to dash off and do other stuff. I was also going out with Chrissy Boy [Chris Foreman] from Madness at the time, and my time was consumed with my new love interest.

Did you meet John Weller at all?

I met John and couple of times and on those occasions he was lovely to me — I get that he was a hard worker and loved his son to bits.

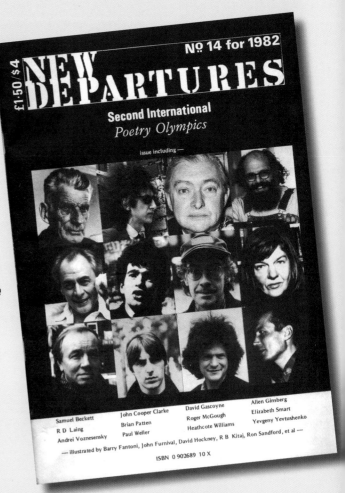

The Best Band in the Fucking World!

My obsession with The Jam had started as soon as I played the *In the City* album on my old record player in my bedroom, with a trusty 2p coin balanced on the stylus ensuring it wouldn't jump (too much). I played the album to death, 'I Got By In Time', 'Away From the Numbers' and 'In the City' blaring through the floorboards so often my mum and dad still know them off by heart.

Fair enough to say that when I heard that The Jam were splitting up, one break time at school, I was devastated. The only band and person I had connected with were going almost as soon as they'd began: 'Town Called Malice' and *The Gift* had both just been Number One! I thought 'The Bitterest Pill' was fantastic, and I really liked the new funky direction of 'Pity Poor Alfie' and 'Fever'. Surely it can't be, someone's on a wind up – but sadly not....

The farewell tour was announced, and I thought that there was no way I'd get to go. I'd just turned 14, and to me being able to go to an actual gig, seeing The Jam at Wembley Arena, just wouldn't happen; there was more chance of Paul Weller turning up at our local youth club on a Thursday night, or so I thought....

It was a normal Tuesday morning before school, eating Weeabix, dreading maths later in the day. My dad walks into the kitchen: "Morning miserable, you're not still moping about that band splitting up, are you? At least you won't have to have a Weller haircut for much longer!" Ha, bloody ha, Dad! Then the moment I'll remember forever: my dad casually drops two tickets for The Jam at Wembley Arena for Saturday 4th December on the kitchen table! My dread of maths later that day seemed irrelevant. There are some things in life you never forget, and that is one of them: cheers Dad!

One of my first memories is of seeing John Weller on the right hand corner of the stage! "Please put your hands together for the best band in the fucking world, The Jam!" Never having been to a gig before I had no idea what to expect – like your first big football match – and most of the lads were taller than me and my mate.

We were carried forward in a giant tidal wave of bodies. 'Start!' boomed out from the massive amps. I looked for Weller, who was a beam of barking energy in a yellow Lonsdale T-shirt (you could still see the fold marks on it, where he must have pulled it out of the wrapping!) and round shades. Jesus, this is mental! The next two hours were a blur of Jam classics: I remember singing my head off to 'To Be Someone' and one of the older lads, who'd kindly been putting a protective arm in front of me to stop me being crushed into the barrier, winking at me saying, "Bloody hell mate, you're into it ain't ya?!"

I remember the security guys trying to hold the metal barriers up, then one of them saying "oh, fuck it", before giving in and letting us all pile through – I don't think my feet touched the ground! I remember feeling more alive and excited than I can ever remember, and I remember coming out of the arena breathless, knackered and covered in sweat. I remember my dad waiting outside for me, he'd been talking to one of the security guards, an old chap. "Guess what," my dad said: "He told me they've had all the greats here – Elton John, Cliff Richard – but this lot are definitely the worst!" Ha, bloody ha! By far the best is what I think he meant to say!

I remember sitting in the back of my dad's Ford Sierra as we pulled away from Wembley Arena. I saw the crowds disappearing into the dark night, and glanced at the huge Jam sign outside the venue, THE FAREWELL TOUR, with the faces from the *Dig The New Breed* album down the righthand side. I remember being pissed off that I'd panicked and brought one of the unofficial tour T-shirts from the street guys outside the venue. I had a tenner for a programme and T-shirt; the official T-shirts were inside, and far better – bollocks! I got a black one with *The Gift* transfer on the front that was knackered after two washes!

The gig had left me elated and gutted, but I knew I hadn't seen the last of Paul Weller, and the huge impression that he and his band had made on my young life.

Martin Carroll

It's early November 1982 and me and a few of the gang are off to Osbourne's Snooker Hall in town, deciding to give school a well-earned rest for the day. I lived a bus stop further down from the rest of the lads, and as I climbed the stairs to hook up with them, I instantly knew something was up. Daz (my Jam partner in crime from the off) just looked at me. "They're splitting up. It's finished." He looked gutted. It must be a joke. Must be. They can't split, they're the biggest fucking band on the planet. MY fucking band. It doesn't make any sense. He passed me a copy of *Record Mirror* and there it was in black and white.

"The longer a group continues, the more frightening the thought of ever ending it, because that is why so many carry on until they become meaningless…. What we (and you) have built up has meant something, for me it stands for honesty, passion and energy and youth. I want it to stay that way…."

It was impossible to make any sense or logic from the official statement at that time. All I felt was a hollow, empty feeling. The band that had informed me as a teenager across all angles, from clothes to politics to literature to poetry to Soul, were soon to be defunct.

As many of you here will have done, I clung to whatever was left of the band prior to the split. The 'Beat Surrender' gatefold package, *The Tube* performance (with the hilarious non-cooperative Muriel Grey interview), the Nationwide windswept interview, *Dig the New Breed*. Tickets sold so quickly for the farewell tour – too quickly for me – and I was left to remember the parting shots from the band on grainy C-90 recordings.

The dust has well and truly settled 30 years down the line, and I look back at the band with nothing but misty-eyed affection and eternal gratitude. That seismic feeling of loss that engulfed me that November day soon evaporated as I fell head over heels for everything The Style Council offered over the forthcoming years; but the love and devotion to The Jam burnt eternally bright. I particularly remember in 1984, when myself and seven schoolmates put together a band and entered a 'battle of the bands' competition for the whole of the Midlands. We were all 16, young, raw and hungry. I spent the whole of the afternoon before leaving for the competition listening to all four sides of *Snap!*, almost as if it would impart a magical power to me that I could transfer to the rest of the band.

The competition? We won it, of course….

SWITCH – What have I learnt?
BELIEF IS ALL!

Andy Nykolyszyn

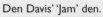

Den Davis' 'Jam' den.

Tracie Young

I'd spent most of my life in Essex, but my mum got divorced and upped sticks and moved to Hereford. So I had to leave everything behind — college, my boyfriend, my friends, etc. I was 17, so it was a devastating age to be dragged away from all the connections I'd formed. I tried getting back down to Essex and London at every opportunity I could.

All I had left of my old life was the music papers that I bought each week. NME, Smash Hits, Melody Maker, Record Mirror. Through these I felt in touch with my old life and I could see when my favourite band, the Q-Tips, were playing, and me and my mates would get to see each other.

I'd seen the ad in Smash Hits a month before I actually decided to reply to it. It said: "Paul Weller is looking for a female singer for his Respond label, aged between 18–22."

Well I was 17 and thought, mmm not going to get away with that and left it. Then the ad appeared again and I was due to come up to London for a gig and I thought, fuck it, might as well go for it. I'm not as old as he wants but, bollocks, let's give it a go.

I just sang into the cassette deck of my Mum's stereo — my mum had one of those old Panasonic music centres, which had a built-in mic. I was trying to think of a great song to sing that would sound good without any musical backing. I had a Phoebe Snow album that I loved, and it had a cover of that fantastic Betty Wright song, 'Shoo-Rah! Shoo-Rah!' on it and I just sang it into the music system in the front room!

I put the cassette in an envelope, copied the address out from Smash Hits, left it in my handbag for a few days, as I was gripped by a strange fear of not knowing whether to send it or not. Days later I went to London to see the Q-Tips at the Venue in Victoria. I had a great night, was on a high when I came out and, as my mate Brian went into Burger King, I saw a post box and just seized the moment and finally sent the cassette.

Now this was a Saturday; by Tuesday I was back in Hereford and I got a call from Gill Price. My mum answered the phone and said, "There's someone called Gill on the phone for you from Solid Bond."

I was like, I don't know anyone called Gill.

I took the call and Gill said, "Can you come to London on the Thursday to meet Paul? He wants to meet you."

It was so surreal, made even more so by the fact that most of my friends were Mods. I wasn't one — I liked the look, the music, and I hung out with people that were into it, but all these fellas idolised Paul and The Jam.

I owned All Mod Cons and Sound Affects and some of the singles, so yeah, I was a fan, but not in the way my friends looked up to him. In fact, I still believe that Sound Affects is one of the best albums I own. I was aware of the enormity of meeting this bloke but more because of the reverential way in which my friends spoke about Paul.

I didn't tell any of them where I was going. Also, I'd had a really nasty infection of the lymphatic system, and was just getting over that and still wasn't right. The infection had started in my ankle, which was still really swollen. I was panicking, thinking what do I wear, what do I wear?!

So I wore thick black tights, a mini skirt and pixie boots (or tukka boots as we used to call them in Essex) to hide the swelling.

My Mum wasn't happy about me going up to London again, so she decided to come with me this time and go shopping with my Auntie Gwen while I did the audition.

I turned up at Polygram (soon to be Solid Bond) Studios with my mum and my auntie and, once they were happy I wasn't going to be sold off to white slave traders, they went off down Oxford Street.

Pete Wilson sat on the piano while I sang, mainly on my own but occasionally with Paul. I did The Four Tops 'Reach Out, I'll Be There' and Freda Payne's 'Band of Gold'.

I did find out later that one of the reasons why Paul liked my tape was because of the song I'd chosen. He was incredibly sweet, and seemed very uncomfortable to be around a teenage girl. Bear in mind he was only in his mid-20s then — it's only when I look back that I think it must have felt as awkward for him as it was for me.

We took a break and as it was a nice day Paul asked me if I would like to sit outside — I remember him saying in the sunshine, and I'm not sure why but hearing Paul Weller say, "Do you want to sit in the sunshine," sounded really strange. We sat and talked about the music we were into. The Friends album by Shalamar and Michael Jackson's Off the Wall, which he was a big fan of. At the end of it, he told me he'd be in touch. So I was waiting by the phone and letterbox for a few days and then got sent a tape with 'The House That Jack Built', demo'd by The Questions.

When did you find out about the split?

It was really strange, I found out through the press. Utterly selfishly, the first thing I thought was, how does that affect me?!

Anyway he phoned and told me he was disbanding The Jam. I asked him where it left me, and he replied, exactly where you were before. The Jam has nothing to do with Respond. He wanted to relaunch Respond and try and realise his vision of being a Tamla Motown-type label, with writers and musicians that all worked with each other.

So he said, I'm going to send you a tape and I want you to learn the backing vocals and I'll put some pointers in as well. It's going to be The Jam's last single and I want you to sing on it. The tape was of 'A Solid Bond In Your Heart'. A week or so later, he'd changed his mind and I got sent 'Beat Surrender'. It was very surreal, to think I'd be singing on a Jam single, let alone their last single.

Would you say that they were the biggest band in the country at that point?

For me, I remember at school we had a lunch room and someone always had a transistor radio, and I can remember two momentous days of being in Room B16. One was when Dexy's went to Number One with 'Geno' and the other was when 'Going Underground' went straight in!

The Jam's legacy was so in me because of my friends, but I was more detached than they were. Suddenly I know this bloke and the group's splitting up and I'm going to sing with them! So I still hadn't told any of my friends, just my family. I didn't tell any friends 'til after I'd come back to London to record 'Beat Surrender'.

What was that like?

It was recorded at Air Studios on Oxford Street. It was the first time I met Rick and Bruce. Jimmy the Scottish organ player was there – keyboards were already becoming a bigger part of The Jam's sound then, it was like Paul was making the shift already.

Dennis Munday was there and was an absolute gentleman and someone I felt I could trust and rely on if needed. I wasn't wrong about him.

Afrodiziak had already done some of the vocals and I was asked to do the straight harmonies on "Come on girl, Come on boy" and double up on the band's vocals. It was winter, and a Sunday morning. I'd been at my friends' Kev and Brian's the day before and told them, there's a reason why I'm here this weekend, and they couldn't believe it. It was hugely significant for me as it was a step nearer to what I wanted to do but, for my friends, it was, "OMG PAUL WELLER!!" That reaction always scared me a bit. . . .

I got on with it and Paul soon became someone I just knew and worked with. I tried hard not to think about how different my friends' perceptions of Paul were. It was too weird.

When we recorded 'Beat Surrender', one thing I had a real problem with was singing "Succumb" the way Paul sang it – pronouncing the hard "B' didn't seem right at all. I didn't get it! The first time I heard the produced single of 'Beat Surrender' was on the radio and that was weird as well! I could hear my vocals so it was thrilling and strange all at the same time.

Did you feel sorry for Rick and Bruce?

No, but I did feel like I was part of something that was being taken away from them and it made me feel very awkward. I heard some of the resentment by some of my friends about The Jam splitting, so I imagined that might be how Bruce and Rick felt, but they certainly didn't show any resentment when I was around. Bruce and Rick were always nice towards me.

Did you see The Jam live?

Saw them at Stafford Bingley Hall on the farewell tour for the only time. Got the train with my cousin and had passes, but the gig was a blur, part of a whirlwind of memories from that time that are hard to distinguish from one another.

Did Weller give off an aura that made people take notice?

To be honest I never saw that, in work or outside it. When we were at Solid Bond, we were forever nipping out to Linda's on the Edgware Road for coffees and sandwiches, and I never noticed people looking at him. He was one of the most famous people at that time and he was hardly ever stopped for autographs when I was with him. Paul was special and talented, but the one with aura was John!

We used to laugh a lot, and he was such a piss-taker. After a while I would give it back to him. He must have thought I was a right gobby mare. Paul seemed very clued in and I was just starting to shape my beliefs, so he was a good person to be around then; he believed in the same things I did and helped me to shape my beliefs, although I was very stubborn and challenging.

TOTP

We recorded it and the week before it was due to be shown the producer, Michael Hurll, knew on presales alone it would be Number One the following week. But the band was going to be away. Again, another surreal time. I remember vividly Lionel Richie walking down the corridor wearing shoulder pads and thinking, I've got loads of your records!

Paul took me out shopping to C&A for the appearance. He pulled out a ski jumper and said, what do you think of this with some ski pants? I said, ok, grudgingly. I then got a pair of leather boots from Kensington market, which he requested, and then he said, "What about wearing ski goggles for a laugh?!"

That's when I put my foot down: "No chance!"

"It'll be really funny!"

"Only for you!"

"Well, just wear 'em round your neck then."

"No bloody way."

It was bad enough wearing the jumper!

On the show, he wanted me to dance side-to-side and follow his movements as we were standing near the back, and look in unison. Of course he didn't do any of the things he said he was going to do, but I just swung my hips side to side like he said and hoped for the best!

The Musicians Union had a rule back then that all TOTP music had to be pre-recorded for performance on the show, and then mimed to. (It was scrapped a few months later – coincidentally, in the week between 'Speak Like A Child' and 'The House That Jack Built' appearing on TOTP). So there was a re-recording session for 'Beat Surrender', which took place at Polygram Studios. Everyone who was appearing on the show had to be there and re-record their parts in the presence of an MU official. The word "Bullshit" had already been replaced with "Rubbish" for the radio version of the single. Now Paul decided to change it to "Bullfrogs". The new recording session completed, the tapes went off to the BBC. But when we mimed to the new version at the TOTP recording, Paul completely forgot about "Bullfrogs"… I can't remember whether he mimed "Rubbish" or "Bullshit", but it definitely wasn't "Bullfrogs"!

When it was transmitted I was back home in Hereford with my mum, my sister, my nan and my auntie, and when it got to Number One my mum and my auntie were going, "Ooh we've met him!"

succumb . . .

to the beat surrender

It's a cold February afternoon in 1982. I've legged it up from school and am now standing outside Selecta Disc record shop on Greenford Broadway. The front of it is completely made of glass yet you can't see in due to the posters and record sleeves blue-tacked all over it. I walk in and the bloke behind the counter looks up briefly then back down at the grot mag he's flicking through. Albums cover the length of both sides of the shop, I make my way down… A, B, C… G, H, I… J – that's what I'm here for.

They have every album they've put out from *In the City* to *Sound Affects*, but the trouble is I don't know which one to buy. There's an old saying, 'never judge a book by its cover' – well, try telling a nine-year-old boy that. The cover was everything to me at that moment in time.

'Town Called Malice' was what done it for me, seeing The Jam on *Top Of The Pops* playing that and how cool Weller looked just blew me away. Others had it with Bowie when he did TOTP – well, I'd found my 'Bowie moment'. I bought the single and played it to death, but now I wanted an album. Woolworths didn't have all the albums but I was told the record shop down the road did.

I was a bit of an early starter: swapped Action Man for girls and I also wanted to get the clothes I saw the older lot wearing. I really wanted a striped boating blazer I saw a boy down our street wearing.

I wanted to be involved in something – anything – and I wanted to get amongst it. So that's how I found myself in a dog-eared record shop in a London suburb looking. *All Mod Cons* called me. The other albums looked great but Weller looked top with those Sta-Prest trousers and white shirt. I liked that cover straight away.

I choose my album and walked up to the fella behind the counter; he puts down his copy of *Razzle*….

The 92 bus drops me at the bottom of my road, I run the length of Bennetts Avenue, sling the key in the door, drag a packet of crisps out of the cupboard and a can of Tizer from the fridge and head straight to my bedroom.

All Mod Cons is taken out of the bag, vinyl extracted and whacked on the turntable. I then jumped up onto my bed to study the inner sleeve. It had caught my eye as soon as I'd seen it. A collection of pictures of the band, an old school badge, a couple of singles and an album, *Sounds like Ska*. There were postcards and old train ticket, loads of stuff, yet it was laid out in such a way I couldn't take my eyes off it. (It's still one of my favourite pieces of art, a nod to Peter Blake but Weller's take on it.)

Looking back I can still picture myself making sense of this new wonder, this vital document, almost an ideal for living. Those 12 tracks still push me into a place that was clear, unique.

'Down in the Tube Station' seems to follow me down the underground system at least once a year. Getting the last train home from the centre of London after a night out back to the suburbs is fraught with danger and there's always a little mob looking to finish off their evening by lobbing a few blows on someone. This song has flashed into my mind on countless occasions. I'm a QPR fan and trips across the capital for London derbies also bring this song into vivid reality as you stand on a platform then suddenly hear a chant echo from above as a firm turns up at the station.

'Fly' is just the oddest record, if you read the lyrics it's like something the Carpenters would have wrote, yet The Jam decide to add spiky Punk-like bass guitar and drums to it…. I fucking loved it. It was simple, almost childish, yet wrapped up in this taunt web of sound. I can just see Weller showing Rick and Bruce the lyrics and them raising their eyebrows before Paul says, "but this is how we're gonna play it", then launching into that tight little riff. Must have blown their minds!

'In the Crowd' is MY song. We've all got a song, well this one's mine. Mine alone. It takes me away somewhere. It's epic. Starting off slow and building, he may be going on about cans of baked beans on toast and ice cream but I get what he's going on about, being part of what THEY want you to be, it made you feel different, individual, apart from the norm, away from the numbers.

It's why some of us chose to dress differently; to listen to music that wasn't *Top Of The Pops*. It spat in the eye of the herd-like mentality of the masses. It was the reason I stood proud, dressed completely differently to those stood around me in the middle school playground, and why to this day choose to dress the way I do. It's that sound of suburban kids kicking out.

From the distant foghorn at the start, 'English Rose' makes you think of lovers. Mine was the girl from the neighbouring school. And it was literally next door. I could look out of my classroom window and see her doing handstands in the playground. I acted all cocky with her and she was all shy and giggly. It was the first time I'd fallen for a girl and I played this and dreamt of holding her hand, kissing her. I played out a thousand scenarios with her to this song. In the end I plucked up enough courage to ask her to the pictures; she was so sweet and innocent that she asked her mum first, right in front of me, who promptly said no, but said it was ok to come round to listen to some records together at their house. But that never happened, the chance was gone. A Saturday afternoon watching Gremlins at the ABC and getting a popcorn-flavoured kiss never happened but the song stayed with me to remind me of my first love. The beauty of great music is its timeless ability to transport you wherever you want to go.

Simon Kortlang

Top left and bottom right: Playhouse Theatre, Edinburgh, 6th April 1982;
Top right and bottom left: Outside the George Hotel, Edinburgh, 7th April 1982.

175

My mate, Pete Barratt, came up with the idea of this gimpy dance troupe, who were going to appear as the special guests of The Jam on the last two dates at Guildford and Brighton. Paul thought it was a great idea, so seven or eight of us were in skimpy clothing, messing about and the audience didn't get it at all. I wouldn't say the abuse we got was really ugly, but there was a lot of testosterone flying about and all I remember is it being like a Benny Hill sketch speeded up, and then a shower of coins coming at us! Getting the train home, I thought it had got too big and the audience had a tunnel vision thing, where it was all about The Jam and nothing else.

Gary Crowley

There seemed to be a lot of bitterness in the venue the more the gig went on, anger that no one could fully understand. More tears of rage from a few, hence the wankers throwing bottles at the stage. When the house lights went up I was talking to some friends I'd made over the years through our shared love of The Jam, and this fella Rob couldn't speak. When I did get him to utter something he just said, "My life's over. What will we do now?" I gave him a hug – I didn't know what to say.

The thing I remember most about the final Jam gig in Brighton was that it was just an anti-climax, really. For this gig we got a coach up there. There was me and some mates from school. I remember I separated from the others inside and found myself just surrounded, and as soon as the band came on the nearby boys had arms and hands everywhere on me – I mean, proper groped up. Then everyone just started bouncing and I couldn't breathe. I remember thinking, oh my god, I'm just going to have to go with this or else I'm not going to survive, so I put my head back to gasp for air and that was that.

I also remember seeing people throwing things at The Jam and it all got a bit sour. I think Weller got annoyed, and quite rightly so. There had been such a feeling that this is the last gig and so it's going to be fantastic – you know that feeling, like on a New Year's Eve, where there is this pressure to enjoy yourself – but it just didn't come off.

At the end the band members came on stage together and stood there all linking arms and bowed; and then that was it. The whole experience was more like the end was being dragged into your mind. It just felt like it was meant to be like this, or what it should have been.

Elinor Crockford

I was in Japan when I heard about the split. Paul sent me a letter to tell me. I remember I cried for few days. I needed to do something, so I went and had another ear pierced!

I remember the last gig in Brighton very well. I was crying after the gig. Kenny Wheeler called me over and asked me to have a drink with them. Then I saw John there. He saw me crying and said, "What's wrong, girl? Paul has a great future now. Be happy for him, ok? He's been making great music already. You would love it! So stop crying and think about the future!"

Then I thought, he's right! I must be happy for Paul.

Keiko

Opposite: Soundcheck – Sheffield Top Rank, March 1982.

'Beat Surrender'/'Shopping' and 'Move on Up'/'Stoned Out of My Mind'/'War'

(Released in November 1982, it reached Number One in the charts. The 12" single included five tracks.)

By the time this song was released every Jam fan knew that this was going to be the band's farewell single. I bought the record knowing this fact and I too felt the sadness and disappointment. However, the song sounded to me like a celebration song – and it still does.

The song opens with a piano roll and Weller announces the song title, then the song erupts into life. It sounds instantly engaging and exciting. The song is full of melody, a driving tambourine beat that gives it bounce and entices the listener to get up and dance. Even today, I can remember me and my mates dancing our best Northern Soul steps in the basement of the youth club we used to frequent on one of the disco nights. 'Beat Surrender' got played over and over again. We danced our farewells to The Jam.

The main body of the song also includes a Hammond organ, more piano, additional vocals from Tracie Young and the soulful sounding horns section. The whole song is energetic and uplifting. Not that I (or any other Jam fan, for that matter) knew it at the time, but Weller's vocal is something resembling what he was going to do with The Style Council.

The picture cover always fascinated me at the time. The shot of Weller's girlfriend Gill seemed to satisfy some kind of curiosity and it gave me some insight into Weller's private life. I had up until that point never seen a picture of Gill. She never struck as being an attractive girl, but then to be fair, I hadn't long put away my tin soldiers.

I also remember reading the words included on the inner sleeve from The Boy Wonder and thinking, what the hell is he going on about? This song remains one of the most memorable Jam songs. Not just because it is a great track but because I bought it at the time knowing it was going to be the last Jam single I would ever buy. There was, for sure, a sense of goodbye….

'Shopping'

This is a jazzy number that is built around a sparse guitar part, a trumpet, Foxton's bass and Buckler's use of the brushes to tap out a jazzy rhythm. There is, however, a nice jazzy guitar solo and also jazzy flute solo that enters towards the end of the song. The lyrics are about going shopping and if there are any deeper meanings, I never got them. I did, however, get the meaning of the importance of going shopping, of searching for that friendly bargain and ensuring that shopping stayed at the top of the list of priorities.

'Move on Up'

This was the A side to the second disc in the EP. By the time this was released by The Jam, I was already fully aware of the brilliant Curtis Mayfield original. I always loved the feel of the Mayfield version and especially its use of congas. The Jam version was also great and included whistles and other percussive instruments that help keep the song alive and kicking. There are some interesting studio effects employed on the song, which helped it sound fantastic coming out of the speakers at the disco. Again, we danced our best Northern Soul steps and shuffles to this song and loved every second of it. Weller and the band seem to charge through the song and breathed a new and original life into it. Job done!

'Stoned Out of My Mind'

This sat comfortably as the opening track on the B side to 'Move on Up'. The song is instantly percussive and keeps the horn section. Buckler pushes the song along using his jazz brushes, and Foxton supports. Weller sings soulfully and again, in my opinion, this song could have been included in any early Style Council set. The song fades, a technique that the band seldom used across their five years of recording.

'War'

The last song in the EP and another well-known Soul classic from Edwin Starr. A version had, of course, already appeared on the flip side to 'Just Who Is the 5 O'Clock Hero', but this version took advantage of some new studio sounds and backing vocals from Afrodiziac. The feel of the song is percussive again and Weller plays a funky guitar part. There is a sense or comparison to the sound attained with 'Precious' and it achieves the feel found on *The Gift* album.

Snowy

Clockwise: Arriving for the soundcheck, The Playhouse, Edinburgh 6th April 1982; Bruce and Rick sign autographs outside the Geroge Hotel, Edinburgh, 7th April 1982; Paul on stage at The Playhouse.

I remember accosting Weller in his car driving out of the BBC studios in September '82. Myself and my old pal Brian would make a habit of climbing over the walls when security weren't looking, and we would randomly wander the corridors to see who we could spot, and also go into the Beeb canteen for a cut price meal.

I think they were recording 'The Bitterest Pill'. So I just waited for his car to come out, and kind of flagged it down, and he wound down the window, and I remember thinking, fuck, what do I say? I then came out with the most ridiculous question ever: "I know you're a busy bloke but fancy a cuppa and a chat sometime?" I still go red to this day…. But speechless as I was, I was totally gobsmacked when he leaned out of the car window and said, "Yeah, what you doing tomorrow morning?" Now I wasn't about to tell him I had double sociology the next day, so I just said, "Err yeah, where and when?"

And so I found myself, after reasoning with my parents that this was too good a chance to miss, and persuading Mum to ring the school with an excuse (they'd grown used to this by now), at a cafe in St Christopher's Place just off Oxford Street the following morning, awaiting every Jam fan's dream, and not expecting for a moment he would actually show up. But he fucking did! Talk about the best moment of your life! Oh my god, I remember the jitters I felt, sitting outside this cafe sipping my cuppa thinking, yeah right, and then he just strolled round the corner and over the road to meet little old me, so surreal.

I couldn't tell you to this day what we spoke about, but I know we had this animated conversation for about 45 minutes about Thatcher mainly, and the state of the music scene; and having Weller ask you how many sugars you want in your tea – I mean, what the fuck? Brilliant that he met me – a treasured memory.

So, Bruce Foxton's shoes… I really do have such happy memories of those days, it always involved a whole day (and usually a call from a parent excusing you from school), but I think me and Brian made an art form of it, from dodging the train inspectors to jumping the barriers at Victoria; anything went really, as long as we achieved our goal, which was getting to Woking and finding out where our heroes lived.

It took us a few attempts but we succeeded. And probably annoyed a few neighbours in our quest! The first time we ever knocked on the door of 44 Balmoral Drive, we were absolutely terrified! "You knock" – "No, you knock"…. One of us eventually did, and when John Weller answered the door we just froze, as you would do. We were all mumbly and dumbstruck, and he just said, "D'ya wanna come in?" And, oh yeah, there we were in Paul Weller's house, with his mum Ann making us tea and biscuits, and John sitting us down in the living room, asking us questions about which gigs we'd been to and where we'd travelled from, and seeing rare videos that only the family had seen. And me and Brian, exchanging 'oh my god' glances! And then, the first time of three lifts for me, he offered us a ride back to Woking station. Top guy, top manager.

We annoyed the neighbours though, who I seem to remember were called the Carvers? I'm pretty sure we pissed them off and I think we badgered them for info. We did, however, through our annoying tactics, manage to find out where Bruce lived, and were up there like a rat up a drainpipe. And eventually, when he got home, we knocked on his door, and asked, is Bruce in? Can't remember if it was his mum or dad that answered, but Bruce appeared on the doorstep, as if it were completely normal to have fans turn up, and, after a few questions from us, asked Brian, "What size shoes are you?" Brian mumbled, "I dunno, 5 or 6". Bruce ran up the stairs, and we kinda gawped at each other for a few seconds. Until he came back down with a pristine pair of his stage shoes. And after a little conversation with Bruce we thanked him and left. So we walked away from Sheerwater with a pair of Bruce's red, white 'n' blue Jam shoes, absolutely high on that memory. I don't know if Brian still has them.

Kate Butcher

The split was a double-edged sword. I didn't cry, moan or want to set fire to my records as some did. The reason was I actually had tickets to see The Jam at Wembley Arena. I have Friday 3rd December 1982 etched onto my heart as it was not only my first time seeing The Jam, but the first time I'd ever been to a gig. (I swerved Abba three years previous and stayed in and watched the first episode of *Minder*). We didn't have good seats, and the sound wasn't the best, but I can say that I saw The Jam. So the following morning I found out that the ginger Mod kid up the road, Shippy, had a spare ticket for that night, too. This time we had even worse seats, and I started to hate the cavernous shithole.

Come Sunday, I was debating whether to go again on my own as I knew it would be the last chance I'd ever get to see the band. I borrowed a tenner off my mum and told my dad I was going to the pictures, as he'd already gone mad that I'd seen them the previous two nights. My mum knew where I was going (mum's always do).

I didn't have a ticket and there were hundreds of older blokes outside the venue, desperately looking for a brief. At one point someone had kicked a side exit door open and about 20 fans bolted straight in before security had to wrestle the door closed. Then out of nowhere this bloke walks up to me and asks me if I need a ticket. I tell him I've only got a tenner (they were fetching £30) and he says, I only want face value (£6). I nearly fainted as he gave me four pound notes back. I followed him in and couldn't believe where the seat was: FRONT STALLS!

I sat there, excited, nervous and enthralled as the support, Big Country, were only 15 rows away from me. The band departed and the DJ played some Northern Soul. Running out for a quick piss turned into a nightmare as the queues stretched down the corridors and people were getting launched out for pissing up the exit doors.

Just as I ran back to my seat, the lights dimmed and the DJ, Tony Rounce, introduced The Jam. ("The best thing on six legs!")

I stayed in my seat, dancing, pogoing and shouting until the encore. And when 'Going Underground' kicked in I raced to the front like someone had just set my Levis alight. I jumped up and down solidly for four minutes, and nearly fainted for the second time. A bloke in front of me was squashed against the stage trying to get Bruce's attention by waving like a beauty queen, and a girl behind me screamed so loud she nearly put my eardrum into next year. It ended with 'The Gift' and a majestic 1–2–3–4! And then they were gone....

I walked out of the Arena, into the damp, bleak Northwest London surroundings dazed, confused and drenched in sweat, but grinning from ear to ear, knowing that I'd seen something that was so worth getting a hard time off my old man about.

Stuart Deabill

Bruce looks on as Paul lands on his backside!
Manchester Apollo, March 1982.

It was on a Sunday morning my dad said to me, "Have you seen this?" Passing the paper over to me and pointing to the headline on about page 30!

"WELLER CALLS TIME ON THE JAM"

I stared at it for what seemed ages. I wasn't reading it right was I, surely? I searched in the other two papers my dad used to get and found an even smaller piece saying the same thing: it read something like, "Paul feels he has taken The Jam as far as he can and wouldn't want them to end up meaning nothing in 30 years' time. He would like to thank the fans for their continued support and wishes them all the best, love Paul."

Well, I wanted The Jam to be around for the next 30 years, that was for sure. I was gutted, no mention of Bruce or Rick wanting to quit, so how could Weller do this to me? After nearly five years of everything I had given him and vice versa, it couldn't be over. Well, the news spread around my area where I lived and at school, too, with people thinking they'd be the first to tell me with a glint in their eye. Bollocks, I thought; Weller will change his mind, I was sure of it.

The gig itself on the 2nd December wasn't how I planned it to be. We had seats nearer the back of the arena, and the sound got lost in this awful place. There seemed to be a lot of fighting in the crowd, too. Different fans from different parts of the UK and beyond, all wishing this wasn't a farewell gig.

As the last song finished I remember staring at Weller as he took the applause and just thought, you bastard, please don't do this, it's not too late. Silly thoughts for a 15-year-old, I suppose, but I was so gutted. Who was I gonna follow now? We made our way to the exits and out into the damp December night air. On the way home me and my mates decided we'd try and get down for the last London date on the 5th, which was a Sunday.

We heard the box office was selling a few tickets on the afternoon of the gig. We got there around 4pm to find a queue stretching around the block. My heart sank: no way were we gonna get tickets now. We still joined the queue and had only moved about 40 feet once the box office opened when someone from the arena came walking along, informing us the show was now sold out completely. As young as I was I could've punched the fuck out of him: that little twat had just ended my chance of seeing the band. We hung around until about 8pm, hoping the touts would take pity and sell at face value. No chance....

Phil Potter

SNAP! store display.

Interview with Caron Wheeler – Afrodiziak

Where did you first hear The Jam and were you a fan?

I first heard The Jam on Top Of The Pops. I wasn't a fan, though!

How did you actually get the gig?

I honestly don't remember, it's forever ago!

How did you feel when you were booked for the 'Beat Surrender' single and subsequent farewell tour?

Excited and ready to go!

How was the tour for you? Culture shock, or had you done touring before?

I recall touring America and Europe with Elvis Costello before working with The Jam. Yeah, it was a bit of a culture shock. Being a Mod/Punk band, the main thing I was fearing was the crowd spitting at the band — eeewww, lol! We didn't get spat on, though, as we insisted on performing on a high riser, way at the back of the stage, so the saliva balls wouldn't reach us. Their tour was wild and crazy!

What were the band like to work with?

They were pretty cool to work with, lovely.

Fave song that sticks out that you sang on?

'Beat Surrender'.

Any gigs that stand out? Glasgow (the first date left people in bits as the band were so powerful, we've been hearing).

They were all pretty hyped — the fans always went nuts!

Any memories of the last gig in Brighton — which wasn't a great gig, due to it being the end?

No, it's soooo long ago.

Did Weller try and tell you what to wear on stage?

No I don't think so, he just loved working with us.

Any funny incidents and memories that stick out?

I remember PW asked me out a few times.

The live performance on The Tube. Were you nervous?

Nah, I love performing live.

THE DREAMS OF CHILDREN

When The Jam split, I wasn't even born. Perhaps this gives me some sense of objectivity about what was too close for some to see or hear. I've never stood in the Sistine Chapel, but when I slid a copy of *Snap!* into my Sony Walkman and pressed play, I felt I was looking-up at the ceiling in the Apostolic Palace.

I came to The Jam backwards – I greatly admired Weller's solo work first of all. Music videos and TOTP performances would pop-up on VH1 Classic – all the great up-tempo singles. But there was one song off the *Extras* compilation that knocked me sideways: 'No One In The World', a song of loss, with the remnants of a past unavoidable.

It's a strange place to start a love affair with The Jam, but the first time I heard 'No One In The World' I didn't move a muscle until it finished. It was one of those moments where everything and nothing made sense.

I was at that age when childhood was behind me and adulthood lay ahead. You want independence but deep inside you cling to the safety of childhood. I was hanging around with my fellow adolescents, and a young boy came out of the local newsagents, his dad's arm around him – they were laughing and smiling. That moment hit like a train – a realisation. The song always takes me back to that moment – I was slowly losing my dad to adulthood. Weller's music draws you into relatable situations and illuminates them.

I had stayed in London when I was a boy/early teen, but when I went back years later, after absorbing Woking's finest – I had The Jam spinning around my head. I don't know what Londoner's think of Paul Weller's portrayal of the city, but it sound-tracked my time there. Coming from a small village, London did appear to be a strange town: a guy with a ferret on a lead; all straight lines; people rushing to get somewhere; people rushing to escape something. Blisters on your feet, christ, I can relate to that one – everything is miles away from each other.

Whenever I hear that crystalline combination of a Ricky and a Vox AC30, it's The Jam that springs to mind: not The Beatles, not Townshend. It's not just a defining rock 'n' roll sound, it's a defining sound – full-stop. Aggressive and at times a sonic tsunami. When Weller hits those isolated chord stabs, it resonated through me.

I wanted to hear everything they recorded. The song, 'Ghosts', just floors me. A song about a person, like all the best songs, all the greatest literature. 'The Bitterest Pill (I Ever Had To Swallow)' – magic does not come close! The Jam are a band with an incredible gift of turning what the heart is feeling into song. 'That's Entertainment', transcending the mundane – music that brings to mind grey skies, beating the odds and being uncommonly beautiful.

When you're a teenager, you are in need of guidance more than any other stage of life. You choose who that guide is. Paul Weller shaped my mindset – he encouraged me to question authority. There was art, craft, and beautiful aggression in his band's work: a band that you'd listen to when getting ready for a night out, for that adrenaline rush. A band which would open up the mind, and with that magic ingredient of music and words, you'd find that you don't have to accept anything – question it!

Was The Jam's look and stance important? Of course it was, but that wouldn't amount to much if their art paled in comparison. Paul Weller has music flowing right through him – you hear it, but more importantly, you just feel it. At his core, he is a songwriter – one of the very, very best. The Jam are there for moments of introspection. The Jam are there for times of directed aggression. The Jam opened up the teenage mind. God bless them.

Michael Patrick Hicks

It's the butterflies feeling in your stomach whenever you here a Jam track played on the radio, or from a passing car, or in the background of a TV programme – anywhere in fact. The joy of seeing new clips on YouTube. The fact that no matter how hard times are – and I've had a few – you've still got every record they ever made (whilst hundreds if not thousands of other records have been bought and sold); still have all the rare imports, the bootlegs, the free flexis that came with magazines; and all those magazines, all the cutout articles from newspapers; the stickers, the pin badges, the sew-on patches, T-shirts, tickets from their concerts; memories from those concerts, the singing of "you'll never walk alone" after the band had left the stage, in their penultimate concert together, Sunday evening at Wembley '82.

What did they mean to me then? On record release day, trying to be the first in the queue at the record shop, and normally succeeding; spending ages looking through every magazine and music paper for articles and mentions; travelling to Carnaby Street to get the latest Mod fashions your fave band were wearing, be it the obvious Jam shoes and the polka dot or paisley Melandi/ cavern shirts, Sta-Prest trousers, boating blazers, etc. When finding out what music and influences Paul Weller had, and learning about them, and furthering your own musical discoveries and knowledge because of these (something that has never stopped for me).

It's hard trying to explain to anyone that has never had a passion for a band, especially trying to explain just how big The Jam were in the UK in those years, but the facts are there: the straight in at Number One doesn't mean much now; but then, when record sales really meant something, it was incredible. And after the split, all their singles released again and getting back in the charts – amazing. They were just that, incredible and amazing.

Richard (Dickie) Lewellyn

WHAM BAM, HERE COMES THE JAM! From the first play of the CD I was instantly transported back in time to the sounds, energy and lyrics of this excellent Weller-led three piece, soon finding out that Bruce Foxton and Rick Buckler made up the band, and realising how relevant and influential they were to the guitar-based bands of the '90s that I had been listening to.

Before too long I'd bought all of The Jam's back catalogue that was available, playing the albums over and over. I remember the excitement I felt in hearing for the first time classics like 'Going Underground', 'Town Called Malice', 'Down in the Tube Station at Midnight' and my personal favourite, 'To Be Someone'. I wished I was old enough to have seen them live but had to make do with the occasional video being shown on TV or magazine feature, if I was lucky.

A few years later Weller started introducing Jam songs to his live sets and in recent years Foxton and Buckler reformed under the name From The Jam, with a 'Weller fella' fronting the band, performing sold-out gigs across the country. I realise this is the nearest I'll ever get to seeing The Jam play live, but for me I'm grateful for what I've seen and heard and the immense contribution to British music this band made.

They touched people's lives with their music and style and the songs are as relevant today as they were when they were first written some thirty odd years ago.

Richard Lewis

As it happens I am a great Jam fan and I regard Weller and The Jam as having provided the soundtrack to my late teens and early twenties. No band, apart from possibly The Specials, captured better the great social changes of the transition from Callaghan to Thatcher. And few writers have understood more astutely than Weller the mad frenzy of thoughts going through the heads of adolescent boys with intellectual pretensions.

Robert Peston

It was 1989 when I first heard The Jam. Sure, before then, I certainly knew of 'Eton Rifles', 'Going Underground' and 'Malice' from constant radio play and various compilation albums I had at home. But it was 1989 when I first truly HEARD them.

My mate and I, it seemed, were the only kids wearing parkas in the late '80s as we naively but fondly tried to recreate and embrace an era that existed long before either of us were born. Whilst my peers seemed to have latched on to a dreary contemporary diet of Five Star, Bobby Brown and Bros, we had taken a step back in time to explore a bygone era that fascinated us and gave us a passion like nothing we had ever experienced before. My cousin, who had been a Mod during the '79 revival, lent me his copy of *Snap!* on vinyl, and I can vividly remember spending many hours reading through the track listing and closely scanning the album pictures. Cool, clean and hard. Three geezers in sharp black-and-white suits, looking the bollocks, serious and authentic. Even on the black-and-white, tongue-in-cheek photo with the bowling shoes placed in the fridge! Who were these blokes? Where did they come from? Why did they split and where were they now?

In '89 music was generally poor and meaningless but The Jam was fresh and exciting – and it was already 12 years old! I wanted to know more about this band, this man Weller in particular, who looked so cool and knew his audience better than they knew themselves. No wonder he was the (reluctant) spokesman for a generation. He spoke our language: from 'When You're Young' to 'Thick As Thieves' (even more so later in life), 'This is the Modern World', 'Mr Clean', etc. I played *Snap!* over and over again, memorised every lyric and every sound, pretended to play the thunderous bass, Foxton style, whilst combing my hair into that classic "curtain" parting of '81 Weller.

'Ghosts' is amazing, a stark, simple ballad that has stayed with me throughout the years. The lyrics became a motto and spurs me on to this day to make the best of things and give it my best. 'Set the House Ablaze' was menacing and powerful and I sang my heart out to it from the comfort of my bedroom on a daily basis. I had the *In The City/This is the Modern World* album on one tape and played it to death, screaming out the words to 'Standards' and 'Time For Truth'. Next, I got a copy of the book, *A Beat Concerto*, for a couple of quid off a market stall and read the whole story over and over again.

Jonny Bance

Searching for the moon underwater?

Defining The Jam in so few words is surely a hopeless task. But maybe that's just the point. The Jam were always about hope, always about a belief that our mundane reality could be overcome with drive, determination and unity. We were all believers... and yet somehow along the way I fear we have lost that youthful courage, that passion, and above all that feeling.

I miss those days; I miss that feeling so I put on the music; the tunes flood over me and it's like being greeted by old friends... I am that kid that punched my bedroom wall in pent-up frustration. I am one of a dozen kids who played football in the streets, pausing only to let cars go by. I am one of a hundred kids who felt a 'Face' in check trousers and black Melandi's bowling shoes. I am one of a thousand kids that cycled to the shops to buy the singles from Woolworths during a school lunch hour and home again just to hear the B-side. I am one of 10,000 kids whose feelings were being better articulated than we ever could do ourselves. I am one of a 100,000 kids who followed the candle that The Jam held in the darkness....

And so I come to *Dig the New Breed* and the live version of 'That's Entertainment'. It ends with the rhythm of a two-beat bass drum pulse and a snare drum kick that to me, always felt like a heartbeat and a punch to the guts – and perhaps it's this that better defines The Jam more than anything I could ever write. That heartbeat will go on forever and no amount of hits we take should ever stop us believing in ourselves.

Jason Brummell

A Saturday's girl's bedroom.

It's a testament to The Jam's importance that 20 years after their split, teenagers around the world are still engraving targets onto their school desks, planning visits to Carnaby Street and trying to work out how to play 'English Rose' on the guitar. With decades of music now available at our fingertips, it shows the power of their legacy, that there is still a passion and interest in a band long departed.

I discovered *All Mod Cons* at 15 and my life changed within days. Cheap parka: check. Chewing gum: check. Moody look: check. I bored my schoolmates senseless about them, making mix-tapes, covering my work books in pictures and I even tied my school tie up the wrong way to make it look thinner. At home I was also the proud designer of my own customised Weller Wardrobe. I may have been decades out but it didn't stop me from being a complete obsessive.

Even more inspiring was discovering a band that cared about their fans so much. A band determined to break down the barriers between performers and audience, a true band of the people. It didn't matter how much of a shit day I'd had at school, because my mate Paul Weller was waiting for me at home: he knew about the girl down the road that I fancied the pants off; he knew about the teachers at school who I despised; and he knew about my old best mate who had since drifted away. He sung about the things that mattered back long ago, and guess what – these things still mattered today.

They were also the band that encouraged me to keep playing guitar until my fingers hurt; they encouraged me to look around for inspiration to lyrics; and in the karaoke age of reality shows and manufactured boy-bands, they gave me a consistent body of work to refer to and take inspiration from.

It's been years since those days. Weller's music is still the primary influence and it was definitely the turning point for me. *All Mod Cons* was the first in a chain of discoveries that without, I don't know where I'd be today. Whether it's jumping madly in a disco hall shouting along to every word of 'Going Underground' at a friends birthday party or sniggering in the back of the classroom when I realised exactly just what 'Billy Hunt' meant, this is a band that gave me music and memories to cherish forever.

Daniel Ash, The Lost Boys

A Butterfly Collection

Clockwise: BPI Gold Award for 'SNAP!'; BPI Platinum Award for 'A Town Called Malice'; BPI Platinum Award for 'Beat Surrender'.

Thanks go to Gavin Frankland for allowing the publisher the rights to reproduce part of his personal Jam collection.

Clockwise: Rick Buckler's BPI Award for 'Town Called Malice';
USA advertising for 'Sound Affects'; rare poster from 1979; early very rare poster.

Clockwise: Rick Buckler's 'boxing boots' as featured on the cover of 'SNAP!'; Rick's boating blazer from 1979; replica Wham! Rickenbacker.

Clockwise: Original poster which used to hang on Paul Weller's bedroom wall; original jacket as worn by Paul Weller for the Strangetown video, 1979; Rick Buckler tour suitcase; detail of Concorde label after band flew back from USA to celebrate first No.1 with 'Going Underground'.

Rick's Sound Affects and Transglobal Express tour jackets.

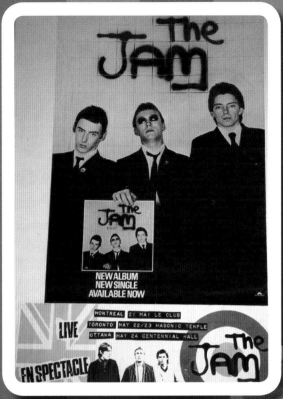

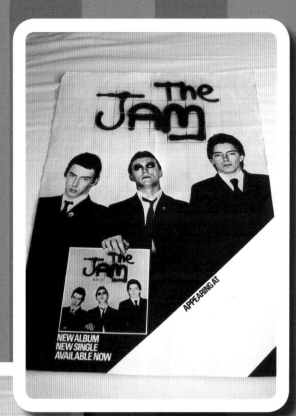

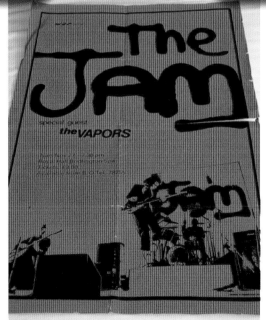

Pages 193–196: Very rare gig posters from around the world.

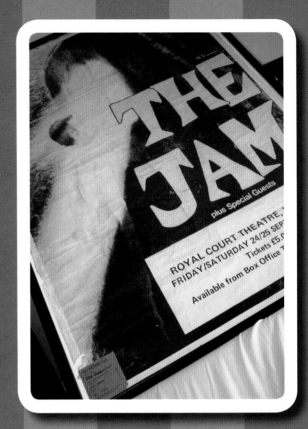

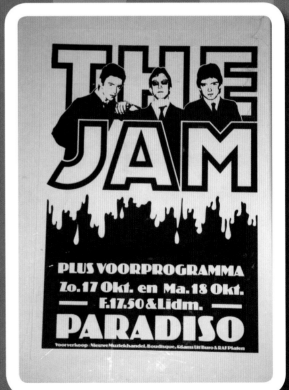

Shop display for 'Dig the New Breed'.

Rare gig posters.

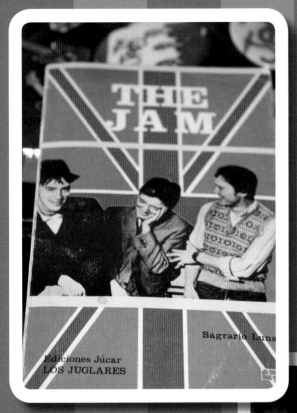

Clockwise: Extremely rare Spanish booklet; various guest passes; Rick's snare drum from the 'Big White' Premier kit.

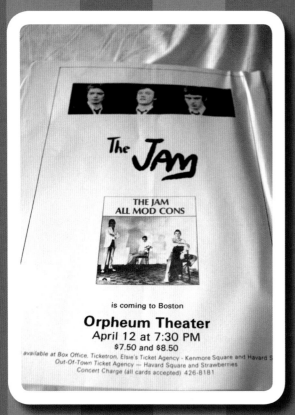

Clockwise: Flyer from cancelled gig; the gig for that date was actually Paradise Rock Club, Boston; guest passes.

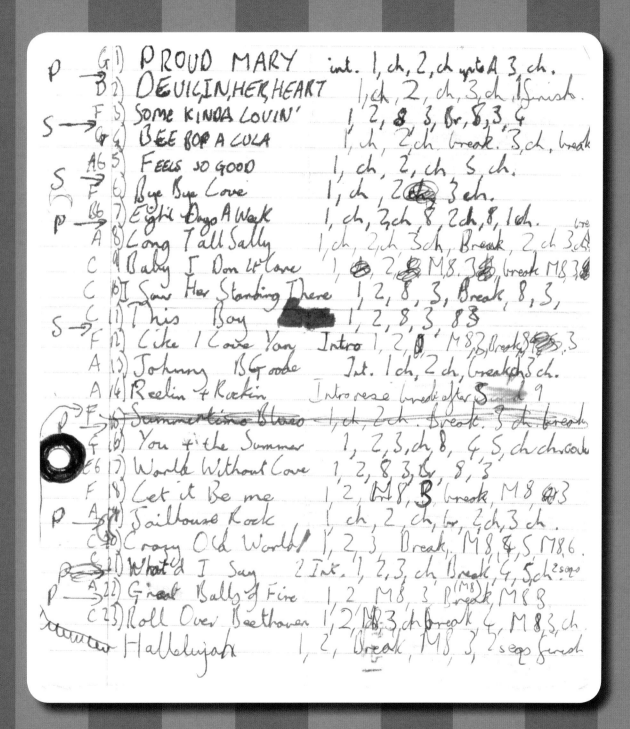

P   G 1) PROUD MARY   int. 1, ch, 2, ch up to A 3 ch.
   B 2) DEVIL, IN, HER, HEART   1, ch, 2, ch, 3, ch, 1 finish.
S → F 3) Some KINDA LOVIN'   1, 2, 8, 3, Br, 8, 3, 4
   G 4) BEE BOP A LULA   1, ch, 2 ch. break. 3, ch. break
   Ab 5) FEELS SO GOOD   1, ch, 2, ch, 3, ch.
S → F 6) Bye Bye Love   1, ch, 2 ch 3 ch.
P → Bb 7) Eight Days A Week   1, ch, 2 ch 8 2ch, 8, 1ch.
   A 8) Long Tall Sally   1, ch, 2 ch 3ch, Break, 2 ch 3 ch
   C 9) Baby I Don't Care   1, 8, 2, 8 M8, 3 8 break M8 3 8
   C 10) I Saw Her Standing There   1, 2, 8, 3, Break, 8, 3,
S → C 11) This Boy   1, 2, 8, 3, 8 3
S → F 12) Like I Love You   Intro 1, 2, 8, M8 break 8 3, 3
   A 13) Johnny B Goode   Int. 1 ch, 2 ch, break ch 3 ch.
   A 14) Reelin + Rockin   Intro vese break after 8 and 9
P → F 15) Summertime Blues   1, ch, 2 ch. Break. 3 ch break
   F 16) You + the Summer   1, 2, 3, ch 8, 4 5, ch ch coda
   Eb 17) World Without Love   1, 2, 8 3, br, 8, 3
   F 18) Let it Be me   1, 2, M8, 3 break, M8 3
P → A 19) Jailhouse Rock   1 ch, 2 ch, br, 2ch, 3 ch.
   C 20) Crazy Old World   1, 2, 3 break, M8, 4 5 M8 6.
P → 21) What'd I Say   2 Int. 1, 2, 3, ch Break, 4, 5 ch 2 sego
P → A 22) Great Balls of Fire   1 2 M8 3 (M8) break, M8 3
   C 23) Roll Over Beethoven   1, 2 M8 3 ch break 4 M8 3 ch.
   Hallelujah   1, 2, break, M8 3, 2 sego finish

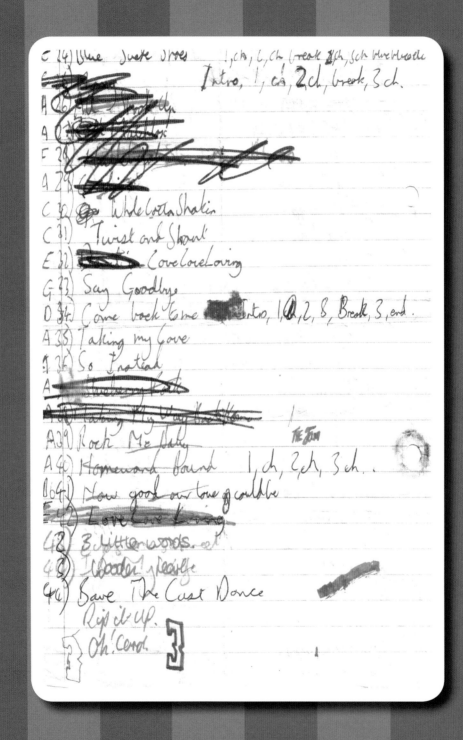

C 24) Blue Suede Shoes   1, ch, c, ch break 2ch, ch blue blue suede
~~C~~   Intro, 1, ch, 2 ch, break, 3 ch.
A 26) ~~Shake it Up~~
A 2~~7)~~ ~~Hanabi~~
E 2~~8)~~ ~~~~
A 2~~9)~~ ~~~~
C 3~~0)~~ ~~Go~~ Whole Lotta Shakin
C 31) Twist and Shout
E 3~~2)~~ ~~~~ Love Love Loving
G 33) Say Goodbye
D 34) Come back to me   ~~~~ Intro, 1, Ch, 2, 8, Break, 3, end.
A 35) Taking my love
~~?~~ 36) So Impatient
A ~~37)~~ ~~~~
A ~~38)~~ ~~~~
A 39) Rock Me Baby   THE JAM
A 40) Homeward Bound   1, ch, 2, ch, 3 ch.
B 64 1) How good our love could be
E ~~42)~~ ~~Love Love Loving~~
~~43)~~ 3 little words ~~ool~~
~~44)~~ ~~Wonderful People~~
45) Save The Last Dance
     Rip it up.
   ~~?~~ Oh! Carol.   3

1) Bye Bye Love. [F] 1ch2 ch, ch.
2) Save the Last Dance [Eb] 1, 2 8, 3 8, 3.
3) World Without Love [Eb] 1, 2, 8, 3, Br 8, 3.
4) Devil In His Heart [D] 1, ch, 2 ch, 3ch, 1finish
5) Crazy Old World [C] 1, 2,3, break M8, 4, 5M8 C
6) 3 Little Words [D]
7) Let it Be Me [F] 1, 2, 8, 3 Br M8 3.
8) Love Love Loving [E] 1, ch, 2 ch, M8 3 M8 3.
9) Proud Mary [G] 1 ch, 2 ch, up to A, 3 ch.
10) So Instead [A] Int, 1, 2 ch, 3 br, ch, 4, 5 Int.
11) This Boy [G] 1, 2 8 3 8 3
12) Remember [G] Int, 1ch, 2ch, M8, 3ch, 1ch, M8 3ch
13) How Good Out [Bb]
14) Wooden Heart [D] 1, 2 M8 3, br, 1, 2, M8 3.
15) You & the Summer [D] 1, 2 br, 2, br ch
16) I Saw Her Standing There [C] 1, 2 8 3 br 8 3.
17) Hallelujah [G] 1, 2, br, M8, 3 2ocq fin
18) Bee Bop a Lula [G] 1, ch, 2ch br, 3ch, break
19) Jailhouse Rock [A] 1, ch, 2ch br, 2ch, 3ch
20) 8 days a Week [Bb] 1, ch, 2ch 8 2ch 8 1ch
21) Some Kinda Lovin [E] 1 12, 8, 3 Br, 8, 3, 4.
22) Little Girl Cryin [C] 1, ch, 2ch, brch, M8 3ch.

23) Love has Died   [A]   1, d, 2 ch, M 8 dbr 3ch
24) ~~Itsons~~ Oh Carol   [A] [G]
25) I am In Love   [A] [G]
26) Rip it Up   [C]
27) Baby I Don't Care   [C]
28) Johnny B Goode   [A] [C]
29) What'd I Say   [C]
30) Great Balls of Fire   [A]
31) Feel's So Good   [A] [G]
32) Like I Love You   [F]
33) Say Goodbye   [G]
34) Takin My Love   [A]
35) Matchbox   [A]
36) Roll Over Beethoven   [C]
37) Whole Lotta Shakin   [C]
38) ~~Come~~ Twist & Shout   [C]
39) Blue Suede Shoes   [P]
40) Reelin & Rockin   [A]
41) Long Tall Sally   [A]
42) Rock & Roll Music   [A]

BBC radio 1

presents

IN CONCERT

THE JAM

DEPARTMENT S

25th August 1978

DAY
TICKET

READING
FESTIVAL

READMISSION

e this portion

READING ROCK '78

Thames side Arena, Richfield Avenue...................August 25.26.27

Admit bearer to ▮▮▮▮▮▮▮▮▮▮▮▮ | On this day

ARENA ONLY	FRIDAY
CAMPSITE ONLY	SATURDAY
	SUNDAY

0927 Issued to ▮▮▮▮▮▮

of NOTTINGHAM QUARTERLY   By ▮▮▮▮▮▮

Odd Fellow Palæet
store sal

International Concert
Organisation A/S presents

The Jam

Tirsdag d. 3. marts 1981
kl. 20,00

№ 2031

Wed. 10th December 1980 8pm
Malvern Winter Gardens

£3.75 Adv. £4 Door

CHERRY BAM PRESENT

THE JAM

THE PHOTOS Dec 20th

HEADS
Cambridge Corn Exchange
Monday 11th February

THE JAM

50
8.00

No 781

GUILDFORD CIVIC HALL

OUTLAW PRESENTS

A special Christmas Show with

THE JAM

Thursday 11th December 7.30pm

ALL TICKETS £3.75

№ 0205

ARMADILLO WORLD HEADQUARTERS
Presents

01486 SEC ROW SEAT
GEN. ADM.
MAR. 22, 1980
ADMIT ONE THIS DATE ONLY

★ THE JAM ★
WITH SPECIAL GUEST
THE BEAT

MAR
22
1980

AUSTIN, TEXAS
SATURDAY
9:00 P.M.

NO REFUND PRICE NO EXCHANGE

$4.00
ADVANCE

SEC ROW SEAT
GEN. ADM. 01486
THE JAM DOOR
$5.00

01486

MAR. 22, 1980.

1451 BCW14
67 LOWER
LOGE

LL ADULT

CHA LBTY1

CC 8.50
price

A

19 23FEB

WARFIELD THEATRE
982 MARKET STREET - S.F

BILL GRAHAM PRESENTS

THE JAM

SAT MAR 15 1980 8:00 P

LEFT ADULT

LL CC 19 $ 8.50

MUSICMACHINEMUSICMACHINEMUSICMACHINE
MUSIC MACHINE
CAMDEN HIGH STREET
FRIDAY 12th DECEMBER 1980
Christmas Show with

THE JAM

LIVE ON STAGE 10 p.m.
Doors 7.30 p.m.
Minimum age 18 years

ADVANCE TICKETS £3.75

№ 699

Mr Lovell.
Recommendations
agreed

M E M O R A N D U M

TO: Director of Entertainments   FROM: Hall Manager, Colston Hall.
    and Publicity   KL/IMT

c.c. Entertainments Manager

Re: THE JAM - 21st MAY 1979

The above concert was the second appearance of The Jam at Colston Hall. Their previous concert on 26th November 1978 passed without many problems, despite rumours that earlier concerts on the tour had turned out unruly and uncontrollable. I had discussed security measures at considerable length with the Tour Manager and agreed to allow a limited number of the audience to stand near the stage, their numbers being discreetly controlled by Security Stewards at the side of platform and three front gangways. The purpose of this arrangement was to avoid the Band calling the audience to the front stage area. On that occasion the Band behaved well, and the audience were easily controlled. My notes on this concert of 26th November 1978 conclude 'Very Good Reaction - no problems!'

For the concert on 21st May 1979 I again discussed security measures at length with the Group's Manager. I made it quite clear that whilst I was willing not to have men lined up against the stage I would control the three front stalls gangways thereby limiting the number of people at the front of stage area. This arrangement was agreed by the Group's Manager on the understanding that the Band would not encourage the audience to move forward.

The Band were introduced by their Manager who announced 'On your Feet, NOT on the Seats, COME DOWN THE FRONT.' This obviously had the effect that we had tried to avoid, the audience surged into the gangways and tried to rush for the front (including people in the Balcony). The Bouncers did well in holding all gangways at the cross-sections in both Balcony and Rear Stalls, but many came over the seats of the first few rows to form an uncontrollable seething mass at the front of stage. Even if the bouncers had been along the front of the stage, this surge could not have been prevented. About a dozen seats fell apart, due mainly to the current state of repair, although a few were vandalised.

I spoke to Mel Bush's Tour Manager of the sheer idiocy of the Group's Manager; both had been present at the afternoon's discussions. The Tour Manager told me that he just couldn't understand him doing it, but he always does!

I understand that The Jam are pencilled for 12th and 13th November 1979. I strongly recommend that this booking is not accepted.

I have spoken to MEL Bush's Office who have asked me not to do anything about these dates until they speak to us later. I have told them that it is your decision ultimately but that I will recommend that the Jam do not appear at Colston Hall again. They say that they will give us assurances but in my opinion the Group's Manager has proved that he is totally irresponsible and that any assurances are not to be trusted.

-2-

With all concerts of this type, it is the performers on stage that have the control, regardless of numbers of security men. The majority of groups that appear at Colston Hall accept this and show a responsible attitude.

The Jams' Manager has shown a total disregard to a sense of responsibility. Had it not been for the quick reaction of the Security Stewards things could have been much worse. I appreciate that we employ Security Stewards to control the audience but I would not expect them to have to deal again with the consequences of the irresponsible action of the Bands' Management.

Hall Manager
24 May 1979.

Naughty boys ...

204

John Weller, Manchester 1982.

JOHN WELLER

This book would not be complete without some mention of Paul's father and The Jam's manager, John Weller. In the course of our research we did not come across one person who had a bad word to say about him. We're sure there were some that didn't appreciate his tough-talking, bluff approach, but we considered this to be a testament to the respect in which he was held. One person even described John as being someone who didn't compromise himself in the cut-throat music industry.

So in John Weller's case all we could find was admiration from people who had at some time crossed his path. During the research for this section we encountered numerous stories from young fans who had met John in soundchecks or in the doorways of venues. One fan said that John "never took the fans for granted". This was something John and The Jam will always be remembered for, and possibly has never been equalled by any other band.

John, once famously referring to the early days, said that he didn't have a thousand pounds to give to the band, but he did have a thousand hours. Over a 30-year history of involvement with his son Paul's musical career, we can only guess how many man-hours John gave to The Jam, The Style Council and Paul Weller's solo career. When John Weller passed on, he was 77 years old.

John was born on 28th November 1931 in Brighton. His parents owned a café. In his youth he took up boxing and went on to become a welter-weight winner of the ABA's Southern Counties Championship.

After school John served a brief apprenticeship as a journalist at the *Chichester Observer* before being shipped off to the RAF to do his National Service. His duties in the RAF included being a physical training instructor (PTI) and boxing for the RAF.

John then met Ann and they were married a year later in the Woking registry office. A year after Paul arrived, and four years later his sister Nicky.

From the family home John provided for his family the best he could. He worked on building sites and in the evenings as a taxi driver. Then he responded to his son's interest in music, purchased a guitar and backed his son's band all the way. Some may even say that John was partly responsible for holding the band together and propping them up at their most vulnerable times and carrying them forward. John's sturdy belief in his son's career and The Jam has always been recognised by those who matter, and rightly so. Of course Ann and Nicky played their parts, too, and made sure no one got ripped off – unlike other fan clubs that were run back then.

The solid bond that developed between John and Paul was often glimpsed by The Jam fans and those around the band. It stood out because it was rare to work with your Dad and even rarer in music. Paul is often quoted as saying that both of them have drank in every airport bar in the world together.

John Weller died on 22 April 2009, after having spent a month in the Runnymede Hospital in Chertsey. He had been suffering from vascular dementia.

At John's funeral on 5th May 2009, Paul's funeral floral tribute was in the design of a pair of red boxing boots in a blue ring. The word "Babe" was also included in the floral design.

John's funeral was held at the Woking crematorium. 'Going Underground' was played. The ceremony was well attended and included relatives, Bruce Foxton, Gary Crowley, D.C. Lee and Mick Talbot. There was also a floral tribute from Roger Daltrey.

Man About Town – Memories of John Weller

John Weller was brilliant to me. In 1980, I went to Brighton to see The Jam on my own. I checked in at a cheap B&B nearby, then went to the venue. John Weller invited me for a drink at the Grand Hotel where the band were camped. John asked me where I was staying? I told him I was staying at the cheap B&B. John told me to stay at the Grand, as they had a spare room. (The person who had this room went home after the gig, so it was empty.) I told him that it was nice of him to offer but I had already checked in to this B&B and my bag was in the room. John said that he'd get someone to come and get my bag. He said, "You can have a good breakfast free, and it's a fantastic room! Don't worry, I'll make sure you'll be safe!" John got this road crew geezer (I can't remember his name) to come with me to my B&B, cos it was late at night, and he carried my bag to the room at the Grand.

John phoned the room as soon as we got there. The guy (road crew) picked up the phone: I could hear John saying, "Is Keiko alright? You just come back here to see me, no messing about, ok?" That was one of my stories, it shows how kind John was: he always looked after me, like a dad.

I remember what he used to say to me:

"I don't like you taking a milk train late at night on your own."

"You pay for the travel, we get you a pass, ok?"

"The boys [road crews] who work for us are good boys, but be careful with them, cos they love women. If they said to you like, offer a meal or drink, just say no – you know what I mean? Good girl!"

"Have something to eat girl – drink after eat, ok?"

John knew my age (I was 19 or 20 at the time), but because I couldn't speak much English, I just understood what people were saying; and I probably looked about 15! He really took care of me. I didn't know Ann personally but John always told me how great she was. No wonder Paul and Nicky are such great people.

Keiko

John Weller was everything that everybody has said about him. He was just a diamond geezer. I remember this time when he really came up trumps. It was at the Michael Sobell gig and I had a broken leg. He came over and he was with Kenny and they just got me a chair and sat me on the side.

There were other times when John would let us into soundchecks (if you got there early enough). That's just what he was like. It was the whole concept of the band. He was all for the fans. I mean all three of the band were approachable back then, but it was John who would do the most.

I think the first time that I met John (and the band) was at one of the Rainbow gigs in 1979. There was me and a few mates and we got in for the soundcheck and it was just fantastic. All the girlfriends at the time, like Gill Price, were there. It was like a mini-gig because there were 30 other people there. The Jam would just carry on with the soundcheck and then at the end they would hang about and sign things for us. It's what they were all about, including John Weller.

Jon Abnett

His unwavering belief in Paul and the band was one of their strengths. He didn't suffer fools, but he was an unbelievable man.

Gary Crowley

John took an interest from day one. He was a really devoted fella. John was also really good at keeping the band together because young bands do have a lot of bust ups.

Steve Brookes

I don't really have much to add about John. Of course I have lots of memories of him but I'm not sure they pertain to The Jam – more to TSC days and my personal memories.

John's love for and loyalty to Paul was immense, I don't know how else to put it. He became my manager by default, really. He offered to look after me and, with no other contacts and no knowledge, I went along with it. There were times when it felt like John and Ann were my favourite auntie and uncle. I don't think John ever made a penny out of me – and of course he looked after Paul first – but he looked after me well, respectful of my age and naivety but always a real devil who gave no concessions when it came to a game of rummy, for example. I used to love to spend time with him on the tours, hanging out on the coach, playing cards, listening to his stories. Bear in mind, I was 18 – someone of that age had to be pretty special to command my attention.

After a gap of many years, I saw John again in 2001 (I think it was the 'Days of Speed' tour), backstage at the Albert Hall and I was quite overwhelmed. Nicky had invited me to John's birthday party but I hadn't been able to make it, so she asked me to come to the gig instead. First, Ann was in the box Nicky had given me tickets for, so that was emotional. Then Ann sent me down to see Paul and John. Lovely as it was to see Paul after a gap of about 10 years, seeing John was even better. The big bear hug, the ripping open of his shirt to show me his operation scar… and everyone – EVERYONE – was asking, "Where's your daughter?" It was very weird at the time that Paul, Ann and John all asked that question, but with hindsight, I realised that these are family people. Family is what matters to them, and if they take you in and treat you as family, they will always regard you and yours as family.

More than anything, John wanted me to grab every opportunity and to make money wherever it was offered. I have to respect him for that, even though I turned down many of the opportunities he got for me and even though our principles weren't the same. He was trying to look out for me and he was smart and, really, he was right – it was a short term thing and he wanted me to make a profit while it lasted. On tour, some of the best nights I had were the ones in the hotel bar with John and Kenny, Dave Liddle, et al.

The first tour I did with TSC, John and Kenny tried to fleece me of all my PDs (*per diems*) on the first day. I let them think I was a novice and won a tidy sum, thanks to my nan, who'd taught me rummy at an early age. I bought a lovely Kodak disc camera with my winnings in Amsterdam. A week or so later, they beat me hands down. I told Ann, with my best, sad, 'I'm only 18' face on, that they'd made me play cards and I didn't know what was going on when they said let's play for a pound a point. She bollocked them both and made them give me my money back.

Another great story about John was also in Amsterdam, the second TSC tour in Europe, I think, because Dee was there. Dee and I were sharing a room and we had a day off. John had been bitching at us both for days about not wearing 'pretty' clothes and not being girly enough. When we arrived in Amsterdam, we had nothing to do until that night, when there was a record company reception in the hotel. So John gave Dee and I £100 each and said, "Go out and buy yourselves something pretty". So… with an extra ton to go with our PDs, we went out, bought a cheap, gaudy, plastic hair slide each, then spent the day on the lash, buying records, and ended up back in the room ordering champagne on room service. We turned up at the reception, trashed and wearing big, plastic hair slides… which we told everyone John had bought for us.

Somewhere, I have a photograph that I took of him on a plane. I was winding him up during some turbulence. His face in that photo is the same as his face when he saw those hair slides and when Ann made him give me my money back.

Tracie Young

I went down to Woking. I was on my own. Now I knew that I was on a lost cause, given that all the tickets had sold out for the Wembley Arena dates, so I did what you do when you are infatuated and obsessed with a band like The Jam, and won't take no for an answer. So, yep, I got on the train and made my way to Woking. And John and Ann just made it seem so normal: "Come in love, where you from?", and half an hour later I was in John Weller's car, listening to tapes of his son aged 14 singing 'One Hundred Ways'. That three minute journey meant so much to me, I can't describe how it felt! A moment and a melody I would never forget, and a song I would hear in my heart for so many years, until someone posted it on YouTube.

But no one can possibly replicate the words John said, as he deposited me at Woking station. It makes me laugh now, but the memory of John Weller in that gruff voice, going, "And make sure you ring your mum!" "Ok, I promise!" Always one to look out for fans, bless him. He also promised me he'd get me +1 on the guest list for all the Wembley gigs. And he did just that!! He got me guest passes into the box by the stage, for all five nights. What a guy, what a memory. Didn't stay in the box much, though!

Kate Butcher

At the beginning Polydor wanted to ease John out and I was told that it would help me if it could be achieved. As there was so much shit going down, I decided to ignore everything they said. John was tight with Paul, Bruce and Rick, and I didn't fancy going to Paul and saying, sack your dad. The replacement they had in mind was a good manager, but not for The Jam and had it happened, Paul would have probably smacked him on the nose. I have never believed that by changing the manager it would have guaranteed The Jam any more success and it might have had a negative effect, with the band imploding.

Over the years, I have read many disingenuous remarks disparaging John, and whilst I don't think he could manage U2 or Radiohead, *nobody* else could have managed The Jam and Paul Weller. Paul wasn't the easiest person to deal with and it didn't make any difference that John was his dad. The musical highs and lows were down to Paul and if John couldn't do anything about them, no one else could. John was an intrinsic part of the success and the last three decades has proved all the doubters wrong, with John having the last laugh on all of them.

I often get asked for stories about John but I don't want him haunting me from his grave!

Dennis Munday

When did you first meet John?

It was at that first gig at the Red Cow.

Was it true that Chris Parry gave John six grand in readies as he didn't have a bank account?

Yes, that's my understanding! John was very working man's club in his style of management early on. It was quite refreshing as he wasn't some sort of middle-class artistic representative and told it like it was. I don't think John knew much about the record industry and it's politics; he had to learn a lot on that score, but he knew about it as much as the band.

I think he did as well by the band as anyone else would have, if not a lot better in some instances. Eventually I think it led to the band being very one-sided, though. They were a band in the beginning, all new to the game, but once Paul started to establish himself as the leader and the main songwriter, the others became sidekicks, I suppose.

Because John was managing it was hard for him not to favour his son, naturally.

Bill Smith

OUTRO

What happened after the band split is well documented. Paul started The Style Council, Rick joined Time UK and Bruce went solo. John continued to manage TSC and some fans even forgave them. All 18 of The Jam's singles re-entered the Top 75 in the January of 1983 as Polydor spotted a good little earner.

For us, we believe that The Jam split at the right time: no other band that we know finished at the top of their game, number one with the nation's youth; and they avoided doing the predictable, boring rubbish that most bands inevitably do when they go past the point of no return.

They've never reformed, and why would we want them to? It's never going to be the same. Although this book is about nostalgia, it's a celebration of a feeling, an ideal, our youth, and a chance to remember the gigs, the records, the clothes and the shared passion. Not to try and recreate the past.

That's just our opinion, anyway.

The Jam changed lives, brought people together, took on the world and left a legacy that keeps a solid bond in all our hearts for the Woking Wonders.

We'll leave the last words for John Weller that greeted many an audience as the band were just about to take the stage.

"PLEASE PUT YOUR HANDS TOGETHER FOR THE BEST FUCKING BAND IN THE WORLD... THE JAAAAAMMM!!!"

THE JAM FAN CLUB

No exact membership figure can be obtained. The fanclub was run from the family home by Nicky and Ann Weller.

Thanks extended to Jon Abnett for allowing the publisher to reproduce part of his collection.

Thank you for your enquiry. Club membership is £2 per annum and entitles you to 6 bi-monthly newsletters which will give you advance notice of The Jam's activities, background information and other specials.

To enrole, please send 6 stamps, along with a £2 postal order to the address below. These will be returned to you via the bi-monthly newsletter etc.

Yours sincerely,

Nikki Weller

The Jam,
44 Balmoral Drive,
Maybury Estate,
Woking,
Surrey.

25

The Jam CLUB
Jon Abnett
Paul Weller Bruce Foxton Rick Buckler

Original introduction fan club letter and membership card, *circa*. Spring 1978. Most subsequent letters were black-and-white photocopies.

Hello,
Welcome to the Jam Club.
Here are a few introductory bits and pieces that we have put together
especially for the club. We will be sending the first news-letter
out, in about Sept. This is the earliest we are able to send them
out due to many printing errors.
The letters will tell you of activities that the Jam will involved
in, and there will also be competitions, special offers, and many other
things, that are being sorted out at this time, all in the interest
of you the members.
Thank you for all your support this year,
From myself and The Jam.
Your's
Nikki Weller (Miss)

The Jam Club
44 Balmoral Drive
Maybury Estate
Woking
Surrey

Nikki Weller

Hello,
Well we've just returned from a new 'sell out'
tour of the U.S.A. The reaction from the audience
was very responsive to say the least! It seems the
States have finally realized that they need new
'live' groups to relate too, not the 'laid back'
bands that up till now have dominated the
airwaves. We might be returning to the States
sometime in September.
We start touring England on May 4TH – 25TH
following that there will probably be some
recording hopefully for a new single.
Take care & thanks

The Jam Club
44 Balmoral Drive
Maybury Estate
Woking
Surrey

Bruce Foxton

To all our friends &
fans out there!
I would just like to
inform you of what the
Jam's been up to over the
past few weeks.
Firstly we've been in the
studio's, recording our latest
single titled 'DAVID WATTS',
coupled with 'A' BOMB in
WARDOUR ST'. We hope you
like it!
Secondly we are to
play a series of 5 shows
at the end of July,
starting at Guildford
Civic Hall on the 30TH July. These will be the
last of our shows until our next album is
completed hopefully, in October. Oh, by the
way, don't forget 'READING FESTIVAL' on the
25TH August! Hope to see you there
All the best
Bruce Foxton

Some 'freebie' offerings ...

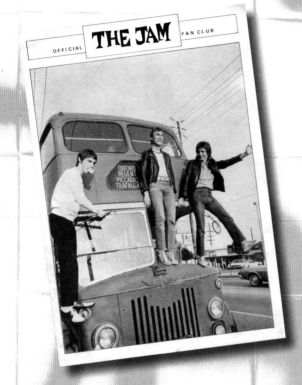

OFFICIAL **THE JAM** FAN CLUB

The JAM

OFFICIAL FAN CLUB BOOK

JAM PACT
SPRING TOUR 1979

OFFICIAL BOOKLET

Coventry, 1978
Pic: Denis O'Regan

Tour Dates

4th May, 1979	SHEFFIELD	University
5th	SHEFFIELD	University
6th	NEWCASTLE	City Hall
8th	SALFORD	University
10th	LONDON	Rainbow
11th	LONDON	Rainbow
12th	LOUGHBOROUGH	Auditorium
14th	EXETER	University
15th	LIVERPOOL	University
16th	LIVERPOOL	University
18th	GLASGOW	Strathclyde University
19th	GLASGOW	Strathclyde University
21st	BRISTOL	Coulston Hall
22nd	BIRMINGHAM	Odeon
24th	PORTSMOUTH	Guildhall

Hope you like/d "STRANGE TOWN + BUTTERFLY COLLECTOR" and thanks (once again) for your support, it sold 100,000 copies in 3 days which was fantastic. "STRANGE TOWN" is a very diverse song, the 1st part starts with the protagonist* wondering in an unfriendly town (not necessarily LONDON) who ends up gaining great confidence from his loneliness and ostracism. But make of it what you will!

We go to the U.S.A. in April for 2 weeks, headlining in 2 to 3,000 seater gigs. Radio wise in the states "ALL MOD CONS" is doing well (46th most played lp or something)

After that we'll be doing a 10 date mini tour around the country (not the only tour this year, must stress) Most of the gigs will be unseated - there's a lot of UNIVERSITIES which will definately be open gigs (not JUST STUDENTS) so write and tell us if you get refused a ticket, and the seated gigs will hopefully have some rows taken out.

Anyway we'll see you then I hope and again (always again!) thank you for standing by us

Best Wishes
Paul Weller.

P.S. All mod cons is almost gold!   * LOOK THEM UP I DID!

Hello,

firstly thanks for buying 'Eton Rifles' and making it a hit! I think its one of the best things we've ever done and I would rank it alongside 'Tube Station'. 'SETTING SONS' the new lp is out on the 16th and Coinciding is our new tour, which starts officially on the 20th, which takes in 28/29 dates.

Obviously its impossible to play everywhere on one tour, but apologies to those people who se towns we arent playing THIS time. We're also going to be recording a few dates which may turn out to be a live lp next year.

The new album is a change of direction (not as radical as 'mod cons' maybe?) with a lot of emphasis on melody and rythmn. The most difficult track to record was "LITTLE BOY SOLDIERS" which was done in 3 stages. "Heatwave" was done live with Rudi (ex-VERY SPEX) on sax and Mick Talbot (MERTON PARKAS) on Piano and "SMITHERS-JONES" has a string section, which makes it sound almost classical!

Anyway I hope you like it and as always thanks for all the support in the year and best wishes to you,

Paul Weller.

Hello

I hope you all enjoyed your christmas and thankatec for a great tour. 'Setting Sons' has gone silver and gold, eton rifles went silver and 'all mod cons' went gold. Hopefully we will be releasing another single soon into the new year, it wont be anything off the album, but some new material. Also a small tour of america is planned. For touring here we would like to do a lot of small ten date tours. A happy new year to everybody and thanks for all the cards.

Rick.

August 80'.

Hello all,

We have enclosed Tour Dates for the October/November Tour,
hope this will help some of you in getting tickets early.

We have also enclosed a list of equipment used by the Jam as a
lot of fans write and ask what equipment they use, so Dave the
Guitar rodie has put a list together.

The Jam have returned from Japan, and were very impressed with
everything, I think next to the British fans the Japanese must
come second in terms of enthusiasm and energy.

As you most probably know the new single 'Start' comes out on the 15th
of August, it is a little different from the last single and the
'B' side is called 'Liza Radley'.

N.Weller.

Recording Details 'Start'.

'Start' was the fourth new song started (in May) in the sessions
for the next L.P., it was written in the morning, rehearsed and recorded and finished by 1.O'Clock. It was one of those songs that
worked like that, much the same way as 'The Dreams of Children!

The overall effect we were going for was one of simplicity, that's
why there are very few overdubs, and the overall theme is basically
communication.

Liza Radley

This was the third sond started in the May sessions. Assorted instruments were used on this amoung some were: Accoustic and Spanish
guitars, assirted bells and Bruce an accordian adding a slightly
French sound to it.

P. Weller.

The JAM

Manager : John Weller

January, 1980.

Hello everybody,

Hope you all had a good Christmas and New year.

As you know the Jams tour was a great success, and we would all like to
thank you for such a good response.

As you can see in Ricks letter, they received some more discs, but this time
two were gold. We hope to have another competition soon, so that is in the
process of being thought up.

We hope to have a new merchandise form for you all this year, so they will be
sent out, as soon as possible.

Thanks for the years support,

Yours,

Nikki Weller.

P.S. <u>Please</u> when writing to the Fan Club, <u>Please</u> quote fan no:

Hello,
We'll be in the U.S. if A by the time
you read this I expect, we're out here
for 4 to 5 weeks, an album is in at 140 in
the Billboard charts, which believe it or not is pretty
good for the states, so things are looking better
there. Hope you like the new single which is out
on the 17th called "GOING UNDERGROUND" and "THE
DREAMS OF CHILDREN" and is a double 'A' side, there's
also a live E.P. containing 'TUBE STATION', 'MODERN WORLD'
and 'AWAY FROM THE No 5' all recorded at the Rainbow.
The first 100,000 will have the E.P. and will cost
£1.49. after that it will just be the single.
We'll be doing some one-off gigs
when we get back, and quite extensive recording
for the next LP. cut hopefully in September.
Also around that time should be a book about us
which is being written at the moment.
Anyway that's about it apart from
saying thanks for the Valentine cards young ladies
sent us and look after yourselves.
all the best and thanks. Paul Weller.

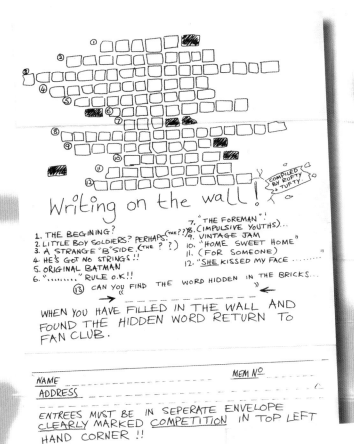

Writing on the wall!

1. THE BEGINING?
2. LITTLE BOY SOLDIERS? PERHAPS (THE??)
3. A STRANGE "B" SIDE (THE ??)
4. HE'S GOT NO STRINGS !!
5. ORIGINAL BATMAN
6. "........." RULE O.K !!

7. "THE FOREMAN":
8. (IMPULSIVE YOUTHS)...
9. VINTAGE JAM
10. "HOME SWEET HOME"
11. (FOR SOMEONE)
12. "SHE KISSED MY FACE ...."

COMPILED BY RUFTY + TUFTY

(13) CAN YOU FIND THE WORD HIDDEN IN THE BRICKS...

WHEN YOU HAVE FILLED IN THE WALL AND FOUND THE HIDDEN WORD RETURN TO FAN CLUB.

NAME _____ MEM No _____
ADDRESS _____

ENTREES MUST BE IN SEPERATE ENVELOPE CLEARLY MARKED COMPETITION IN TOP LEFT HAND CORNER !!

237.

Hi,

The Jam's new single will be out on the 16th October 1981 and it is called Absolute Beginners, with Tales from the River Bank on the flip side. The photo on the sleeve was taken by Derek D'Sonza who is a fan club member, we thought we would give him a chance..

The Xmas dates are 12th and 13th December at Sobell Centra, London, 14th and 15th December at Hammersmith Palais. Tickets are not available from the fan club, but members can get tickets by sending a cheque or postal order to the value of £4.50 to:

M.C.P.,
P.O.Box 124,
Walsall,
West Midlands.

Also enclose a S.A.E. for reply before November 15th 1981. Hope this helps you to obtain your tickets easily.

Competition Time

A word puzzle called 'Writing on The Wall' is this month's comp. Prizes will be six pairs of tickets for the London gig's of your choice. If any of the winners cannot for some reason get to the London Gigs (ie too far) the tickets will be valid for the Major British Tour, in the New Year, which will hope-fully be nearer to you.

Your competition form must be sent on it's own in a seperate envelope clearly marked Competition.

The Jam have been doing some T.V. programmes for Swedish and Belgium television. Also they will be doing Swop Shop on the 20th October and the B-15 Radio Show on 25th October, doing 4 live numbers.

Don't forget the C.N.D. march on the 24th October along the Thames Embankment. The Jam will be performing along with other top groups. Hope you can make that date.

Nikki Weller.

p.s. Quote membership number when writing to fan club.

Greetings Earthlings!   1/2/82

Hope you are all well
and in fine spirit. Find enclosed a flexi-
disc of "Tales from the Riverbank", its a re-rec-
orded version we did originally for the LP but
eventually decided not to use. I suppose the
main difference is the added brass (sax + trumpet)
which is how we've been doing it live. Anyway
I hope you like it, I personally really like the
song and feel it was a bit 'overlooked' on the
B side of A. beginners.

We're using the brass players
on the forthcoming tour, I think they're the only
other instruments we can add without losing
any of our own sound. That is they (hopefully)
add to our sound and not water it down.

The sax player's name is Keith and the
trumpeter is Steve, both great geezers. We've
used a lot on the LP, which brings me to :—

The LP is out 12th March, called →

→ "THE GIFT". Its got eleven tracks which are —

SIDE 1

1. HAPPY TOGETHER.
2. GHOSTS.
3. PRECIOUS (Re-mix sort of!)
4. JUST WHO IS THE 5 o'CLOCK HERO?
5. TRANS-GLOBAL EXPRESS.

I will elaborate
nearer the time!

SIDE 2

1. RUNNING ON THE SPOT.
2. CIRCUS (Bruce's song)
3. THE PLANNERS DREAM GOES WRONG.
4. CARNATION.
5. TOWN CALLED MALICE.
6. THE GIFT.

All the rest of the songs are mine. I suppose
the over all sound / effect is quite soul influenced, but not necessarily Tamla Motown. I really
wanted to try and create a 1980's brand of
soul. That is music to set your soul on fire!
Most of the songs have a happy feeling which
makes a bleedin' change! I've kept the lyrics
fairly simple and straightforward no arty/farty

Stuff but obviously you will make your own
minds up.

I'm also looking forward to the tour,
it'll be great to play some new songs, that
was what was missing in the summer '81
& fun (what fun!?) tour. After the U.K tour
we're off to Europe (dates of which will be passed
onto you in case you can make any of them)
then a few dates in the U.S.A (cheeeeeesss
johhnnnyy!) then Canada and Japan and
then home. We're also trying to fix up a big
gig in the summer which will be a C.N.D.
gig. No details as yet of that though.

I was genuinely surprised at the N.M.
polls, I didn't think we had done enough
last year to get anywhere. But to anyone who
did vote for us - Ta! I don't know about
'most wonderful human being' though, I've a long
way to go yet! I have given up drinking though!

Lastly, I will leave you with the →

→ overall ~~ideals~~ behind the Gift — that is the next
time you think "is it worth it?" I hope the songs
will MAKE you feel, no, know that it is! and
that it is within our grasp to change this
society, maybe even this world. One person can't
do it alone, at least no 'ordinary' person, but together
oh, that is another story! We can only do this
by joining together, so its up to you to get other
people involved as well as us. Young people should
always be (they have to!) the resistant wall of hope.
Otherwise — who else is there. Thatcher certainly
aint gonna help no one except her greedy
bleedin' lot.

I don't mean all this as a bloody lecture
its just I have the opportunity to speak my feelings
and I'm using it.

Keep the faith!
love Paul

THE GIGS

1976

March
9   Greyhound, Fulham
20   Greyhound, Fulham

May
8   Hope & Anchor, Islington

June
6   Windsor Castle, London
7   Kensington, London
16   Windsor Castle, London (Unconfirmed)
17   Greyhound, Fulham
29   Hope & Anchor, Islington (Unconfirmed)
30   Teacher Training College, Canley

July
5   Windsor Castle, London (Unconfirmed)

September
8   Upstairs At Ronnie Scott's, London
17   Greyhound, Fulham (Unconfirmed)

October
16   Soho Market, London
21   Queensway Hall, Dunstable

November
9   100 Club, London
16   100 Club, London
23   Upstairs At Ronnie Scott's, London

December
13   Greyhound, Fulham
14   100 Club, London
28   100 Club, London

1977

January
11   100 Club, London
22   Marquee, London
25   100 Club, London

February
2   Nashville, West Kensington, London (Unconfirmed)
3   Nags Head, High Wycombe
7   Nashville, West Kensington
11   Roxy Club, Covent Garden, London
19   Hunt Hotel, Leighton Buzzard
21   Nashville, West Kensington
24   Roxy Club, Covent Garden, London
25   Greyhound, Fulham
26   Hunt Hotel, Leighton Buzzard

March
1   Railway Hotel, Putney
2   Red Cow, Hammersmith
5   Leicester Polytechnic
9   Red Cow, Hammersmith
11   University of Kent, Canterbury, Kent
15   Hope & Anchor, Islington
16   Red Cow, Hammersmith
18   Hope & Anchor, Islington (Advertised, but later changed to Southbank Polytechnic, London)
22   Roxy Club, Covent Garden
23   Red Cow, Hammersmith
24   Rochester Castle, Stoke Newington
25   Royal College of Art, London
28   Palais De Glace Punk Festival, Paris
29   100 Club, London
30   Red Cow, Hammersmith
31   Rochester Castle, Stoke Newington

April
1   Leeds Polytechnic
5   Nashville, West Kensington
6   Hope & Anchor, Islington
7   Manor Ballroom, Ipswich
9   Rochester Castle, Stoke Newington
12   Nashville, West Kensington
15   Embassy Cinema, Brighton
16   Rochester Castle, Stoke Newington
17   Roundhouse, London
19   Nashville, West Kensington
20   Roundabout Club, Newport
22   North London Polytechnic, Kentish Town
23   Marquee, London
26   Dingwalls, Camden (Cancelled)
28   Hope & Anchor, Islington
29   Royal College Of Art, London

May
3   Dingwalls, Camden
5   Oaks Hotel, Chorlton, Manchester
7   Playhouse Theatre, Edinburgh
8   Electric Circus, Manchester
9   Rainbow Theatre, Finsbury Park
12   Nag's Head, High Wycombe
20   Newcastle University (Cancelled)
21   Town Hall, St Albans (Cancelled)
22   Civic Hall, Wolverhampton (Cancelled)
23   Top Of The World, Stafford (Cancelled)
24   Top Rank, Cardiff (Cancelled)
25   Woking Park Swimming Pool Area (Cancelled) [The Woking Conference Of Youth Organisation's 'Jubilee Youth Week' held a "Fashions Of Yesteryear by Sheerwater Youth Club with rock bands." The local paper reported that The Jam was unable to appear.]
25   Brighton Dome (Cancelled)
26   Colston Hall, Bristol (Cancelled)
27   West Runton Pavilion (Cancelled)
28   Odeon, Canterbury (Cancelled)
29   Chancellor Hall, Chelmsford (Cancelled)
28   Portsmouth Polytechnic (Cancelled)
30   California Ballroom, Dunstable (Cancelled)

June
4   Nag's Head, High Wycombe
7   Barbarella's, Birmingham
8   Winning Post, Twickenham
9   Winter Gardens, Eastbourne
10   Corn Exchange, Cambridge
11   Bristol Polytechnic
12   Stamford Bridge (Chelsea FC), London (Cancelled)
13   Top Rank, Reading
14   Locarno, Portsmouth
15   Village Bowl Discotheque, Bournemouth
16   Leeds Town Hall, Leeds

17 Seaburn Hall, Sunderland
18 Civic Hall, Poplar, London
18 UCL, London
19 Electric Circus, Manchester
20 Outlook Club, Doncaster
21 Top Rank, Cardiff
22 Lafayette, Wolverhampton
23 Huddersfield Polytechnic
24 Brunel Rooms, Swindon
25 Winter Gardens, Malvern
26 Greyhound, Croydon
27 Battersea Town Hall, London
28 Drill Hall, Lincoln (Cancelled)
29 Cat's Whiskers, York
30 Rebecca's, Birmingham (Cancelled)

July
1 Mayfair Ballroom, Newcastle
2 Middleton Town Hall, Manchester
4 Unknown venue, London
5 Top Rank, Brighton
6 Top Rank, Portsmouth
7 Mr Digby's, Birkenhead
8 Middlesbrough Town Hall
9 Harrogate Spa Hall (Originally advertised but later changed to the California Ballroom, Dunstable)
10 Top Rank, Sheffield
12 Tiffany's, Shrewsbury
13 Shuffle's, Glasgow
14 Maniqui Hall, Falkirk
15 Clouds, Edinburgh
16 Eric's, Liverpool
17 Maxims, Barrow-in-Furness
22 West Runton Pavilion, Cromer
23 High Wycombe Town Hall, High Wycombe
24 Hammersmith Odeon, London

August
8 Punk Rock Festival, Mont de Marson, France (Band arrived but didn't play)
16 100 Club, London

September
10 Nashville, West Kensington
11 100 Club, London
17 Chelmsford City FC, Chelmsford (Afternoon)
17 Roxy Theatre, Harlesden, London
23 Malmo, Sweden
24 Ronneby, Sweden (Gig abandoned after crowd invaded stage and smashed up equipment)
25 Stockholm (Cancelled)

30 Paradiso, Amsterdam

October
8 Whiskey-A-Go-Go, LA
9 Whiskey-A-Go-Go, LA
10 Rat's Kellar, NY
13 Rat's Kellar, NY
15 CBGBs, NY
16 CBGBs, NY

November
17 Huddersfield Polytechnic, Huddersfield
18 Mayfair Ballroom, Newcastle
19 Leeds University
20 Empire Theatre, Liverpool
22 Top Rank, Cardiff
24 University of Leicester, Leicester
25 Kings Hall, Derby
26 Friars, Aylesbury (Afternoon and evening shows)
27 Top Rank, Sheffield
28 Top Rank, Birmingham
29 Apollo, Manchester
30 Apollo, Glasgow

December
2 Bracknell Sports Centre, Bracknell
3 Civic Hall, Wolverhampton
4 Locarno, Bristol
5 Bournemouth Village Bowl, Bournemouth
7 Top Rank, Brighton
8 Locarno, Coventry
9 Odeon, Canterbury
11 Greyhound, Croydon
14 Lancaster University
15 Victoria Hall, Stoke Hanley
16 Corn Exchange, Cambridge
18 Hammersmith Odeon, London

1978

February
13 L'Ancienne, Brussels
14 Le Sporté Hall, Paris
16 Salle de Concerts, Le Mans
18 Palais des Sports, Lille (Tickets stated 13th but clashes with Brussels gig, and may have been postponed until 18th)
24 Marquee Club, London
25 Marquee Club, London
27 100 Club, London

March
2 Music Machine, London
16 University Of Bridgeport, CT, USA (Supporting Blue Oyster Cult)
18 Tower Theatre, Philadelphia, PA
19 Agricultural Hall, Allentown, PA
20 Four Acres Club, Utica, NY
21 Colonial, Toronto
22 Colonial, Toronto
24 Hammond Civic Centre, Hammond, IN
25 Richfield Coliseum, Cleveland, OH (Supporting Blue Oyster Cult)
26 Civic Centre, Wheeling, WV (Supporting Blue Oyster Cult)
27 Coliseum, Fort Wayne, IN (Supporting Blue Oyster Cult)
29 Paradise Rock Club, Boston, MA
30 CBGBs, NY, NY
31 CBGBs, NY, NY

April
2 Rupp Arena, Lexington, KY (Supporting Blue Oyster Cult)
3 River Daze, St Louis, MO
4 Bunky's, Madison, WI
5 BJ's Concert Club, Detroit, MI
6 Bogart's, Cincinnati, OH
7 Riviera Theatre, Chicago, IL
11 Celebrity Theatre, Phoenix, AZ (Supporting Be Bop Deluxe)
12 Celebrity Theatre, Phoenix, AZ (Supporting Be Bop Deluxe)
14 Starwood, Santa Monica, CA
15 Winterland, San Francisco, CA
16 Exhibition Hall, San Jose, CA

June
1 BBC Paris Theatre, London
12 King George's Hall, Blackburn
13 Victoria Hall, Keighley (Cancelled)
14 The Pier, Colwyn Bay (Cancelled)
15 Barbarella's, Birmingham
16 Barbarella's, Birmingham
17 Friars, Aylesbury
18 Lyceum, London

July
30 Civic Hall, Guildford
31 Town Hall, Torquay

August
1 Fiesta Club, Plymouth

2   Village Bowl Discotheque, Bournemouth
4   Brunel Rooms, Swindon
13   Bilsen Festival, Limburg, Belgium
25   Reading Festival, Reading
27   Groningen Festival, Holland

October
20   Top Hat Club, Dublin
21   Leisureland, Galway

November
1   Empire Theatre, Liverpool
2   De Montfort Hall, Leicester
3   St George's Hall, Bradford
4   Newcastle City Hall, Newcastle
5   Apollo, Glasgow
6   Capitol Theatre, Aberdeen
7   University of St Andrews, Fife
10   Sheffield Polytechnic, Sheffield
12   University of Leeds, Leeds
13   Apollo, Manchester
14   Odeon, Birmingham
15   Coventry Theatre, Coventry
17   Corn Exchange, Cambridge
18   ABC Cinema, Great Yarmouth
20   Cardiff University
21   Dome, Brighton
22   University Of Kent, Canterbury (Cancelled)
24   Guildhall, Portsmouth
26   Colston Hall, Bristol
29   Great British Music Festival, Wembley Empire
     Pool, London

December
7   University of Kent, Canterbury
21   Music Machine, London

1979
February
16   Reading University
20   Metropole, Berlin
21   Star Club, Hamburg
22   Star Club, Hamburg
23   Wartburg Wiesbaden, Germany
26   Stadium, Paris
27   L'Espace Club, Rennes
28   Le Royale, Lyon

March
4   Marseille, France

April
10   Rex Theatre, Toronto
11   Unknown venue, Chicago, IL
12   Paradise Rock Club, Boston, MA
13   Tower Theatre, Philadelphia, PA
14   Palladium, NY, NY
16   Agora Ballroom, Cleveland, OH
17   Punch & Judy Theatre, Detroit, MI
20   Auditorium, Oakland, CA
21   UCLA Royce Hall, LA, CA
24   Commodore Ballroom, Vancouver

May
4   University of Sheffield, Sheffield
5   University of Sheffield, Sheffield
6   Newcastle City Hall, Newcastle
8   Salford University
10   Rainbow Theatre, Finsbury Park
11   Rainbow Theatre, Finsbury Park
12   Loughborough University
14   University of Exeter, Exeter
15   University of Liverpool, Liverpool
16   University of Liverpool, Liverpool
18   University of Strathclyde, Glasgow
19   University of Strathclyde, Glasgow
21   Colston Hall, Bristol
22   Odeon, Birmingham
24   Guildhall, Portsmouth

June
9   Saddleworth Arts Festival, Saddleworth

August
29   Moonlight Club, West Hampstead (Cancelled)
30   Bridgehouse, Canning Town (Cancelled)
31   Nashville, West Kensington (Cancelled)

November
2   Marquee Club, London (Secret gig, billed as
     John's Boys)
3   Nashville, West Kensington (Secret gig, billed
     as The Eton Rifles and La Confiture)
17   Friars, Aylesbury
18   Poole Arts Centre, Poole
20   Apollo, Manchester
21   Apollo, Manchester
22   Civic Hall, Wolverhampton
23   Gaumont, Southampton
24   Gaumont, Southampton
25   Bingley Hall, Stafford
26   Trentham Gardens, Stoke-on-Trent
27   Royal Spa, Bridlington

29   Deeside Leisure Centre
30   Lancaster University

December
1   Sophia Gardens, Cardiff (Cancelled)
2   Rainbow, Finsbury Park
3   Rainbow, Finsbury Park
4   Rainbow, Finsbury Park
6   Newcastle City Hall, Newcastle
7   Newcastle City Hall, Newcastle
8   Apollo, Glasgow
9   Caird Hall, Dundee
10   Odeon, Edinburgh
11   Queen's Hall, Leeds
12   King George's Hall, Blackburn
13   Sophia Gardens, Cardiff
15   The Brighton Centre, Brighton
16   Guildhall, Portsmouth
18   De Montfort Hall, Leicester
19   De Montfort Hall, Leicester
20   Pavilion, Bath
21   Pavilion, Bath

1980
February
11   Corn Exchange, Cambridge
12   University of Kent, Canterbury
13   Winter Gardens, Malvern
15   Woking YMCA Centre, Woking
27   Emerald City, NJ
28   Stage West, Hartford, CT
29   Palladium, NY, NY

March
1   Triangle Theatre, Rochester, NY
3   JB Scott's, Albany, NY
5   Motor City Roller Rink, Detroit, MI
6   Park West, Chicago, IL
7   Old Chicago Amusement Park, IL
9   St Paul's Civic Centre, Minnesota, MN
13   Shoe Box, Seattle, WA
15   Fox Warfield Theatre, San Francisco, CA
16   Santa Monica Civic Centre, CA
21   Palace, Houston, TX (Cancelled)
22   Armadillo World Headquarters, Austin, TX
27   Ontario Theatre, Washington, DC (Cancelled)
28   Capitol, Passaic, NJ (Cancelled)

April
7   Rainbow, Finsbury Park

8   Rainbow, Finsbury Park
18   Civic Hall, Guildford

May
17   Pavillion Baltard, Paris
26   Pink Pop Festival, Holland

June
2   Civic Hall, Wolverhampton
3   King George's Hall, Blackburn
4   Victoria Hall, Hanley, Stoke On Trent
21   Loch Lomond Festival, Scotland

July
3   Mainichi Hall, Osaka
4   Kaiken Hall, Kyoto
6   Nakano Sun Plaza, Tokyo
7   Nihon Seinenkan, Tokyo
8   Nihon Seinenkan, Tokyo
10   Unknown venue, Tokyo (Cancelled)
22   Civic Hall, Guildford

August
2   Friars, Aylesbury
3   Poole Arts Centre, Poole
9   Ruisrock Festival, Turku, Finland

October
18   Technical College, Bromley (Charity event organised by Wing Music, Bromley, for Save the Children Fund)
26   Top Rank, Sheffield
27   Newcastle City Hall, Newcastle
28   Newcastle City Hall, Newcastle
29   Playhouse, Edinburgh
30   Apollo, Glasgow
31   Apollo, Manchester

November
1   Apollo, Manchester
2   Leisure Centre, Deeside
3   Queen's Exhibition Hall, Leeds
5   Brighton Conference Centre, Brighton
6   Brighton Conference Centre, Brighton
7   Bracknell Sports Centre, Bracknell
8   Bracknell Sports Centre, Bracknell
9   Poole Arts Centre, Poole
10   Sophia Gardens, Cardiff
11   Bingley Hall, Stafford
12   De Montfort Hall, Leicester
13   De Montfort Hall, Leicester
15   Rainbow, Finsbury Park
16   Rainbow, Finsbury Park

18   Hammersmith Odeon, London
19   Hammersmith Odeon, London
22   Unknown venue, Gothenburg
23   Christiana Centre, Stockholm
24   Unknown venue, Oslo (Cancelled)
25   Gota Lejon, Stockholm
26   Gota Lejon, Stockholm
27   Unknown venue, Lund, Sweden
29   Carregat, Eindhoven, Holland
30   Westfalenhalle, Dortmund

December
1   Vredenburg Concert Hall, Utrecht
2   Oosterpoort Groningen, Holland
3   Hof ter Lo, Antwerp
6   Fort Regent, Jersey
8   Coliseum, St Austell (Cancelled)
9   Colston Hall, Bristol
10   Winter Gardens, Malvern
11   Civic Hall, Guildford
12   Music Machine, London
14   Coliseum, St Austell

1981

February
14   Cricketers Pub, Westfield, Woking (Secret gig billed as The Jam Road Crew)
16   Woking YMCA, Woking
17   Sheerwater Youth Club, Woking
21   UEA, Norwich
22   University of Nottingham, Nottingham
23   Crawley Leisure Centre, Crawley
26   Pavillion Baltard, Paris

March
1   Olympen, Lund
2   Oddfellows, Copenhagen
3   Oddfellows, Copenhagen
5   Market Hall, Hanover
6   Markthalle, Hamburg
8   Metropole, Berlin
10   L'Ancienne, Brussels
12   Tivoli Hall, Strasbourg (Cancelled)
13   Paradiso Club, Amsterdam
14   Paradiso Club, Amsterdam
15   Palais St Sauvre, Lille
16   Studio 44, Rouen

April
27   Royal Court, Liverpool

May
13   Aichi Kinro Kaikan, Nagoya
14   Mido Kaikan Hall, Osaka
15   Nakano Sun Plaza, Tokyo
16   Nakano Sun Plaza, Tokyo
21   Le Club, Montreal
22   Masonic Hall, Toronto
23   Masonic Hall, Toronto
24   Technical High School, Ottawa
26   Ritz, NY, NY
29   Channel Club, Boston, MA

June
10   Grona, Lund
12   Unknown venue, Borlanger, Sweden
17   Rainbow, Finsbury Park
20   Festival Pavilion, Skegness
22   Granby Hall, Leicester
23   Guildhall, Portsmouth
25   Coliseum, St Austell
27   Bingley Hall, Stafford
30   Magnum Centre, Irvine

July
2   Royal Hall, Bridlington
4   Market Hall, Carlisle
5   Guildhall, Preston
7   Civic Hall, Guildford
8   Civic Hall, Guildford

October
23   Rainbow, Finsbury Park (CND Benefit)
24   Embankment, London (CND Benefit)

December
12   Michael Sobell Sports Centre, Finsbury Park
13   Michael Sobell Sports Centre, Finsbury Park
14   Hammersmith Palais, London
15   Hammersmith Palais, London
19   Hippodrome (BBC TV Theatre), Golders Green, London

1982

February
24   Central London Polytechnic

March
6   Guildford Civic Centre, Guildford
11   Canterbury (Cancelled)
12   Guildhall, Portsmouth

13 Brighton Conference Centre, Brighton
14 Brighton Conference Centre, Brighton
15 Fair Deal, Brixton
16 Alexandra Pavilion, London
17 Royal Bath & West Showground, Shepton Mallet
18 Afan Lido, Port Talbot
20 Bingley Hall, Stafford
21 Bingley Hall, Stafford
22 De Montfort Hall, Leicester
23 De Montfort Hall, Leicester
25 Apollo, Manchester
26 Apollo, Manchester
27 Leisure Centre, Deeside
28 Opera House, Blackpool
29 Top Rank, Sheffield
30 Top Rank, Sheffield
31 Top Rank, Sheffield

April

1 The Queens Hall, Leeds
3 Newcastle City Hall, Newcastle
4 Newcastle City Hall, Newcastle
5 Playhouse Theatre, Edinburgh
6 Playhouse Theatre, Edinburgh
7 Apollo, Glasgow
8 Apollo, Glasgow
16 Johaneshov's Isstadion, Stockholm
18 Olympen, Lund
20 Falkoner Theatre, Copenhagen
21 Vejlby Risskov Hall, Arhous, Denmark (Cancelled)
24 Paradiso Club, Amsterdam
25 Paradiso Club, Amsterdam
26 De Vereniging Nijmegen, Amsterdam
27 L'Ancienne, Brussels

29 Pantin Hippodrome, Paris
30 Palais D'hiver, Lyon

May

14 University Of Maryland, Washington, DC
15 Palladium, NY, NY
16 North Stage, Long Island, NY
18 Palladium, NY, NY
19 Trenton Hall, NJ
20 Orpheum Theatre, Boston, MA
22 Verdun Auditorium, Montreal
24 Coliseum, Toronto
25 Michigan Theatre, Ann Arbor, MI
26 Aragon Ballroom, Chicago, IL
29 Perkins Palace, Pasadena, CA
30 Perkins Palace, Pasadena, CA
31 Perkins Palace, Pasadena, CA

June

2 Fox Warfield Theatre, San Francisco, CA
5 Kerrisdale Arena, Vancouver
11 Kosei Nenkin Kaikan Hall, Tokyo
14 Nakano Sun Plaza Hall, Tokyo
15 Mainichi Hall, Osaka
16 Seinenkan Hall, Tokyo
17 Kinro Kaikan, Nagoya
26 QPR Football Ground, Shepherds Bush, London (Cancelled)

July

10 QPR Football Ground, Shepherds Bush (Cancelled)

September

20 Leas Cliff Pavilion, Southend
21 Showground, Shepton Mallet
22 Brighton Conference Centre, Brighton

23 Granby Halls, Leicester
24 Royal Court, Liverpool
25 Royal Court, Liverpool
27 Ingliston Highland Centre, Edinburgh
28 Whitley Bay Ice Rink, Whitley Bay
29 Whitley Bay Ice Rink, Whitley Bay
30 Queen's Hall, Leeds

October

1 New Bingley Hall, Stafford
9 Gloucester Hall, Jersey
11 Beau Sejour Leisure Centre, Guernsey
13 Paris (Cancelled)
14 Strasbourg (Cancelled)
15 Genk, Belgium (Cancelled)
16 Popperinge, Belgium (Cancelled)
17 Amsterdam (Cancelled)
18 Amsterdam (Cancelled)

November

25 Apollo, Glasgow
27 Poole Arts Centre, Poole
28 Coliseum, St Austell
29 Afan Lido, Port Talbot

December

1 Wembley Arena, London
2 Wembley Arena, London
3 Wembley Arena, London
4 Wembley Arena, London
5 Wembley Arena, London
6 Royal Spa, Bridlington
7 Apollo, Manchester
8 Bingley Hall, Stafford
9 Civic Hall, Guildford
11 Brighton Conference Centre, Brighton

Bibliography

The following books and websites were used as an invaluable resource when writing *Thick As Thieves*.

Books

About The Young Idea by Mike Nicholls
Keeping The Flame by Steve Brookes
Paul Weller: My Ever Changing Moods by John Reed
The Jam: A Beat Concerto by Paolo Hewitt
The Jam: Shout To The Top by Dennis Munday
The Jam: Sounds from the Street by Graham Willmott
The Jam Unseen by Twink
The Modfather: My Life with Paul Weller by David Lines

Websites

www.zani.co.uk
www.thejamfan.net
www.thejam.org
www.thepublicwants.com
www.fridaystreet.com
www.ourgenerationpunkandmod.co.uk
www.heavysoul.co.uk
www.wholepointpublications.co.uk

Acknowledgments

Snowy would like to dedicate the book to Rich and Craig (just one gang of many Saturday's Kids) and New Rose (let us pray for another).
   He'd also like to thank Bax at Mono Media, Adam at Heavy Soul, Michael at Time for Action, Chang for the Chelsea days out, Aunt Nelly and Tim the band slag, Richard for the Brighton days, Kent Soul Clubbers, Baz and Dan for the Weller gigs and Iain at Wholepoint.

Stuart would like to dedicate this book to the new breed, Issy, Edward, Ethan and Elliot – may your dreams as children be fulfilled – and to my wife Paula, who knew I had a good book in me. Once I stopped talking about it.

Big thanks go out to Phil Potter for the initial phone call and a point in the direction of Mr Jam and Meds, who seconded the motion. To Andy Nyko, who's help was immediate, invaluable and steered me off the moors and onto the safe path more than once. Matteo Sedarazzi and John Reed for their direction and encouragement; Mick and the Hotel Pelirocco, Brighton; Stuart Sons, Neil Phillips, Nigel Tufnell, Jonny Bance, Tommy Holt and Steve Jones, who's enthusiasm, support and belief has carried me through. Tracie Young for getting the attention of the big man. Bax, for whom the expression 'diamond geezer' was invented. Gavin Frankland for letting us into his abode and pulling his gaff apart. Twice.
   Derek D'Souza for his trust and sharp eye; Jon Silwood for his contribution to early design and general monkey behaviour. Debs and Anita for the stories, laughs and abuse.
   Rory Blaney, Simon Kortlang, Mark Lock, Al Peasey and Sean Robbie, who I'm proud to call my brothers; and to Georgia and family, a longstanding support system when days lost their names. To the Away From the Numbers/PWC mob – thank you for sharpening my wit and knowledge. To Simon Kelly for being Simon Kelly! Billy Spitfire and Dan Lost Boy – this time next year, Rodders! To my Mum, Dad, Nicole and Rob – Love ya. To all my Kings of Europe – Reece and Pat, John Smith, Gav, Lammo, the Kingston & Guildford mobs, Ginger Tel and the pups, the Phillips clan, Keith and Gary, the Haynes dynasty and the North Stand, Stamford Bridge. To all the brothers and sisters from the people's-republic of Northolt; big love to the outlaws, Toni, Dave, Farren, Chris, Tina, Maz, Steve and the wonderful Lorna. Turn that fire up, girl!

And finally a special thanks to Chris at Marshall Cavendish for his enthusiasm for the book, Mike Spilling for his help beyond the call of duty and Jon Abnett, whose energy, sweat, passion and blood flows throughout the book.